A Modern Maistre

OWEN BRADLEY

A Modern Maistre

THE SOCIAL AND
POLITICAL THOUGHT OF
JOSEPH DE MAISTRE

University of Nebraska Press
Lincoln and London

Publication of this book was assisted by a grant
from The Andrew W. Mellon Foundation.

♾

Library of Congress Cataloging-in-Publication Data
Bradley, Owen, 1960–
A modern Maistre: the social and political thought of Joseph de Maistre / Owen Bradley.
    p.   cm.—(European horizons)
Includes bibliographical references and index.
ISBN 0-8032-1295-x (cl.: alk. paper)
1. Maistre, Joseph Marie, comte de, 1753–1821—Contributions in political science.
2. Maistre, Joseph Marie, comte de, 1753–1821—Contributions in sociology.
I. Title.   II. Series.
JC179.M28B73   1999
320.52′092—dc21
98-43636   CIP

CONTENTS

Preface

Surprising as it may seem, there exists as of yet no comprehensive account of Joseph de Maistre's social and political philosophy, despite his tremendous influence upon the modern European intellectual tradition. There are, of course, a large number of works devoted to Maistre and his place in history. Yet these accounts have been either of an entirely biographical nature, tracing the narrative of Maistre's rather tumultuous life story, or of a primarily ideological bent, treating him as a merely representative mouthpiece of the forces of reaction. Often, these two approaches are combined to present Maistre's thinking as no more than an ideological superstructure built up upon the narrow base of his aristocratic material life interests.[1]

The chief exceptions to this style of interpretation have been several able studies of Maistre as a religious thinker that, however, leave the modern resonance of his social and political ideas unexamined.[2] One significant anomaly to this silence is found in Carl Schmitt's pregnant misreading of Maistre's theory of sovereignty, which I will have cause to examine at some length.[3] Finally, a host of valuable essays on specific aspects of his life and ideas has appeared over the last two decades in a journal devoted solely to Maistrean studies.[4] Still, there has been no systematic study of his social and political thought, much less an extended consideration of its modern character.

My interpretation avoids the common strategy of starting from Maistre's negative response to the French Revolution and deducing therefrom the reactionary character of his thought as a whole. Instead, I start from a close reading of his ideas, often upheld long before the Revolution, in order to grasp the internal coherence of his philosophical conservatism. Only in light of that philosophy can we make sense of his response to events in France, a response that was in fact much more nuanced than received interpretations would allow.

The organizing factor upon which my own work relies is Maistre's theory of sacrifice, a cultic practice of which he was the first European to offer a comparative cross-cultural analysis. Around this theme gravitate all the major themes of his intellectual production: power and victimization, religious customs and institutions, social norms and transgressions, legal sanction and criminal punishment, war, revolution, and the sacred bases of political authority. The issues raised by Maistre's analysis resonate strongly with twentieth-century continental philosophy, much of which itself emerges from an awareness of conceptual impasses insurmountable by the canons of the Enlightenment, especially the questions of language, difference, and power, which were at the heart of Maistre's intellectual project.

The Maistre that thus emerges is less an irrationalist than a theorist of social irrationality, less a lover of paradoxes than a philosopher of paradoxical situations. For all his emphasis upon moments of excess and extremity and for all his royalist allegiances, Maistre was a voice of moderation in his day and one of the most moderate defenders of the French monarchy, of which he was often highly critical. Maistre's doubts about popular sovereignty and the rational organization of society themselves remain important for the effort to understand the potential abuses unique to modern democracy, an effort that has become all the more pressing in the twentieth century.

It is a pleasure to acknowledge a few of the many people who in one way or another have assisted in the long gestation of my argument. Dominick LaCapra watched over its early growth as a doctoral dissertation at Cornell University, as did Steven Kaplan and Satya Mohanty. Since that time, correspondence with Richard Lebrun and conversations with Jean-Louis Darcel and George Steiner have contributed greatly to whatever merits may be found in the result. I would also like to thank the entire University of Nebraska Press staff and Mary Hill for their exceptional editorial work. Finally, a faculty development award granted by the University of Tennessee allowed me to investigate archival sources in Chambéry, Turin, and Paris during the summer of 1995. None of these individuals or institutions, of course, is responsible for the risks or limits of my interpretation, sometimes maintained against their better judgment.

Introduction

At first glance, and even perhaps at second glance, no one would seem farther from our horizons than Joseph de Maistre. If he is known at all to contemporary readers, it is as the ultraconservative defender of Catholicism against the Enlightenment, monarchy against democracy, tradition against innovation, the advocate of the executioner, sacrifice, and papal authority. Each of these claims will have to be considered closely in the following chapters, where it will be seen that Maistre's arguments were neither so one-sided nor so backward as they might appear and that they may indeed provide insight into some of the defining themes of modern thought.

Such an interpretation goes very much against the grain of received scholarship, which has consistently pictured Maistre as the last spokesman of a bankrupt old regime. Influential readings have portrayed him as "a blind traditionalist and reactionary" whose political thought "appears feeble and thin," a writer "as dogmatic, intransigent, absolute, and violent as possible" who "called for a return to absolutism, with the Pope as the final arbiter and the executioner as his henchman."[1] These extreme evaluations are understandable when viewed with historical hindsight. Maistre was among the first and most forceful critics of nascent modern democracy, and his ideas have proven serviceable in France to one regressive political force after another. Any critical study of Maistre's ideas must carefully sift what remains valuable for thought from what is useful merely for a reactionary politics. Yet Maistre's position is far more complicated and far more interesting than a narrow ideological reading, whether from the Left or the Right, would allow.

If Maistre were as feeble, thin, and dogmatic a philosopher as his critics contend, he could hardly represent much of a threat to what they hold dear. It is only because his understanding of political authority was as profound as it was that the translation of his theory into political practice could be a danger to democracy. For if Maistre was an ideologue of sorts, he was far more of a philosopher than a rabble-rouser. Like all conservatives, he emphasized the limits human irrationality places upon progressive social change. His writing does stand out, however, for the depths of human depravity it portrays.

This portrayal certainly has its dangers. Thus his close attention to social irrationality could be transformed into a call for irrational social action, his emphasis on the symbolic bases of social order into an assertion of the legitimacy of a merely symbolic order, of the mere illusion of good government. His attack on Jacobinism and his call for a royal restoration could be transformed into a rejection of all progressive reform, a violent denial of the Left that encourages scapegoating and social violence. These steps were taken much more by Maistre's posterity than by Maistre himself. They are forcefully contested by other elements of his thinking. Nonetheless, the step from a theory of violence to an affirmation of violence was prepared by him, for which he must bear some responsibility (just as Nietzsche must bear some responsibility for the misappropriation of his thought by the Nazis). I am convinced and mean to show, however, that in no sense did he simply venerate violence.

A danger equal to reading Maistre uncritically would be to believe that the social irrationality and symbolic violence that so concerned him have been put behind us and thus may be safely ignored. His work illuminates a class of social and political facts generally ignored by the tradition of political thought inspired by the Enlightenment he opposed. Early conservatives like Maistre, critics of revolution and rationalization, provide essential material for understanding the irrational bases of domination and social order, of the theological dimension of politics, of the Mysteries of State. Shaken by the French Revolution, they were constrained in defense of their own political world to voice those "political secrets" the very essence of which is to remain unexamined and accepted without reason. It is this sacred or irrational element of social and political life that is the guiding thread of all their meditations on politics. Maistre is arguably the most sophisticated of these early conservative philosophers. As a mere denunciation of democracy Maistre's thought would be of little value (unless as a pretext for noble indignation). He *is* of value to the extent that his criticism is founded on a critical analysis of irrational social forces too often left unanalyzed by critics working within liberal horizons.

Latter-day silence on Maistre is especially surprising given the similarities between the world of his thought and the world in which we live. The modern world, one might well say, has shown itself to be all too Maistrean. It would be a gross understatement to say that the horrors that have punctuated the twentieth century have shaken our faith in the progress of enlightenment and darkened our view of humanity.

George Steiner, lamenting the lack of attention to Maistre's work, presents it as an "essential reference" for contemporary reflection:

> Joseph de Maistre's "night-vision" . . . may well be the principal feat of precise foresight in the history of modern political thought and theory. It makes the "futurology" of Rousseau, of Hegel and Marx look utterly shallow. The age of the Gulag and of Auschwitz, of famine and ubiquitous torture, of Idi Amin, Pol Pot and of Ceaucescu is *exactly* that which de Maistre announced.

Maistre's stark view of mankind's fallen degradation, Steiner argues, kept him from the facile meliorism of the Enlightenment and allowed him to "predict" the atrocities of the modern age.[2] To be sure, Maistre possessed an exquisitely refined sense of the nearness of human atrocity, a perennial capacity for barbarism barely held within bounds by institutions, ritualized behavior, and myth. This awareness made him a conservative. His alertness to the interplay of transgression and limits, order and disorder, law and violence led him to a conservative defense of limits, order, and law as the lesser of necessary evils.

If Maistre's dark vision of humanity and the world presaged our own, his response to that darkness is surprisingly even-handed for a writer of his reputation. It is as a rule less "dogmatic, intransigent, absolute, and violent" than what passes for politics in our day. We will see that he rejects not only revolution but counterrevolution, that he insists one must embrace the movement of history at work in one's time, and that his work seeks not to further but to understand the disorder of his day.

Maistre's absence from current debates is a yet much greater surprise given the uncanny resemblance between his work and dominant trends in recent French thought. Bataille on the sacred as the defining feature of human existence, found in sovereignty and sacrifice; Blanchot on the dissimulated yet essential violence of all speech and writing; Foucault on the social function of punishment in prerevolutionary Europe; Derrida on violence and difference; Castoriadis on the social imaginary; Girard on the scapegoat—all these themes of contemporary theoretical debate were anticipated and extensively elaborated in Maistre's writing. Particularly contemporary is his belief that the key to the "normal" functioning of society is to be sought in the "abnormality" of social excess and that social theory must therefore consider not only moments of stability but also moments of transformation and transgression.

Equally fashionable is his thesis that the moorings of order are found in the spheres of language, the imaginary, and the symbolic.

No less an expert in things postmodern than Philippe Sollers has written of Maistre that "this writer of the first order has been one of the most calumniated of men and most unjustly so, because he was one of the very few to reveal the secret destiny of the Revolution." Maistre discovered that the Revolution was "a crisis in the symbolic itself" (strong words for a Lacanian). For Sollers, Maistre's great achievement was to answer the question of how the French Revolution's discourse of liberation was capable of underwriting the most excessive tyranny.[3] Maistre thus anticipates the current suspicion that revolutions are not necessarily liberating and that, on the contrary, the bulk of existing institutions deserves to be conserved—or at least must be conserved if chaos and bloodshed are to be avoided.

Chantal Mouffe has already remarked upon the affinities between postmodernist and conservative critiques of the Enlightenment. These affinities, she asserts, are

> to be found not on the level of the political but in the fact that, unlike liberalism and marxism, both of which are doctrines of reconciliation and mastery, conservative thought is predicated upon human finitude, imperfection and limits. This does not lead unavoidably to a defense of the status quo and to an anti-democratic vision, for it lends itself to various forms of articulation.[4]

Mouffe's emphasis on a shared philosophy of limits seems on the mark. Yet the question remains of just how supple and how binding these theoretical resemblances might be. This question will be a guiding concern of my investigation.

Perhaps the resemblance between postmodern and early conservative thinking ought to come as no surprise. It has been the central theme of the attack on contemporary criticism by Jürgen Habermas, for whom these affinities are not only theoretical but political. To simplify his well-known argument, Habermas identifies modernity with the extension of the rational norms of the Enlightenment. Any questioning of the one entails the rejection of the other, and either critique would thus be equally reactionary. Every variety of recent French thought and much of the Frankfurt School to boot are thus revealed to be at bottom antimodern and conservative.[5]

Habermas is right to point out certain resemblances between contemporary theory and the counter-Enlightenment tradition. He is right to infer from these resemblances the potential dangers of postmodernism: a nihilistic fascination with irrationality, violence, and transgression. This lack of critical distance from unreason has been all too common and all too recuperable by reactionary forces. Yet, on the other hand, these affinities that Habermas and others have pointed out may also imply that traditionalism has been in some sense creative and forward-looking, something more than the threadbare ideology of an impotent aristocracy.

Indeed, Maistre wrote at a time when the traditional verities could no longer be taken for granted. Unlike what one might call a "traditional traditionalist," he was sharply aware of the present as a time of strife, as a combat of reason and unreason, order and disorder, each always present in the other. If the experience of strife was universal in his day, his effort to theorize it was not. We shall see that the central question of that theory was how dualistic structures (order and disorder, the sacred and the profane, the spirit and the flesh, sovereignty and abjection) are created and undone. As a conservative, he defended the old against the new and endeavored to include strife within a higher and broader symbolic unity. There is no denying his antagonism to the discordant new world emerging around him. Yet he altogether rejects the efforts of his contemporaries to step out of the tension between past and present that defined his era. He rejects out of hand both the overweening rationalism of the revolutionaries who would have done with the past and the ignorant fanaticism of their counterrevolutionary opponents who would have done with the present. It is indeed remarkable how Maistre flourished within the revolutionary epoch, as though he only there found who he was.

Maistre's work could only be the product of a situation in which tradition had been thoroughly destabilized. This was the result not only of the French Revolution but also of his previous close involvement in Masonry, *parlement*, and the republic of letters: three central sites of the emergence of critical public opinion within the old regime. His *mal du siècle* represented something more than a passive or reactive reflection of existing anxieties. On the one hand, he critically engaged the most forceful intellectual tendencies of his day: Locke and Hume, Rousseau and Montesquieu, Vico and Warburton. On the other hand, his use and defense of tradition were something more than an appeal to established authority. Plato and Paul, Plutarch and patristics: these classical sources emerge from Maistre's pen transformed by his concern with the present moment, placed as they are among the contemporary discourses of Masonry, ethnography, and political theory. While Maistre's intellectual sources do point to the particular historical conjuncture of his late-eighteenth-century context, the resulting hybrid, dialogue, or montage is anything but traditional, much less a mere catalog of counterrevolutionary clichés.

If despite all this Maistre remains a somewhat scandalous figure within modern European intellectual history, it is not because of his vehement defense of tradition alone. Burke, after all, is equally firm and more vitriolic in his loyalty to the past and yet has his assured place within the modern canon. Rather, what makes Maistre such an ambivalent figure is the very subject matter of his thought. Those things that stand in the way of rationalization and Enlightenment, violence and the sacred in particular, represent the very epitome of the loaded or equivocal subject. The great question here is what one makes of that equivocal remnant: whether one succumbs to the seductive fascination of the irrational or rather maintains a detachment that allows for critical reflection upon it.

This issue of critical as against symptomatic responses to social irrationality is nowhere more evident than in Maistre's theory of sacrifice, according to which ritual violence and legitimate authority are closely, even inextricably, bound up together (though by no means, as some critics would have it, identified). George Brandes long ago touched upon the heart of the matter in observing that "all this is undoubtedly an offense to reason."[6] Sacrifice is indeed an offense to reason; but this is precisely why, given its general predominance in the history of human culture, it must be understood. The question, then, is whether Maistre's *theory* is an offense to reason. In its moments of mysticism, perhaps it is, especially those when he seeks in sacrificial violence some higher meaning or redemptive value. Yet Maistre's theory is anything but a threat to reason in its general aim of accounting for social irrationality. The existence of sacrifice cannot be deduced from the Enlightenment's presuppositions of the social contract and man's inherent benevolence and reasonableness. This, however, is no reason to ignore the existence of ritual violence. On the contrary, "Enlightenment on Sacrifices" (the title of Maistre's essay with which I begin) is a necessary component of the general project of Enlightenment: making what is obscure in man's life open to knowledge.

Maistre's effort to develop a critical theory of social order and disorder distinguished him sharply from other royalists of his day. One finds in his work a critique of extremist politics, whether revolutionary or counterrevolutionary. Rather than simply restate the claims of throne and altar, he developed a general theory of extreme situations, of wars, revolutions, usurpations, capital punishment, and, tying all these together, a theory of sacrifice. This recourse to theory was itself an untraditional gesture, and the contents of that theory—a sociological approach to sovereignty and the sacred—anticipate central themes of modern European thought.

But surely, one might quite properly reply, Maistre was a conservative, a traditionalist, an opponent of the modern world emerging around him. Indeed he was. He denies the basic claims we have come to associate with the Enlightenment as the birth of the modern age. Like the conservative tradition as a whole, Maistre everywhere stresses the limits of self-determination. He ridicules the autonomy of the rational subject that for Kant defines Enlightenment as freedom from self-incurred tutelage.

Yet Maistre offers us not simply a defense of the irrational against the rational, the sacred against the secular, order against disorder. At times he does give us just that, and to that extent he is indeed a conservative in the narrow sense. But at other times, most times it seems to me, he gives us to think that these very oppositions are neither so stable nor so readily distinguished as all that, that every order has its elements of disorder and every disorder its broader order. In providence and punishment, sovereignty and sacrifice, he discovers a general order or rationality within what appears most disordered and an essential kernel of disorder in the most ordered or rational social practices. This effort to theorize a general economy of human existence that includes both order and disorder, reason and savagery, marks Maistre as our contemporary.

Here I must face one last objection. Perhaps Maistre does resemble us more than we thought, but this might not be such a good thing. This is the position of two of the most influential readers of Maistre's work, Isaiah Berlin and E. M. Cioran, both of whom see him as all too clearly anticipating or even personally embodying what is worst about our era in all its violence and extremity.

Isaiah Berlin approaches Maistre as an important historical and essentially modern figure—important and modern as the great theoretical precursor of fascism. Berlin's interpretation deserves careful attention. Throughout his most distinguished career, he has shown a close interest in and even a certain sympathy for the critics of the rational pluralism of the Enlightenment that he himself upholds, notably Vico,

Hamaan, Herder, and Tolstoy. Yet for Berlin, Maistre simply seems too much. He presents Maistre as the figure who pushes counter-Enlightenment thinking from a study of irrationality and human limits to an advocacy of violence and human powerlessness.

This interpretation is not altogether without its grounds. To trace the sources of fascism back to Maistre, however, is quite another thing, least of all perhaps for its anachronism. Maistre's deep lifelong interest in violence and irrationality, which might indeed be called an obsession, does not at all necessarily imply he praised them. The step from the one to the other, which Berlin nowhere doubts, is in Maistre's case quite precarious.

Berlin summarizes Maistre's rejection of the Enlightenment's view of human nature with his characteristic clarity and directness:

> Men are by nature aggressive and destructive; they rebel over trifles. . . . When the destructive instinct is evoked men feel exalted and fulfilled. Men do not come together, as the Enlightenment teaches, for mutual cooperation and peaceful happiness; history makes it clear that they are never so united as when given a common altar on which to immolate themselves. This is so because the desire to sacrifice themselves or others is at least as strong as any pacific or constructive impulse.

One may well disagree with Maistre's description of history and human existence. Yet it remains a description rather than a prescription. Thus the reader should remain skeptical when Berlin concludes that "these gloomy doctrines . . . inspired nationalism, imperialism, and finally, in their most violent and pathological form, Fascist and totalitarian doctrines."[7] On the contrary, we shall see that Maistre's dark vision encouraged him instead to defend every limit against the spread of that darkness. He in fact offers trenchant criticisms of nascent nationalism and imperialism alike as consequences of democracy that destroy cultural traditions. The above passages come at the end of an important essay on the counter-Enlightenment in which Berlin had in some fashion praised every other member of that school whom it mentions. Maistre here seems to carry off on his shoulders all their historical sins.

The same misprision is found in an essay on Sorel in which Berlin presents Maistre as an example of "the violent rhetoric of the extreme right" against "*déraciné* intellectuals, or Jews without a country."[8] This is to ignore that Maistre himself was an émigré intellectual who showed an admiration of Judaism extremely rare within the Catholic tradition and wholly lacking, for example, from Burke. That "the barbarism of the Hebrew people is one of the favorite theses of the 18th century" was for Maistre a sure sign of that century's nullity.[9] Above all, these charges ignore his unrelenting hostility to right-wing revolutionaries.

All this comes to a head in Berlin's major essay on Maistre, written in 1960 but only published thirty years later, "Joseph de Maistre and the Origins of Fascism." Here again we have the same clear summaries of Maistre's view of man and the same odd attribution of fascist tendencies. This extended interpretation, in which Berlin argues rather than merely asserts Maistre's fascist leanings, itself reveals how Berlin's own argument makes room for a very different reading of his abiding significance.

At a central juncture of his argument Berlin cites Maistre's gloss on the powers vested in the general will by Rousseau. The authoritative voice of the general will intones, "You believe that you do not want this law, but we assure you that you do. If you dare reject it, we shall shoot you down to punish you for not wanting what you do want." Berlin comments that "no clearer formula for what has rightly been called *totalitarian democracy* has surely ever been uttered."[10] The evidence provided, however, would seem to argue Maistre to be an outspoken critic of what was to become fascism, not its precursor. Berlin here attributes to Maistre the danger that Maistre perceives in Rousseau. Maistre neither invented, advocated, nor condoned the unvoiced violence of the general will that gives democracy a "totalitarian" potential. Democracy's penchant for violence and its inability to restrain it, we will see, were more than anything else what turned Maistre against it.

To blame Maistre for the dangers he perceived in our disenchanted world has been the error of almost every rejection of his thinking. Berlin repeats it when he tries to connect him more directly to twentieth-century cultural politics:

> Orwell's *1984* merely re-echoes [Maistre's] crucial thesis that control of language is essential to control of lives, even though the means chosen by [Orwell's] elite, whose aims are somewhat different than Maistre's, is a language not traditional, but artificial, specially constructed—in fact the object of Maistre's attack.[11]

One might well argue to the contrary that if the principles upon which the language of Big Brother is constructed are those that Maistre attacks, this would mean he could not simply be included on the bad side of the fascist/antifascist divide. Moreover, to argue that *1984* is "merely" an echo of Maistre's claims about ideological hegemony is to confirm their critical potential. In turn, the existence of those evils that Berlin seeks to trace back to Maistre would themselves seem to imply that Maistre was all too correct that political order is irrationally maintained and underwritten by cultural discourses—by language, Maistre would say—and that the achievements of the Enlightenment have done little enough to change that so far.

An interesting variant of this way of reading Maistre as a precursor of twentieth-century evils is provided by E. M. Cioran in one of the most insightful essays of all the Maistrean literature. Cioran's own dark view of human finitude and perversity has much more in common with Maistre than with Berlin's liberal pluralism. He tells us he will have nothing to do with that idealism and nobility of soul that has refused to enter into dialogue with Maistre and yet, despite this lack of engagement, has shaped all along his received reading.

On the contrary, he holds that Maistre is a uniquely modern writer, and he is modern precisely in his "monstrosity" and "odiousness." This assertion is marked by the same virulent tone for which Cioran and others reproach Maistre; nonetheless, it raises forcefully the transferential dynamic at the heart of all receptions or refusals of Maistre's thought. As Cioran observes, "To combat a *monster* it is necessarily to possess some mysterious affinities with him, it is likewise to borrow from him certain character traits." The monstrous unity of guilt and innocence, identity and difference, legitimacy and violence will be an ever-recurrent theme of this work. Here I would only add that it is the duty of interpreters to take some distance from this talk of monstrosity, particularly if they uphold the right to criticize Maistre's unsettling vision of politics. Rather than engage again in a spiral of accusations, surely it is more useful to consider carefully what Maistre gives us to understand and thus to help establish a further distance between political discourse and political violence. The fundamental aim of this work is to make of Maistre the ambiguous, equivocal, undecidable figure I believe he ought to be for modern thought rather than a monster plain and simple. As Cioran points out, Maistre is far more troubling in his proximity to us than in his distance.[12]

The initial temptation when faced with such an ambivalent figure is always to ask "But was Maistre good or bad? benign or dangerous? friend or foe?" Perhaps if one had to decide once and for all, it would be for the latter. Perhaps. More likely, this is the wrong question. The task of the interpreter is to avoid and to question the stark alternative between total friendship and total enmity, for such an alternative only confirms Maistre's political vision at its very worst: scapegoat that ye be not scapegoated. The only way out of the spiraling violence that Maistre finds at the foundations of social order entails negotiating a path between unmitigated acceptance and unmitigated rejection of those differences that most challenge us.

My reading of Maistre has thus meant to follow his own advice on reading "the ancients." It is necessary, he tells us, to avoid two errors. "1) Not to believe that the ancients, even the most celebrated, were oracles: for they said some very stupid things. 2) Not to reject brusquely their observations under the pretext that they conflict with some of our current ideas; this would be another error perhaps more dangerous than the first."[13] In tracing this path, finally, we may even confirm what is best in Maistre's politics, as expressed in his motto "enemies become friends." To be sure, Maistre's thought represents on many levels a challenge to the legitimacy of the modern age. Yet perhaps the best gauge of that legitimacy is the manner in which the age responds to such challenges. To listen and respond is a more legitimate response than to close one's ears and to damn. This latter response would indeed hardly be modern. More to the point, it would fail to live up to the example that Maistre's own investigations of the equivocal have set for us.

Having raised the question of Maistre's place in modern European thought, I will close this introduction with a few words of biography in order to sketch the setting within which his ideas developed. This bare outline, meant to provide some initial historical orientation, will be fleshed out in the following chapters as we investigate Maistre's response to the age in which he lived and wrote.

Joseph de Maistre was born on 1 April 1753 in Chambéry, the capital city of Savoy, a French-speaking province of the kingdom of Piedmont-Sardinia. The Maistre family history tells us a success story of the ancien régime. Rising from trade and commerce to law and public service, the family was granted noble status in 1778 for the work of Maistre's father, François-Xavier, a senator and the second president of the Savoy *parlement*, in drafting a new royal constitution. Of his two parents, however, it was probably Maistre's mother, Christine Demotz, also from a family of magistrates, who exercised the stronger influence on Maistre's early religious and literary views.

While no evidence survives of Maistre's schooling, there is no doubt that the Jesuits played a major role in his early development, notably through a religious confraternity he entered at age nine. Another important religious influence was the order of the *pénitents noirs*, into which he was initiated in 1768. Both of these confraternities taught a rather grim Christianity, centered on notions of guilt, death, and fear of God. In 1769 Maistre left Chambéry to study law at the University of Turin. Maistre's youth, then, seemed to presage the life of traditional piety and legal work for which his parents had prepared him.

Such expectations appeared to be confirmed by Maistre's career as a magistrate. From 1772 until 1792 he rose steadily in the ranks and was ultimately named a senator of the Savoy *parlement* in 1788. In 1786 he married Françoise de Morand, the daughter of an ancient noble family who would bear him three children by 1793. This outwardly conventional life was qualified, however, by cultural and intellectual engagements that were hardly traditional. Maistre's personal library, one of the largest in Savoy, was extraordinarily wide-ranging. Only a small fraction of his collection, which was especially strong in contemporary arts and sciences, was devoted to professional or pious concerns. Before becoming one of the Enlightenment's most forceful critics, then, he had been one of its most avid followers.

From 1772 to 1793 Maistre participated closely in the life of the Masonic lodges. His later description of this involvement as merely a social game would seem to be belied by his 1778 initiation into a highly esoteric and illuminist lodge, in which he rose to the highest grades. Masonry encouraged Maistre's interest not only in Orientalist mystical cosmology but also in the ritual organization of social groups.

Thus, alongside a personal and professional trajectory squarely located within the ancien régime, Maistre participated closely in three of the most modern tendencies of his day: the legal and political discourse of the *parlements*, the cosmopolitan readership of the Enlightenment, and the sociability and preromanticism of the Masonic lodges. This balance was ruptured by the French invasion of Savoy in September 1792, which broke the traditional framework within which Maistre had lived and turned him against the enlightened opinions of his youth.

Thus began Maistre's twenty-five years of exile, which were to prove the most creative period of his life. For several years he worked as a correspondent and counterpropagandist for the Sardinian monarchy in Lausanne, Turin, Venice, and Florence. From the start, Maistre's activities were looked upon with distrust by his government, both for his earlier reformist views and for his insistence on the need to face the realities of the French Revolution with sobriety and flexibility. In 1800

Maistre was transferred to Sardinia itself, where mutual exasperation between him and his superiors grew as he criticized the court's petty tyrannies and was criticized in turn for insubordination.

Finally, in 1802 Maistre was appointed Sardinian ambassador to Saint Petersburg, other than London the only remaining source of aid for the counterrevolution. There he frequented the court and the Francophone salons, maintained an immense diplomatic and personal correspondence, continued his encyclopedic reading, and produced his greatest works. Perhaps what is most remarkable about Maistre's life of exile was how he experienced it as a freedom of sorts, a cultural liberation from the mediocrity of provincial life into the greater European world. Indeed, it was only with quite some reluctance that in 1817 he returned to his native land. His last years in Turin were devoted primarily to arranging the future of his children and the publication of his works. He died on 26 February 1821, surrounded by his family and the rites of the Roman Catholic Church.

These brief biographical remarks already intimate how decisive the experience of exile proved for the development of Maistre's work. My investigation thus begins with the emergence of French conservative thought among the émigrés from revolutionary France, the cultural and intellectual setting within which Maistre wrote.

A Modern Maistre

Chapter 1
French Traditionalism

Thus the aristocracy took its revenge by singing lampoons on their
new master, and whispering in his ears sinister prophecies of coming
catastrophe . . . at times, by its bitter, witty, and incisive criticism,
striking the bourgeoisie to the very heart's core; but always ludicrous. – Marx and Engels, *The Communist Manifesto*

Counterrevolutionary thought has not yet become enough of a problem for us. As the royalist historian Blanc de Saint Bonnet already had
to put it in 1872, "It is most comfortable at this hour to anathematize
Kings!"[1] Historical memory since has treated the outsiders of the
French Revolution as though one could do away with a problem, a veritable impasse for thought, by doing away with half of the terms that
make up the problem. Memory thus repeats the deed of exclusion from
the fold. The elimination of strife has not been altogether complete,
however. Were it so, the Revolution would then likely be a simple fact
as unproblematic for the French and their historians as the American
Revolution is for most Americans.[2] Indeed, without resistance to the
revolutionary project, there would have been no original "problem"—
no French Revolution. That it was resisted is a fundamental part of
what makes the Revolution one of the most fruitful subjects of historical reflection. Because the counterrevolution was a chief partner of that
decisive sociopolitical transformation, its critical perspective upon the
emergence of modern politics in the Revolution plays a decisive part in
the dynamic of the Revolution itself, a part we must recall whenever
that tremendous event is to be treated as a problematic, as an occasion
for thought, and not simply as a fact.

The counterrevolution is more question-worthy yet, for while its
politics has been dismissed as ridiculous presumption, its interpretation of the Revolution is still very much with us, by no means only
among the lunatic fringe. Under the influence of Furet's ironic dis-
missal of revolutionary gains, we have come to accept as an historical
commonplace that the Revolution was essentially Jacobin and that Jacobinism is essentially hostile to liberty. The predominance of this view
over the course of bicentennial reflection compelled Régis Debray, an

ardent defender of the Jacobin republic, to conclude that "unbe-
knownst to ourselves, we have become counter-revolutionaries."[3] The
strange combination of scorn and emulation in our dealings with the
counterrevolutionary argument demands careful consideration.

Those who defended the French monarchy against the Revolution
have continually been dismissed as the representatives of ignorance, intolerance, and inequality. There are good reasons for this charge. Yet
these traits were neither all there was to the counterrevolution nor its
monopoly. One often finds in these denunciations, moreover, a certain
philistine excessiveness that points toward dogmatism rather than the
open rational dialogue they explicitly uphold against their foes.

If the counterrevolution and its close relation the counter-Enlightenment were incompatible with all change and all thought, there would
indeed be little motivation for reading these writers. That they are not
read today is only in part a matter of well-deserved censure. As Maistre
often remarked, it is not a book's merit but the power of the interests behind it that makes for its celebrity. In contemporary scholarship there is
certainly no profusion of voices waiting the chance to speak out for the
Bourbon monarchy. I do not at all intend to raise any such cry. Yet I
hope to show that the question of allegiances may not be quite so simple as it would appear at first sight.

This chapter aims to provide a context for Maistre's thinking by describing the nature and development of French traditionalism. This
will entail a brief discussion of the counterrevolution and the experience of exile within which the traditionalist argument was elaborated.
The account is not meant to be exhaustive but only to establish a frame
of reference within which Maistre's ideas can be understood. We will
see as we go on that Maistre was quite an unusual figure within that setting, but to understand this we must first see what that setting was.
Once that is accomplished, the chapter will conclude with a consideration of the legacies of French traditionalism and its stance toward the
modern world.

Resistance to the French Revolution was as diverse as the society the
Revolution replaced, a fact only lately granted by studies of the period.
A recent essay on the counterrevolution by Roger Dupuy has shown
how designations of ignorance and fanaticism, as well as an alleged barbarism or stupidity arising from peasant isolation in western France,
are commonly used to lump together and dismiss all resistance to revolutionary progress. The continuing dominance of this way of thinking
over the discussion of the counterrevolution, when such a discussion

takes place at all, "corresponds to a profound conviction of a large section of French historiography, which perceives itself and wishes itself to be the heir of Enlightenment, and finds itself corroborated by much current research, preoccupied with measures of literacy and inquiring about possible criteria of acculturation."[4] Yet, Dupuy argues, models of culture derived from the Enlightenment and deployed by the Revolution cannot be very helpful for understanding what these sought to undo. The "ignorance" argument indeed derives from revolutionary discourse as a rhetorical strategy to conserve its appearance of cohesion before the event of a populace not spontaneously patriotic and republican; "it must be then that they are stupefied by a fanaticism which keeps them from having a clear awareness of their true interest, which cannot but be the same as that of the urban patriots" (39).

The history of both elite and popular resistance to the Revolution was determined in large part by the history of the Revolution itself. What the Revolution perceived as its "enemies" varied significantly over its course: in 1789 only the most obstinate defenders of royal absolutism, with the rise of sans-culotte populism the wealthy bourgeoisie, and in 1793 any defenders of sociopolitical moderation or other forms of "incivism." Indeed, over the course of first five years of the Revolution virtually everyone was at one time or another "counterrevolutionary." There was thus no single counterrevolution. Its inner conflicts were virtually as acerbic as its outward ones: those who called for compromise against the intransigent, theorists of social order against advocates of White Terror, those who rejected the Revolution in toto, those who accepted 1789 or 1791, the Thermidorean reaction, the Consulate, or the Empire.

As new social strata entered the counterrevolutionary camp they brought with them new interpretations and new rejections of the Revolution corresponding to their various motivations for resistance. Claude Mazauric, aware of this fundamental heterogeneity, defines the counterrevolution as an "ensemble of political strategies" that "amalgamates all the varieties of political opposition, of resistances, . . . of indifferences even or again of distances taken at such or such a moment."[5]

In spite of this broad definition, however, Mazauric proceeds to reduce the aristocratic counterrevolution to a political attack on the Revolution in defense of royalism, order, and elite privilege and then proceeds to indict their political tactics. The nobles failed to provide a "coherent strategy." Had they consistently upheld an "anti-liberal, anti-bourgeois, anti-urban discourse," he argues, they might have obtained broad mass support (241–42). One finds the same claim in God-echot's *La Contre-Révolution*. This is to argue that the nobility should have become populists, promoted a purely negative politics based on resentment, and embraced the demagogic politics of mass insurgency, the dangers of which had turned them against democracy in the first place. To succeed, in short, they would have had to stop being what they were and become something perhaps far worse.

It is necessary to remark, however, a certain *pride* in failure on the part of the counterrevolution: not simply a disdain verging on disgust toward events in Paris, but a pride in not being understood as the trait of a superior sensibility. Among the émigrés one not seldom finds a willful foolhardiness in the espousal of the irretrievable, of the norma-tive power of what is now taken as irrelevant, of what does not conform to rational procedure, against the victorious champions of a mandatory progress. This blessed ignorance of reified thinking (but too often along with it a refusal of what is simply reasonable) was carried over into the proud retreat into provincial silence of the high aristocracy of the later nineteenth century. This note of pride is sounded in an early text by Maistre, who later came to paint a much darker picture of aris-tocratic resistance:

> The cry or the arms of Europe will perhaps return them the patri-mony of their fathers; but whatever their fate, all the sufferings to which a horrible cruelty could condemn them could not vanquish them, still less humiliate them; from the very table of the poor with whom they share dry bread, they will take their place around the throne, and all grandeur will bow before their proud poverty.[6]

Here one finds a refusal of the bourgeois–utilitarian criterion of success or profit as a measure of value; indeed, from this perspective, tragic self-loss may represent the highest of values. It is in this status of the willing victim (a phrase that dominates Maistre's work) and of proud marginalization that the antagonists of the Revolution retain their in-terest, above and beyond the pathos of exile. It is their affirmation of a different world and worldview that continues to speak to us and not their resentment, a resentment in which too many counterrevolution-aries remained wholly negative, passive, and uncreative within the new world emerging around them. Both these tendencies of early French conservatism, proud marginality and resentment, first made them-selves felt in the experience of exile, an experience that fostered both modern and antimodern attitudes.

Exiled Thought

Exile is at once both central to the modern imagination and as old as the world. History has always produced exiles. Intolerance of difference is found at all levels of culture and indeed at all levels of animal life. On the "giving" end, banishment and ostracism are primordial punishments, reserved for fundamental crimes like sacrilege, murder, or treason. On the "getting" end, exile is commonly conceived as expiation or trial. That all human beings are in this sense exiles is a basic Christian dogma, whether formulated as exile from Eden or from some heavenly origin; this doctrine is shared by all varieties of Gnosticism (Maistre's bête noire), which only distinguishes itself by its advocacy of a *politique du pire* as the best way home. But if exile is thus among the most ancient of themes, it is also among the most modern.

In the idea of exile we find the typical modern themes of anonymity, alienation, displacement, and marginality. The power of the metaphors of exile, of life in the meantime, of life as a stranger in a temporary state of affairs, is gauged by their penetration throughout both popular and elite modern cultures, from Pascal to Jack Kerouac, from Schubert to George Jones. We moderns are thus all familiar with the romantic figure of the artist or creative thinker outcast in his or her own culture, a stranger among philistines.

All these themes make themselves felt among the French emigration. The experience of exile provided a sociological impetus at work in their fascination with victimization and sacrifice, with origins, language, and cultural specificity, and also in their tendencies toward nostalgia or resentment. In short, exile made them romantics.

The transition from an enlightened to a romantic sensibility among the exiled French nobility is well documented in Fernand Baldensperger's *Le Mouvement des idées dans l'émigration française.* His central claim is that the exiles, in their loss of society, came to identify romantically with the "savage" or "primitive." The rupture with traditional aristocratic sociability encouraged a "mysticism of the me" that culminates in a full-fledged Romanticism. Eighteenth-century classicism, as a confident application of order to experience, became a much more difficult attitude to uphold in emigration. The sole remaining classicists at exile's end were the philosophers, whose sense of order was wholly intellectual; the disorder of the everyday life of exile left little for the classically minded pragmatist or aesthete.

Baldensperger estimates the number of émigrés departing France between 1789 and 1797 and returning between 1797 and 1815 at 180,000, among them the majority of the previous French elite (1:iii). These men and women, cosmopolitans in spite of themselves, developed "dispositions more docile to the diversity of the world" through contact with other national traditions whose untaintedness by the French Enlightenment, now blamed for the Revolution, impressed upon the émigrés the value of local customs and traditions, so-called superstitions and anachronisms. The very disarray of the émigrés in their new surroundings made their experience of cultural difference far more dramatic and often more fertile than that of the Napoleonic armies, bearers of a triumphant Enlightenment universalism.

The émigrés' experience of other cultures, as a rule less modern than their own, provided the French traditionalists with a supply of ancient truths and old certainties as yet immune to criticism. It also provided them with a sense of distance from which to judge events in France. In a text addressed at once to the French inside and outside France and to his fellow Savoyards, Maistre offered the perennially useful advice that "if you want to know how posterity will judge you, listen to the foreigners who are for you a contemporary posterity" ("Lettres," *OC* 7:77). History itself is just such a seeing from afar. Among the exiles, the historical present was thoroughly and uniquely historicized, that is, rendered distant and problematic and demanding to be understood.

As Baldensperger demonstrates, the great lack experienced by the displaced nobility was that of the *soirées* and *causeries*, the disappearance of the sociability of the salon that so marked the *belle époque* of the ancien régime in France. "The English," according to Madame de Staël, "have retired into their families, or gathered into public assemblies for national discussions. The intermediary one calls society barely exists among them."[7] In Germany the nobility was found to be too uncultured, the intellectual elite too bourgeois, although some recompense was found among German Jewish families, whose education and culture were widely admired. "What is a Sabran going to do in Rheinsburg, a Delille in Brunswick, a Genlis in Bath, a Chateaubriand in Suffolk?"[8]

In the wake of this collapse of an accustomed society one finds a multiplication of memoirs, memorials, recollections, journals, voyages, in short, of novelistic histories of private lives. This proliferation transgresses the prohibition upheld by classicism and salon sociability alike against the egoism of the reiterated, insistent use of the "I." The narcissistic undercurrent of this romantic tendency comes to light above all in Chateaubriand, who himself remarks that "the me is to be noted among all authors who, persecuted by men, have passed their lives far from them. The solitaries live off of their heart, like those kinds of animals who, lacking exterior nourishment, feed themselves with their own substance."[9] The author, need one add, is speaking of himself.

Bonald writes of the emigration that "the civilized man sees his homeland only in the laws that rule society, in the order that reigns there, in the powers that govern there, in the religion one professes there, and for him his homeland cannot always be his country."[10] This loss of a homeland may result either in the *mal du pays* of a Chateaubriand, "that languor of the soul which one experiences outside one's homeland," which confronts us as something half kitsch and half sad,[11] or in a theoretical reconstruction of the ancien régime, its laws, order, and religion, that sets it off from the new France. Even in the second case, however, it is sometimes difficult to distinguish which ideas represent *theories* and which *reassurances*, reassurances as to one's past innocence, present legitimacy, and future well-being, to distinguish between claims based on principles and those based on hopes or resentments. The same holds for the various ways in which these counter-revolutionaries interpreted the Revolution.

The least nuanced, most absurd, but very widespread explanation of the Revolution attributed it to some murky but delimited philosophic "sect," though not to the more general philosophic critique of religion and society in which many émigrés had themselves taken part. The most common variant of this tendency emphasized the alleged role of secret societies, above all of Masons. Again, however, since frequent noble membership in the Masonic lodges had familiarized them with Masonry's decidedly vague philanthropy and hope for progress, this claim limited itself to some hidden conspiracy of a discrete body of philosophes, Masons, and German Illuminati. The apogee of this tendency is found in the works of Barruel.

Those dissatisfied with conspiracy theories inclined toward a general disavowal of the Enlightenment and its spirit of examination. This direction of thought resulted either in a general obscurantism and disavowal of reason per se or in a spirit of self-criticism for the nobility's dabbling participation in Enlightenment culture as sorcerer's apprentices. In this vein, Ségur wrote that "we marched gaily along over a carpet of flowers concealing an abyss." The nobility was

> beguiled by every seductive dream of a philosophy that was about to
> secure the happiness of the human species. Far from foreseeing misfortune, excess, crime, the overthrow of thrones and principles, the

future disclosed to us only the benefits which humanity was about to
derive from the sovereignty of reason . . . Never was a more terrible
awakening preceded by a sweeter slumber or by more seductive
dreams.[12]

For the laconic Bonald, "power doubted, it was lost."[13] This self-in-
dictment on the part of the nobility resulted at the same time in a rethinking of intellectual history and in a posture of expiation for an aristocracy that by its own principles was responsible as social exemplars of
duty and service for the moral fiber of those below them. The providentiality of this expiation is emphasized by Maistre in one of his more
penitential moments: "in placing the good man in the grips of misfortune, God purifies him of his past faults, puts him on guard against future ones, and prepares him for heaven."[14]

Finally, attempts to account for the monarchy's collapse, in the absence of particular causes of an adequate magnitude to explain the event
and in the desire to form expectations as to an uncertain future, encouraged more intellectual émigrés to develop theories of history and the
deep structure of society. These philosophies, faced with an unprecedented reversal of fortunes perceived as utterly iniquitous, were driven
by the extremity of the observable facts of the Revolution themselves to
extreme formulations of fatality, providence, and "the force of things"
that ranged in a broad spectrum from sheer lunacy to veritable forerun-
ners of sociology and historicism. Maistre, I mean to show, represents
the summit of this tendency.

Paul Beik remarks of Baldensperger's book how the experience of
exile produced "the most pathetic delusions" among the émigrés.[15]
While there is ample evidence to support such an argument, to attribute
backwardness and delusion to the vanquished of history only serves to
further remove them from our sight. Any critical reconsideration of
their ideas must therefore distinguish carefully what is creative and
what reactive, what represents intellectual advance and what intellectual retreat or retrenchment.

This essential distinction leaps to the eye in the juxtaposition of two
commentaries on exiled thought, the first by a Pole living in Argentina
and the second by a German in Italy. Witold Gombrowicz, criticizing
émigré Polish literature of the mid–twentieth century, emphasizes its
debilitating tendency toward nostalgia, self-pity, and escape. "When
they throw you out of your home, what are you supposed to do? 1)
Moan and groan. 2) Reminisce. 3) Inveigh against others. 4) Proclaim
your innocence."[16] This romantic yearning in bad faith and resentment

for the roses of yesteryear is a danger underlined by Nietzsche in his effort to present a more modern version of exiled wandering or "homelessness." In the following passage from *The Gay Science*, exile becomes a precondition of being modern.

> If one would like to see our European morality for once as it looks from a distance . . . then one has to proceed like a wanderer who wants to know how high the towers in a town are: he leaves the town. . . . The human being of such a beyond who wants to behold the supreme measures of value of his time must first of all 'overcome' this time in himself—this is the test of his strength—and consequently not only his time but also his prior aversion *against* this time, his suffering from his time, his untimeliness, his *romanticism*.[17]

Kicked over the border, the émigré must think, feel, and write from outside his or her own culture. Perhaps because too specific a milieu is irreplaceable, the more provincial and less enlightened members of the French nobility were not up to the task. Some of the more cosmopolitan among them, however, experienced a loosening of cultural norms that was highly conducive to theory. As Nietzsche would have it, some such distance is necessary to every intellectual, for an event must be experienced as at least somewhat foreign to be critically thought through.

This idea guides Karl Mannheim's *Conservatism*, the most insightful study of the ideas of the early continental conservatives, in which he asserts their decisive contributions to modern European historical and sociological thought. Without desiring something from society or from history, Mannheim argues, no sociohistorical comprehension whatsoever is possible. The study of history "only turns into historicism when historical facts are not just passionately invoked against the facts of the present, but when the process whereby things have come about is experienced with feeling." The same holds for sociology, which likewise requires a sense of distance, "a fruitful angle of vision which is existentially created." If some French counterrevolutionaries were so intellectually creative, it is because "France alone provides an example of a nobility which itself became aware of its own conditions of existence. This is without doubt explained by the fact of their emigration."[18] Early French traditionalism should not therefore be seen as a simple falling back on a would-be stable continuity. It rather implies a rupture with tradition, a rupture that was lived by the exiles and that made history an essential existential concern. Only when tradition ceases to be an unquestioned norm does curiosity as to its structure and its normativity itself become possible. The French exiles' loss of their accustomed life-world brought into relief as daily concerns several central questions of cultural theory: how identity is culturally determined, how meanings are culturally bound, how such cultural identities are displaced and appropriated, and how one becomes oneself again in a wholly new set of cultural coordinates.

This radical experience of decontextualization produces a certain vertigo, an unavoidable *phenomenological epoche*, on the part of the exile whether willing or no. The émigré's exile from the everyday domain of the lived-through and taken-for-granted acclimatizes him or her (by way of disacclimatization) to perceive the elements of culture that produce the ordinary and quotidian: symbols, rites, customs, prejudices. This liminal experience may produce either romanticism or theory, either resentful plaints of rootlessness or an embrace of its new possibilities. While some of the former may no doubt everywhere be found among the French émigrés, Maistre himself emphasizes the latter: "I never think without admiration of that political whirlwind which has uprooted from their places thousands of men destined never to know one another, to make them swirl together like the chaff of the fields . . . We are painfully and justly pulverized; but, if miserable eyes like my own are worthy to glimpse divine secrets, we are only pulverized to be mixed" (*Soirées, OC* 1:169, 171).

Early French Conservatism

Now that we have examined exile as an existential precondition of early French conservatism, a few words of definition are in order. To understand the varieties of conservative criticism, and Maistre's place among them, we need to distinguish among its three primary intellectual currents: counterrevolution, counter-Enlightenment, and traditionalism.

The term "counterrevolution" refers to any of a very broad range of resistances to the social and political consequences of the French Revolution, especially of its atheism and egalitarianism. The counterrevolution particularly attracted outsiders and anachronistic classes at the very top and bottom of society, those outside the universalism of the Revolution or Empire; one thus finds very strange allegiances established between peasants, lumpen proletarians, and aristocrats against established powers (and later against the Charter). Against the innovations of the Revolution, the counterrevolutionaries generally defended a decentralized or even preindustrial economy, a likewise decentralized and traditional structure of authority and privilege, Catholicism, and a traditional worldview. Because at some point in the 1790s almost every Frenchman resisted the Revolution in the name of one of these principles, counterrevolution was a part of the Revolution itself. Its chief failing was to underestimate or to ignore the social, political, and economic inequities of the ancien régime that had not a little to do with the revolutionary excesses it decried. Exemplary here is the remark of a moderate critic of the Revolution, Staël: "Where did the disorderly tendencies of the early years of the Revolution come from, after all, if not from a hundred years of superstition and arbitrary rule?"[19] This simple question pulls the rug from beneath much counterrevolutionary discourse.

In the most general sense, the "counter-Enlightenment" criticizes the Enlightenment's understanding and use of reason because of its egalitarian, atheistic, or mechanistic implications. Often but by no means always, this critique was motivated by a defense of received ideas along with the interests they represented. At its worst, the counter-Enlightenment was a rejection of reason and self-determination plain and simple. At its best, in Vico for example, the counter-Enlightenment provided a theory of what was unaccountable on the basis of Enlightenment presuppositions: the fundamental and decisive role in social life played by myth, language, and other forms of behavior that fall outside the sphere of enlightened self-interest. To the extent that it thus participates in extending human self-understanding, above all in the development of history and sociology, the counter-Enlightenment was an integral part of the general project of Enlightenment itself, even while contesting the philosophy of the age that goes by that name.[20]

"Traditionalism" in the French revolutionary context refers to a historical hybrid of counterrevolutionary and counter-Enlightenment tendencies. In the wake of the Revolution it defended traditional ways of thought (and secondarily the social structures that support them) against the incursions of Enlightenment. It was capable of a broad variety of manifestations among social groups from peasants and artisans to archbishops and Masons. There was, accordingly, a very broad range of notions of just what the tradition was: for some the narrowest possible definition of Catholicism, for others a variety of traditional ways of life. For Maistre, tradition included Greek philosophy, Hindu cosmology, Christian heresies, alchemy, and scholasticism; his defense of tradition extended to traditional societies ravaged by Western expansion. At its worst, traditionalism defended received oppressions and the biases that underwrote them. At its best, it was a philosophical position that held that tradition *is* normative, that the past gives the present its consistency, and not merely the political position that it *should* do so. This attitude was tremendously important for the development of historicism in France.[21]

One can perceive in the above definitions significant room for both agreement and disagreement among parties. The various facets of these three varieties of conservatism in France interact within the work of individual conservatives in ways that are sometimes surprising and sometimes ruthlessly predictable. As we proceed, two things must be borne in mind. First, although largely on the defensive, early French conservatism nonetheless posited its own particular vision of the world, a vision that radically questioned the individualist, rationalist, and voluntarist ideals of the Revolution. Second, the counterrevolution must be understood as itself a part of the Revolution, sometimes mirroring its excesses, opposing a White to the Red Terror, sometimes providing an understanding of social order proportionate to the challenges that the Revolution offered to that order. These two horizons define at once the scope and limits of early French conservatism.

The theoretical confrontation between Revolution and counterrevolution was before all else a conflict between two opposed visions of history. Where the Revolution pictured the present casting off a superfluous past in order to become the future, conservatives saw only the continual self-transformation of the past. The minimal condition of the conservative outlook, first formulated against the French Revolution, is the belief that all historical transformations must occur within the framework of tradition, that in politics as in surgery "one cuts only when one has to."[22]

More specifically, the great intellectual divide between these two camps was that between rationalist and historicist philosophies. In historicist fashion, conservative thought everywhere emphasized the primacy of being over thinking, of practice over theory. Thus, against the Enlightenment's rationalist procedure of deducing the norms governing a particular case from general rules of universal validity, it stressed the qualitative and irrational dimensions of reality, in light of which the particular case must dictate the terms for theory, not vice versa.

The Revolution was perceived by its opponents as the direct practical application of a theoretical reason made absolute that would allow no practical resistance. To combat the actions of the Revolution it was thus necessary to combat its ideas by developing what one might call a "counteranthropology" that would question the autonomy of individ-

ual reason from sociocultural traditions and challenge the Enlightenment's assumption that the human lot is infinitely perfectible through
education, technical progress, and the application of natural laws to society.

The conservatives' critique of natural law arguments derived at once
from this denial of the infinite powers of reason and from Catholic ideas
of just what a natural law is.[23] Following the Thomist tradition, they
argued that the natural order is first and foremost teleological rather
than mechanical; it is a cosmos, a meaningful and evolving totality, not
a sum of masses and forces. The nature of a given being is thus defined
as the ensemble of its essential qualities, those that are proper to it and
lead to its perfection and that can only be known through the observation of its development. Man's history shows him always in society;
from this one may conclude that society is *necessary*, that is to say, *natural* to man, it is a *law* for man, as is everything necessary for the conservation of society. Society here *is* man's "state of nature," it is not something one may choose. There is no natural man prior to society on
which to model timeless universal legislation, for it is society that
makes man, not man society.

On the basis of this claim that human nature is a product of institutions, the conservatives rejected social contract theories and thus the
constitutional projects of the Revolution. Society, they argued, necessarily implies sovereignty, because sovereignty represents the very
unity of action and of will that defines every society. Because sovereignty is necessary to society (and hence to man), it cannot be the product of voluntary agreement. Law cannot be the will of all, the product
of majority opinion, since it is to be the rein on all wills and opinions.
Neither is the constitution of a nation to be found in its written laws,
for what is written today may be erased tomorrow, but rather in the ensemble of its mores and traditional usages. In short, the constitution is
the product of tradition and history, not of rational deliberation.

Concordant with their idea of society as a well-ordered cosmos, conservatives find the proof of the illegitimacy of revolutionary democracy
in its instability, excess, and disorder. This instability leads to a self-
centeredness, a protection of one's own, and morality becomes only a
private affair. Democracy in practice thus becomes an unlimited despotism: reason, norm, and justice are only what the sum of egotists called
"the people" wants at a given time. This lessening of the social authority of established norms entails an increase in the reliance on force to
maintain and apply the law. The individual and the authority of the

state thus grow hand in hand. By destroying all the traditional institutions intermediary between these two poles, the new regime has become more tyrannical than the old.

Such are the main outlines of the traditionalist argument. We now turn to individual variations on these shared themes in the work of three major traditionalist philosophers: Bonald, Lamennais, and Ballanche. A rapid overview of their social and historical ideas will both flesh out the unity and variety of French traditionalism and allow us to better understand Maistre's place within it.

Bonald, Lamennais, Ballanche

Of all the counterrevolutionary philosophers of social order, Louis Gabriel Ambroise, vicomte de Bonald (1754–1840), was the most systematic and consistent. In his work society is always treated in historical terms, and history is always structured, sometimes extremely so, by the necessities of society. After a brief survey of Bonald's social ideas, a few words will be said about his interpretation of the French Revolution and the limits it reveals within his version of traditionalism.[24]

Bonald describes social order as "the union of like beings by laws or necessary relations, a union the goal of which is their production and mutual conservation." Necessity and conservation are the key terms in both this sentence and Bonald's philosophy as a whole. What he calls a social law is precisely a necessary relation, one that "could not be otherwise without disturbing the nature of the beings concerned." The sum of these necessary relations is conserved in a nation's constitution.[25]

A constitution is for Bonald irreducible to an abstract code or even to government in the narrow sense. It is a society's way of life, its deep structure, a unity prior to any particular administration.[26] Before any given law, the constitution holds a nation within necessary limits, preventing the emergence of "political monsters," political "giants" and "midgets," tyrants and their playthings (Bonald, *Théorie* 324). Constitution is a normative concept for Bonald, a body not of statutes but of mores. It is civil society's principle of unity.

The task of civil society is to conserve fallen man, a task both political and religious. Because civil society is much more a grouping of minds than of bodies, its unity must be found in the intellectual sphere, in religion. Religion conserves intelligent man by "repressing his depraved volitions"; politics conserves physical man by "repressing the exterior action of those depraved volitions" (Bonald, *Législation primitif* 75). Religion clearly has the primary role. Without it there would be no duty, no reason for obedience. Religion is thus "the fundamental con-stitution of every state of society" (Bonald, *Législation primitif* 141).

Because all societies are by definition established for the general rather than a particular good, every society is a "republic," a *res publica*. Only the misguided eighteenth century has limited this name to the popular state, the one in which "each is most occupied with himself, and where all are least concerned with the public" (Bonald, *Législation primitif* 231–32). Society cannot do without unity of power, however, and in democracies it is found in majority will. Yet majority decisions can create only political statutes, not the necessary relations that are truly law. Democracies thus lack a constitution.

Lacking a general order, democracies lapse into egoism, a constant "state of war or invasion of property" that goes by the name of com-merce. With the bourgeoisie ("sometimes those of the best standing") concerned with profit rather than virtue, "one has before one's eyes, in reality and without metaphor, the hideous spectacle of a band of sav-ages" (Bonald, *Théorie* 423). The enlightened legislation of the eigh-teenth century has thus been fundamentally misguided: its social order of individual reason guided by self-interest is "a blindman led by a cor-rupt judge" (Bonald, *Théorie* 431).

Against these misguided assumptions Bonald brings the claims of history. History for Bonald is a unitary and structured process, a lawful development of given principles, the gradual perfection or constitution of society according to its truth. For tradition is precisely the sum of those truths that history has confirmed while shedding all mistaken and harmful opinions.

Such philosophy of history leads Bonald to extreme monist conclu-sions. As tradition is identified with the general, fundamental, and nec-essary truth, there is ultimately only one tradition, only one true phi-losophy, shared by all men in all times and places despite their errors and ignorance. "Every modern doctrine that is not as old as man is an error," partial and sectarian (Bonald, *Législation primitif* 8). By breaking from the necessary truths of tradition (notably the Catholic monarchy), the French Revolution assures its fruitlessness, for a new constitution is a contradiction in terms.

In Bonald's writing apocalyptic tableaux of revolutionary scandal abound. France, "the center of Europe and the bosom of civilization," has fallen into total anarchy spread from a corrupt city "once the first town of the universe": "there will be no place on the whole surface of this vast empire that is not the theatre of a crime, no man who is neither victim nor accomplice." If the European powers do not perform their duties of conservation, the "final catastrophe" will begin, the end of society as a whole (Bonald, *Théorie* 397–400). The Revolution does have a value for Bonald, however, as it must for every traditionalist who identifies truth with history: to test empirically the so-called values of the Enlightenment. He describes the Revolution as a "crucible" in which those values "have melted away like a light fog." It proves the inadequacy of human reason before the forces of tradition and social necessity (Bonald, *Théorie* 391).

The repressive tendencies of such an argument emerge in its reduction of history to a single necessity, on the one hand, and fruitless revolt, on the other. History thus becomes a reserve of quasi-geometric political truths. The "parallel" between political and geometric truths is indeed "perfectly exact": just as there is no circle without a center, there is no society without a king, no intellectual order without God. "This truth is as evident as the propositions of Euclid" (Bonald, *Théorie* 49–51). This picture differs radically from Maistre's picture of society as an acentric structure defined by its margins; where Bonald seeks a social statics, Maistre finds a social dynamics.

In Bonald's identification of history and reason, each of them bearers of the same single truth, we find the positivist dimension of traditionalism and its resemblance to right-wing Hegelianism: what is, is true, is necessary; what is not is false and ultimately impossible. This is the legitimation strategy of conservatives of all stripes and parties: to pass from the description of a state of affairs to its prescription. Ultimately only one constitution is possible for Bonald, where law, truth, order, necessity, tradition, unity, monarchy, Catholicism, and the good of society are all identical.

Here one might wonder how much of a "traditionalist" Bonald really is. His emphasis on the stable self-identity of social forms severely downplays the mutability of historical tradition. In its insistence on system, Bonald's thought always focuses on an arrested object, and historical dynamics can only appear as transgression. He thinks only of those elements that make up a stable and uniform society and of the bad that results from their absence. Society as a well-constituted and self-identical system would have no history: Catholic monarchy is eternal, and only nonconstituted societies have histories in the dynamic sense of the word, as they struggle toward this eternal form.

The rigidity of Bonald's doctrine severely limits its modern relevance. While he laid some of the foundations of what later became sociology (see below), his insistence on a single possible political form does not speak to a situation in which that form has become obsolete. He thus offers us little for understanding a specifically modern political life, even from a critical perspective. That traditionalism does have a critical potential becomes clear in the next figure on our itinerary, Félicité de Lamennais.

Lamennais (1782–1854) thought Bonald the greatest philosopher of his day. He borrows and develops Bonald's social perspective on religion, his insistence on social and religious unity, the universal truth found in tradition, and his often Manichaean conception of politics.[27] To this he joins an interest in the irrational bases of authority derived from an enthusiastic reading of Maistre. For our guiding concern with the historical significance of traditionalist thought, Lamennais is crucial for how he carried over a consistently traditionalist set of ideas from a defense of Catholic monarchy to the invention of Catholic socialism and liberation theology.

Where Bonald is chiefly concerned with structures of power, Lamennais emphasizes the structure of authority and the moral order that supports it. His insistence on the priority of intellectual to political order is thus more forceful: "No government, no law, no order would be possible, were men not previously united in bonds which already constitute them in a state of society . . . by common beliefs conceived as duties; and this spiritual society is the only true one, for no other, without this, can establish itself or subsist."[28] Lamennais's theocratic position is found in his argument that political order requires moral order, and moral order in turn requires an unquestionable religious authority. "Everything man has made he can unmake. . . . Every durable legislation, like every legitimate power, descends from heaven."[29]

Laws, in short, demand sanction. The certitude of the law rests on faith in authority, on obedience of the will rather than rational comprehension. It is thus religion that "makes the government gentle and strong, and the people free and submissive."[30] In its absence, politics is reduced to brute power, to a state of unending war between sovereign and subjects, without any higher guarantee or criterion of justice.

Lamennais has not the least confidence in regimes founded on the principle of enlightened self-interest. No idea is further from the obligations toward others on which society must rest. In a passage from *Essai sur l'indifférence* that reveals the full pathos of his prose and the abidingness of his social vision, Lamennais describes how, under the rule of self-interest, democratic fraternity is thoroughly subordinated to liberty in pursuit of one's own happiness:

> One invents a thousand pretexts to exempt oneself from helping the suffering. To give alms to a beggar is to favor vagabondage, idleness. Is he hungry, naked? Let him work. But he is old: at all ages one can find something to do. He is a child: do not support his laziness, it's never too early to combat vicious habits. She is a mother charged with a large family: she says so, but is she telling the truth? Before gratifying a few liars, one must make inquiries: one does not have the time. (Lamennais, *Essai* 1:40)

The sciences themselves demonstrate their charity by determining how little a person can live on. Finally, one puts the poor behind bars, out of sight and earshot, "taking away the liberty of those who have nothing left" and "treating as criminals those whose only crime is to suffer" (Lamennais, *Essai* 2:401).

This general reign of indifference reflects a drastic loosening of the bonds that link the person to society, a decline of moral authority that results in both social and intellectual disorder. The only alternative is a return to the certainty of tradition, a common consent resting not on rational argument but on faith. Lamennais here rejects the rationalist Cartesian tenor of eighteenth-century Catholic apologetics much more thoroughly than does Bonald. Tradition alone, the testimony of all times and places, provides religious certainty. Tradition indeed perfects religious truth: "each dogma is the occasion of a particular heresy, for it is required that all be proven and consolidated. The proofs multiply themselves with the objections, and Christianity develops all of a piece" (Lamennais, *Essai* 1:xix). Tradition is thus the sufficient proof of Catholicism, since eighteen centuries of a consistently false belief would be "the most extraordinary, the most inexplicable moral phenomenon imaginable" (Lamennais, *Essai* 1:212–13).

How then account for Lamennais's eventual break from throne and altar politics? His political radicalization was the result of the very intransigence of his traditionalist position, his refusal to compromise with a compromised monarchy and papacy. He passionately indicted what he saw as the feeble, irresolute, and unfulfilled character of the Bourbon Restoration, too willing to compromise with the incompatible. Lacking the political and religious culture of the traditional Catholic monarchy, the Restoration is an empty fiction. Kingship is merely "the inscription from an ancient temple placed on the façade of a different, completely modern building. . . . France is nothing but a vast democracy" (Lamennais, *Essai* 2:ii–iii). From this morally bankrupt monarchy, Lamennais turned to the papacy as a guardian of tradition and came to place his hopes for Catholic regeneration in the people rather than the government. He thus broke with the political counterrevolution independent of any liberal inspiration. He supported his shift of allegiances with arguments drawn from Maistre's *Du pape*, of which he was one of the only early defenders, precisely during his struggles first with the Bourbons and then with the papacy.

Lamennais was scandalized by the French clergy's cleavage to the so-called Restoration, a misalliance threatening total mutual collapse that must be resisted at all costs. "To endure everything, rather than abandon the least part of the doctrine that Christ sealed with his blood."[31] No matter how ill-disposed toward Gallicanism, however, Gregory XVI was little inclined to "endure everything." The language of apocalyptic salvation had gone out of style with a return to throne and altar as usual and a desire for maintaining its welcome stability. Again, Lamennais was scandalized by tradition's compromise with the new society: "there is no more papacy."[32]

He now likened Rome to the synagogue of Christ's day, in need of a new Gospel that would preach social redemption. The voice of this new creed was to be sought in the general reason of the people, now judged to be a higher authority than the compromised Church. The unrelenting logic of Lamennais's position thus drove him steadily to the Left. His demand for human redemption from the thinglike existence of modern society remained a constant, but salvation now came to be sought not in the preservation of kings but in the progress of peoples. Christianity would underwrite revolution rather than reaction. Redemption, however, remained a notion that derived all its meaning from the traditions of the early Church. Lamennais now came to identify the republicans of his day with the most ardent of Christ's first disciples. While demonstrating his allegiance to the liberal cause, this comparison cuts both ways: the model for a legitimate society was always for him the moral purity of the early Church.

Lamennais's guiding desire for complete community, moral purity, and religious unity sometimes led him, like Bonald, to ignore the needs of individuality and the right to differ. "Constitution, laws, mores: there is all of society. . . . Mores finish what other laws began, and put in order secret actions most independent of human justice, by regulating everything in man, even his thoughts and desires" (Lamennais, *Es-*

sai 1:278). Here the understanding of social mores seeks only to uphold
a monolithic social order. Lamennais often goes so far as to define difference from this order as madness: "madness consists of preferring
one's own reason, one's individual authority to the general authority or
to common consent."[33] Yet on this argument, from the perspective of
present day liberal-democratic common sense, traditionalists like
Lamennais themselves would be the very embodiment of those "sick
minds, intelligences in delirium, monstrous beings that no longer belong to the universe," whom he dubs "mad" (Lamennais, *Essai* 2:30). If
there is only one possible norm, a unitary tradition outside of which lies
depravity, then either modernity is simply madness or, if not, that
norm cannot account for it.

Lamennais and Bonald are both limited in their response to post-
revolutionary society by their acceptance of only an unchanging, single, and absolute tradition. Neither Bonald's system nor Lamennais's
passion is flexible or perhaps ironic enough to match the new dispensation. Ballanche, our third traditionalist, is extremely flexible. His tradition would be as plural, mutable, and relativist as possible, while still
remaining essentially one. It would be so, however, without the very
least tinge of irony.

In the work of Pierre-Simon Ballanche (1776–1847), traditionalism
becomes romantic. As a philosopher Ballanche was most significant as
a relay between what are commonly viewed as incompatible intellectual positions: the philosophy of history and language, neo-Catholi-
cism and Neoplatonism, liberalism and utopian socialism, Orientalism
and theosophy. He was himself a tireless expositor of an allegedly single and identical truth of all philosophy. He has thus been described as
the great exemplar of "that vast romantic heterodoxy . . . which grafts
onto the Christian trunk a literature of religious synthesis, of human
progress and universal redemption."[34] As a preparation for reading
Maistre, Ballanche's heterodoxy is highly relevant, yet one must hesitate to apply the title of synthesis where that of pastiche might be more
fitting.

Ferdinand Denis, a mutual friend of Lamennais and Ballanche,
noted in his journal that Lamennais "reads everything, he gladly reads
an almanach, but he could never read Ballanche." Denis himself describes Ballanche, piquantly but appropriately, as "a melange of Fénelon and the Incas."[35] In fact, Ballanche attempts to amalgamate the
work of Vico and of Bonnet, an equally unlikely mixture. From Vico,
Ballanche borrows (to use a kind word: Ballanche himself was quick to

charge others with plagiarism) the ideas of the three ages of history, of history as a study of languages and symbolic practices, and of myth as the key to prehistory. Vico's great contribution for Ballanche was to have demonstrated "the marvellous and indefinable cosmogonic and synthetic faculty" of all languages.[36] Vico's explanation of history as a product of successive misunderstandings, however, he rejects as atheistic, and he attempts to correct it with odd borrowings from Maistre and Lamennais, Herder and the Schlegels, and above all Bonnet. The Swiss nature philosopher had argued that a person attains perfection through the development of spiritual "germs" that are the imperishable element within each individual's bodily frame. Ballanche extends this claim from the individual to society and thus attains a vision of history as progressive spiritual perfection or gnosis.

Ballanche's central historical idea is that of providential progress through human tribulation. History is suffering. Yet suffering is the source of progress, not the result of obstacles to progress as the Enlightenment had maintained. World history is the history of humanity's fall and rehabilitation, a gradual process of redemption through successive trials and expiations. Where Bonald sees history as the perfection of constitutions, Ballanche sees a history of gnosis, of illumination and eventual return to Adamic powers. History is a series of initiations, "each initiation preceded by a trial, and every trial inflicted as an expiation" (Ballanche, *Essais* 17).

Ballanche envisions history as a progress across dichotomies, as a passage from fall to redemption, through trial and expiation. Thus man passes from Orient to Occident, patriciate to plebianism, fatality to will, destiny to providence, pessimism to optimism, potentiality to act, diversity to identity, from "the force of things" to "the generation of human destinies," in short, from traditionalism to liberalism (Ballanche, *Essais*, 62f.). The great trial and expiation that prepares this new age of a redeemed humanity is of course the French Revolution.

Where those one might call "traditional traditionalists" sought the long-term origins of the Revolution and agonized over its unforeseen end, Ballanche understood it as bloody but brief, an unprecedented catastrophic birth yet a crisis that has wholly passed. Initially he believed the Restoration of 1814 to be the beginning of a redeemed history, the end to all struggles; after 1830, he remarked that the Restoration failed its mission "in trying to make the initiation retrogress." Now it is with the revolution of 1830 that "a great social deed has been brought to conclusion; we have aged an entire palingenetic cycle."[37] Whatever the date, the crisis has passed, and the bonds with the fallen and now irrelevant past have been completely broken.

Such an interpretation allows Ballanche to neatly resolve the intellectual conflicts of his day. Traditionalist social theory has its truth, he argues, but it holds only for the past, for tradition. It is progressive social thought that is true of the future and of the present that is already a part of that future.[38] For having failed to embrace these glad tidings, Maistre (whose work on sacrifice Ballanche rifled in the act of condemning it) is but an "impious Jew of the ancient Law" (Ballanche, *Essais* 197).

The pains of history as a process of expiation are over. We now await the initiation that will culminate our rite of entry. "In effect, we march toward a time when the identity of cosmogonies will be proven. . . . Are we destined to re-create this history, are we called to reassemble with a thousand pains the lost science?" (Ballanche, *Essais* 41). In effect, yes. Although the painful passage from past to future has been completed, a poet is still required to preach the new dispensation. For it is always poets who are the founders of nations, "but only those who are instructed in the profound mysteries of morality and politics" (Ballanche, *Orphée* 5:100). Ballanche is plainly the man for the job. He is to be the modern Orpheus or, more modestly, the modern Dante (with Madame Recamier as Beatrice), or, once again, a latter-day Saint John: "I am there, I am the solitary of Patmos. I know myself the interpreter . . . of a tribe which is the elite of the human species."[39]

Much of his work as initiator into the new social mysteries, playing Christian to Maistre's Jew, consisted of giving happy endings to classical tragedies. This is how he substitutes the reign of providence for that of destiny. The lives of Oedipus and Antigone indeed represent the trials and expiations of humankind, but the plot of their stories must be rearranged to comply with progress, not with old Sophocles' vengeful fate. Ballanche's biographer comments: "To this end, certain changes had to be made. The Sphinx is not a monster to be exterminated, but a divine creature. Oedipus did not die; he disappeared from the summit of Mt. Cytheron. Hemon, of course, could not commit suicide, nor could the long-suffering Antigone be submitted to the garotte."[40]

Ballanche self-consciously set out to adapt tradition to modern needs. His eclectic vision shared none of the unbending monism of a Bonald or a Lamennais. Like them, however, if from an inverse angle, he sees no tension between ancient and modern, no grounds for a mutual questioning of tradition and modernity. By relegating every conflict, impasse, and aporia to a bygone past, Ballanche loses not only their tragic sense of human finitude but also their critical perspective on the present. Much of Ballanche's "modernity," highly touted of late,[41] is simply consent to a new order other traditionalists refused, a replacement of criticism with complacent sentiment. Traditionalism does not so much become modern in Ballanche; it becomes kitsch.

Conservatism and Critique

"Morasses, however noxious they may seem, have, nevertheless, very important uses."[42] What Chateaubriand says here of amphibians and reptiles must be asserted as well of the early-nineteenth-century conservatives; unattractive as they often are, they play an ineluctable role in the life-world of modern thought. The pertinacity of their claims must now be addressed and some provisional conclusions hazarded, prior to a more expansive treatment throughout the work on Maistre.

Pareto informs us that "to characterize dangerous men, given over to wrong-doing, there used to be employed the terms *heretic* and *God-accursed*; in our day such men are labelled *reactionaries*."[43] Pareto, identifying with this tradition of excluded thought, seems to exult in these charges. In doing so, he reveals both the force and the dangers of conservative critique. To grasp the specific dangers of counterrevolutionary ideas, it is useful to distinguish between the threats these ideas posed as criticism of a newly established order and those that result from unyielding insistence upon the older dispensation, that is, between conservatism as the quite literally fugitive discourse of social outsiders and as the belief system of an entrenched dominant class. It is in their fugitive and critical guise that the early conservatives remain modern, both in their creativity and their dangers. This is simply common sense: the relevance of a defense of a given state of affairs disappears with the state of affairs it defends. The abiding significance of early conservatism is to be found, first, in its criticisms of the then emergent and now established order of liberal capitalist democracy, and, second, in its general theory of society and history insofar as this theory is something more than a defense of the now virtually extinct class of the French nobility. As is only proper, let us begin with these positive contributions before considering their limits.

Tradition is an idea necessary to any historian. Downplayed by the Enlightenment, the continuity and legitimacy of the historical tradition was the cornerstone of the conservatives' argument. The development of a specifically historical way of thinking, of the idea that history has a force and logic of its own, was in large part the work of those opposed to the universalizing tendencies of the Enlightenment. Where the Enlightenment, pursuing its task of rational criticism, would judge the legitimacy of a given state of affairs by reference to universal norms that transcend it, traditionalism judges it according to its derivation from the past or, as Bonald would put it, its process of constitution.

The concepts of order, cohesion, dependency, status, norm, symbol, and ritual, all central to any sociology, are all conservative ideas, ideas that refer to conservation and that were elaborated initially by conservatives. Out of these elementary concepts were built up the idea that society is something more than an aggregate of persons, something prior in history, logic, and morals to the individual; the idea that social phenomena are necessarily interdependent, not to be treated in isolation but always within the constellation of historically given beliefs, customs, norms, and institutions; and finally, the idea of the fundamental value of the sacred, nonrational, nonutilitarian aspects of social existence. This latter contribution has been stressed by Robert Nisbet in his work on conservatism. Nisbet, like many modern sociologists, however, tends to emphasize the "usefulness" of this nonutilitarian dimension for the maintenance of social order. The traditionalists themselves argued not that a thoroughgoing rationalization would be unproductive but that it would be ultimately impossible.[44]

The traditionalists were among the first to identify the social with the political realm. Although we may well disagree with their conclusions, they insisted early in the nineteenth century that customs and habits, gender and family relations, religion and economics are all political questions. They further recognized that such social institutions are not merely superstructural elements but rather fundamental social forces, that the symbolic makes up a significant part of any social infrastructure. The philosophical opponents of the French Revolution, moreover, were obliged to approach the question of social chaos more than the supporters of the Revolution, who either did not see the chaos so sharply or felt less threatened by it. In their sense of the closeness of the arbitrary, of violence and excess, shielded only by an ensemble of habits, mores, and dogmas, the early conservatives opened the highly modern thematic of man's capabilities for disorder as a being always on the brink of disequilibrium.

Traditionalist thought shows us children of the nineteenth century our origins at their most august and sovereign moment already rebuked, scoffed at, and explained. Its lasting significance in the history of political philosophy was to have subjected the new order, which would soon become as bent on order as the old, to a fundamental critique at the very moment of its charismatic emergence. The role of a certain French *delicatesse* in the formation of socialism is hinted at in Lamennais's remark, a propos of the contribution of the aristocratic to the popular critique of capitalism, that "the vice of the bourgeoisie, its smallness, narrowness, paltriness and ridiculousness, was always strongly felt among us. Elsewhere one was not shocked at all, so that this meaning of the word 'bourgeois' would be untranslatable."[45] And so it has remained. Traditionalist thought should be understood not only as a failed attempt to reenchant a bygone politics, as is usually the case, but also as an effort to disenchant the charismatic triumphalism of the new regime.

The second generation of philosophical and social conservatives inspired by the traditionalists was among the first to call for the organization of labor against capitalist exploitation. This call was voiced, with varying emphases and motivations, by Lamennais, Berryer, Tocqueville, Veuillot, Chambord, Le Play, and Durkheim. All of them defended a society of corporate groups with collective rights and duties, at a time when the guild system had been abolished and unionization was still illegal. The early conservatives broke with the tradition, stretching from Hobbes to Rousseau and culminating in the Le Chapelier Law of 1791, which held that society is made up of the individual and the state, nothing more, and proscribed every intermediary institution that would come between them to limit the free intercourse of citizen and government. The traditionalists dampened the celebration of this new-found freedom by attacking individualism and "statism" as mutually implied developments.

What Nisbet claims of Bonald may be said of the traditionalists generally: they "must be seen as the first of those attacks upon the conception of the unitary state which were to become so distinctive in the nineteenth century." Nisbet, writing in 1944, went so far as to see traditionalism as a prophecy of the ever-present danger totalitarianism would offer to democracies.

> It is a commonplace that the totalitarian leader flourishes among the rootless, undifferentiated mass, among aggregates whose customary relationships of family and religion have been attenuated and destroyed. The issue that totalitarianism has raised is not simply that of freedom versus authority. Authority any society must possess. The issue is between a society in which the maintenance of social order

shall be a function of free social groups, and one in which all authority is concentrated in the state, democratic or otherwise.[46]

The traditionalists provide a critical perspective not only on this sociological background of totalitarianism but also of its privileged ideologies, those of nationalism, charismatic leadership, the uses of terror,
and overweening faith in technology and rationalized management.

The general question addressed to the new order by the traditionalists is that of when the rationalization of politics advocated by the Enlightenment becomes an *over*rationalization itself culminating in irrational excesses. They stress the limits of the project of Enlightenment,
its inevitable fragility, against the dangerously implacable faith in Reason's infallibility. In particular, they offer a biting critique of the Revolution's ideal of transparency, of a "pure political reason" wholly adequate to political reality. Against this ideal, the conservatives uphold
the categories of the concrete, the lived, the historical. Often, they confront higher reason with its low others: unreason, the organic, violence, the peasantry with its coarse religion and mores.

As Mannheim explains in *Conservatism*, conservative thought "represented the first opposition to capitalism's spiritual universe, and takes
to itself all the psychic and spiritual contents which would be displaced
if the bourgeois/rationalist world were to rule alone" (67). Against the
depersonalized and alienating tendencies Mannheim believes common
to capitalism and modern rationalism, he stresses early conservatism's
"almost empathetic experience of the concrete" (*Conservatism* 88). "The
repeated insistence, by Marx and others, on the abstractness of human
relationships in the capitalist world was originally the discovery of early
estate-based Conservative thought" (*Conservatism* 90).[47] Marxists and
traditionalists use the term "concrete" in rather different senses, however. Among the former it refers to the economic order and the class
struggle that takes place on the basis of its contradictions, whereas among
the latter it is presented as the social unity founded upon mores. Yet it is
significant that both do seek the "concrete" reality of sociopolitical life in
the relations among men and not in the relation between man and the government, as is the wont of liberal political theory.

This revaluation of early conservative thought has its limits however, both philosophical and practical. First, conservatism generally
does not aim at the eradication of *all* illusion and reification but insists
on the maintenance of those that support order. It may be that man cannot live without illusions of some sort, that his status as the political animal is intimately bound up with being an animal capable of illusions,

but the determined teaching of a one-sided illusion is philosophically unacceptable (to anticipate, the almost extravagantly hybrid character of Maistre's thinking will locate him in this problematic far from the "average" conservative).

In the sphere of practical politics, the conservative criticism of mass democracy presupposes a responsible and rational conservative ruling elite (as does the liberal-democratic defense of enlightened government by elites). This supposition was quashed, by and large, by the machinations of monarchists within the democratic framework of modern French politics, by MacMahon and the "Moral Order," by Maurras and the Action Française, and even as early as the Restoration with its appropriation of Napoleonic techniques and agents (Falloux, Fouché) of surveillance and control. Conservatives here become the very image of the extremists and schemers they denounce among the democrats. It may be argued, though, that they thus cease to be traditionalists, *philosophical* conservatives, to become political conservatives who accept the bases of the new order's political worldview.

In the eyes of history, what has compromised early French conservatism more than anything else is its posterity. Two moments of their inheritance in particular, while often serving in condemnations of the tradition of the French Right, may also begin to show its complexity: the Restoration and the Action Française.

The Restoration initially understood itself as a providential new beginning, a starting up again of what always should have been. As Remond explains, "France, washed of her Jacobin contamination and restored to her true Christian and royal inclinations, was going to learn again to love its princes."[48] In 1814 the Revolution might well have seemed an utter failure, a temporary aberration returned to normality with the reestablishment of legitimate authority. The Restoration could do little, however, to reverse the Revolution's social, cultural, and economic transformation of France, so that much of the Right was correct in observing that Louis XVIII mounted the throne of Napoleon, not of the Bourbons. Those most unhappy with this situation and most loyal to the ancien régime formed the bulwark of the Ultraroyalist party, the Ultras, among whom, however, there were deep-seated differences between the intransigent (La Bourdonnaye) and the liberal (Chateaubriand), the Catholic (Lamennais) and the anticlerical (Montlosier).

The Ultras, or the Legitimists as they were also known, thus began in opposition to the king and the Charter; their slogan, indeed, was

"Long live the king in spite of himself" (Remond 37). In this period it
was the liberals who called for increased royal power, while the Ultras,
now in the majority, called for greater power of parliament. The Ultras'
political bases were primarily the aristocracy and clergy, but these were
plainly a minority; the Ultras, however, "always felt they could count
on the lower classes which had remained sound, as against the commer-
cial bourgeoisie or the liberal professions which were quite infected
with the Jacobin spirit" (Remond 59). Only the royalist Right sought
an extension of the franchise. One of the more able historians of the
Restoration thus feels able to remark without the least irony that "it
was to the happiness of *all* the subjects of the king of France that the
counter-revolutionaries methodically consecrated their efforts."[49] The
Left was hostile to the extension of suffrage to women and to peasants,
who, it was believed, remained hostages of the priesthood. And indeed, in the still largely traditional society of the West and the Midi, the
Ultras hoped that the highest and the lowest classes would again make
common cause against their common enemy, the middle classes. This
populist strategy was abruptly dropped by the Legitimists after the
success of the plebiscites of Napoleon III. Maistre, who witnessed the
first years of the Restoration with great consternation, shared the Ultras' allegiance to the Catholic royalist ideal. Yet he thoroughly derided
their romantic picture of the old regime, their populism, and especially
their all-or-nothing, us-versus-them political style. He was perhaps
less the first of the Ultras than the first of their critics.

What has tainted the French conservative tradition above all else is its
supposed culmination in the twentieth-century fascist sympathies of
the Action Française, the Ligues Patriotes, the Faisceau, and the Croix
de Feu. These political forces, however, only took up the phrases of the
counterrevolutionary tradition in a piecemeal fashion, borrowing the
most fervent expressions while putting aside what was fundamental
and fundamentally incompatible with their views. In fact, traditionalism and fascism were in many important ways antithetical.

Relations between traditional conservatism and emergent fascism
were anything but cordial. One finds occasional alliances between
them in the years after 1900 in times of crisis, as one does between Social
Democrats and Communists. Yet both parties were strongly conscious
of the gulf that separated the traditionalist Right from the radical and
populist Right that emerged in the late nineteenth century. The hostility of traditional French conservatives to the amalgam of nationalism
and socialism offered by fascist politicians has been well described by

Sternhell: "Respectful of forms and legality, detesting agitators, particularly proud of their respectability, they were concerned above all with preserving the existing structure of society."[50] Destruction of the given order at any cost is a position a traditionalist cannot accept without ceasing to be a traditionalist or even a conservative in the traditional sense of the word.

This antagonism was mutual. Thus the ardent nationalist Maulnier wrote: "Conservative, now there's a word that's bad from the start. We are not the splendid young people that have been hoped for, the 'milice sacrée' that the traditional right hopes will arise so it will be able to prolong the age of horses and carriages, to defend Tradition, Property, Family, Morality."[51] Fascism affirms the new, the modern (although in a grotesquely distorted form), the age of youth and electricity, not traditional custom. Thus for Drieu La Rochelle, "a monarchist is never a true fascist. . . . A monarchist is never a modern: he does not have the brutality, the barbaric simplicity of a modern."[52] Certainly, there was very little aristocratic about the fascist leaders in comparison to an FDR or a Churchill, who were far more traditional in their political appeal.

Demagogic charisma is altogether incompatible with the foundation of legitimacy in tradition, seeking it instead in the alleged will of the people. In this it depends on the revolutionary heritage as Bonapartism had. Of this it was well aware. Thus Valois explained that, "with regard to the movement of 1789, it is a tremendous mistake to think that fascism opposes it, misconstrues it, and seeks to reverse it. . . . We continue the movement of 1789 with the cry *Down with Parliament! Long live the Nation!*"[53] Fascism's nationalist and antiparliamentary doctrines are absent from traditionalism (totally so from Maistre, a senator and the son of a president of one of the *parlements* of that hybrid kingdom Piedmont-Sardinia). The royalism espoused by the Action Française, writes Remond, was "another royalism with only the name in common" with the royalisms of the nineteenth century (237). Indeed, Sternhell again and again insists that it was precisely the abiding strength of the traditional Right into the twentieth century and its adherence to parliamentary government that most impeded the growth of a popular fascist movement in France; throughout Europe it was the weakness of the conservatives, their readiness to panic and to place their destinies in equivocal hands, that "proved to be the essential precondition for the success of fascism. This situation, however, did not exist in France" (118).

The Limits of Traditionalism

One fundamental liability for conservatives, despite all their talk of the concrete, is the danger of a fundamental loss of reality brought on by a denial of change in a world that does change. The category of the concrete itself becomes an abstraction when the given, the fact of a given tradition, is raised to an absolute status. This insistence on how things are and were lapses into idealism. The fact becomes an idea, a value: the fact for its own sake. This is the mental posture proper to conservative politics as a rearguard action. The raising of an idealized situation to transcendent heights tends to encourage an undervaluation or ignorance of the day-to-day concrete needs of most people, particularly of those damaged by the order, authority, and hierarchy conservatives so adamantly defend.

In this sense, one can say that traditionalism does not remain a merely theoretical assertion of the existence of some eternally self-sustaining tradition. Rather, it represents specifically an awareness that tradition has ceased to maintain itself and a project to resuscitate it. It is a choice against modernization, an ideological project of traditionalization veiled under the claim of timelessness. As well as a theory, traditionalism is the tactic of a political and cultural elite that finds itself in a defensive position and wishes everyone to act in a traditional way, in deference to their traditional superiors. This is the source of the activist, even violent kernel of all traditionalism, its inherent counterrevolutionary tendency. Even when remaining at a distance from White Terror, it seeks by means of the "force of tradition" (reinforced by police powers) the same quiescence that Terror brings.

Yet these voices from the past do remain of no small significance for a present that only grants a reality to the individual, a reality that society ostensibly lacks. Modern scholars are only recently coming to understand the Western subject as a social and historical product, the construction of a relatively recent constellation of forces. This tendency to question the premises of individualism—the subject's autonomy, timelessness, and self-mastery—is evident in structuralism (for which, however, the sociohistorical production of meaning disappears in the prestidigitations of the combinatory) and in the current critiques of psychologism, substantialism, and presentism in favor of a theory of the *ensemble*. The apogees of contemporary theory and of traditionalism seem to touch at many points: in their mutual interest in the "structurality of structure," their search for a fundamental anthropology and theory of culture, their study of social representations, myth, and ideology, and finally in their blurring of the lines between the social, the cultural, and the political. In both one can observe the exotic mythological coloring that marks all new beginnings.

What I have meant to stress is the value of the conservative tradition for *knowledge*, not for politics. This tradition has opened up all these intractable questions only to close them, the sooner the better. The mutual shaping of society, language, and history is only posited to be subordinated to *this* society, to some norm embodied only in this one society (the Catholic monarchy of the ancien régime). To remain productive, this thought must be maintained in its moment of openness and indeterminacy. To argue that the order of society is more significant than the liberty of the individual is at once the foundation of conservative practice and the necessary first step of any critical social theory. While the latter must argue that society is prior to and determinate for the individuals within it, it cannot accept the claim of many conservatives (and not a few Marxists) that these individuals are wholly reducible to social determination: practical political dangers aside, such a complete reduction would imply an impossibly complete knowledge of the social, or a closure and covering over of the aporias that society poses for knowledge.

The following chapters seek to contribute in a small way to a rethinking of the historical and modern import of philosophical conservatism. They do so by presenting Maistre as one of the first, following Vico, to propose an anthropology of European culture and to provide a critical theory of ideology grounded on cultural anthropology. If he remains significant for our age, it is because he thus offers us not just another oppressive ideology of order but an understanding of how ideology and social order work, in often uncanny, troubling, and oppressive ways. Let us now at long last turn to Maistre's thought, beginning with what he believes to be the dynamic basis of all social order, sacrifice. We will find that here, where one would expect the greatest danger, is announced something enlightening in the fullest sense of the word.

Chapter 2

Sacrifice

That others should have shown, and still show, the same attitude of rejection surprises me less. For *little children do not like it* [Goethe] when there is talk of the inborn human inclination to "badness," to aggressiveness and destructiveness, and so to cruelty as well. – Freud, *Civilization and Its Discontents*

Why should a modern historian speak of something so archaic and so unpleasant as sacrifice? A first clue is offered by Hegel, who, one year after Maistre's death, told us that "the slaughterbench at which the happiness of peoples, the wisdom of states, and the virtue of individuals have been sacrificed" is *history*. Hegel's philosophy of history is laden with sacrificial overtones, notably his very idea of the dialectic as negation of the negation, simultaneous cancellation and preservation, through which Spirit enters the world and the horrors of history take on a higher meaning. Yet in Hegel the "most fearful picture" of the "monstrous sacrifices" of which history is made remains merely a "panorama" to be "contemplated." Left unanalyzed, the notion of sacrifice continued to inflect modern thought in highly questionable ways.[1]

Thus such an otherwise careful thinker as Merleau-Ponty was able to defend Stalin's show trials by placing them within an historical dialectic that is frankly sacrificial. His premises are indeed wholly Maistrean: "Inasmuch as we are incarnate beings, violence is our lot. . . . Violence is the common order of all regimes." Every politics, he argues, rests upon an imposition of values that entails violence against the bearers of other beliefs. Stalin's trials thus become a ritualized staging of this founding violence. The only question then becomes whether the future history of Russian communism will redeem this ritual violence shared by every regime: if it creates a lasting society, it will have become acceptable. There seems no suspicion that a regime begun in this manner could never become legitimate. The example of Merleau-Ponty's *Humanism and Terror* shows the power of the idea of sacrifice both to disrupt comfortable political assumptions and to encourage an uncritical acceptance of political violence as somehow possessing a higher meaning.[2]

More broadly, sacrifice has served as a guiding theme of modern po-

litical discourse, especially among advocates of a return to stability, order, or unity. Nineteenth-century German reactionaries did not hesitate to take up the vocabulary of sacrifice (blood, soil, and devotion) in
the interests of the Fatherland and a politics based on victimization.
Needless to say, little philosophical reflection accompanied this victimization, which was hardly holy. French conservatism too played upon
the terminology of sacrifice, above all with regard to the regicide, yet
this remained largely a rhetorical device suited to the politics of the Legitimist party or to the reveries of romantic primitivism. Neither has
the liberal tradition proved immune to the charms of sacrificial language. Thus Constant: "Friends of liberty . . . Liberty is fed by sacrifices. Restore the power of sacrifice to the exhausted race which has lost
it, . . . give them the strength to become martyrs."[3] Herzen, disgusted
with all this talk of political devotion, drew the conclusion that "to subordinate the individual to society, to the people, to humanity, to the
Idea, is merely a continuation of human sacrifices, . . . of the crucifixion of the innocent for the sake of the guilty."[4] If such is the case, however, one wonders if we are left with any alternative. This is Maistre's
question.

Yet the idea of sacrifice has guided not only ideologists but also
many a modern intellectual seeking to understand the power of ideology, myth, and religion to shape social action. The sociology of religion became one of the grand genres of nineteenth-century thought, as
writers from Vico to Freud sought the origin of society in sacrificial rituals. Late-nineteenth-century British anthropologists gave special attention to sacrifice in their efforts to explain the origins of religion.
Thus Tylor, placing it within an animist context, understood sacrifice
as a gift, a propitiation or inducement of the ruling spirits. Robertson
Smith, in his work on primitive Judaism, approached sacrifice as a form
of communion conducive to the establishment of social bonds, unity,
and solidarity. Frazer, who did most to popularize interest in archaic
life, viewed sacrifice as a form of sympathetic magic that aimed above
all to induce fertility or to defuse evil influences.

All these late-nineteenth-century models treat sacrifice as a more or
less socially efficacious form of masquerade and imply the absurdity of
the beliefs it implies. One is tempted to say of all of them what Wittgenstein said of Frazer: "his explanations of the primitive observances
are much cruder than the sense of the observances themselves."[5] The
rehabilitation of ancient religious beliefs and practices as bearing truths
still relevant to the modern age was the accomplishment of Durkheim

and his followers. Until the emergence of the Durkheim school, however, no one treated the subject of ritual violence so seriously as did Maistre, for whom the theory of sacrifice formed a basis for all his social and political meditations.

Sacrifice and Social Theory

The study of sacrifice is equally relevant for cultural historians concerned with the social role of symbolic processes and for cultural theorists concerned with ideology, both interested as they are in the binding nature of collective representations. For nowhere so much as in sacrifice do we witness the power of ideas over life. In sacrificial rituals commingle the daily life of society and its ultimate values, social order and the order of representations, violence and religion in such a way that the latter shapes the former.

Cultural historians have recently come to emphasize the ritual dimensions of popular culture: the festivals, riots, and carnivals of early modern Europe. Sympathy for traditional thoughtways displaced by modern life and a desire to reawaken the critical potential of popular culture, however, have continually run up against the existence of ritual barbarities, notably the formation of social unity through victimization. Nothing, Maistre tells us, has been so popular or so universal in human history as sacrifices: a remark to give any populist pause.

Cultural theorists, in turn, speak often nowadays of "the life-world of the sign" to describe the sphere of ideological influence. Yet for the world of signs to have life it must be brought in contact with the living. This is one reason why sacrifice can be "good to think." Indeed, ideology would perhaps be powerless without its sacred aspect of incomprehensible compulsion. Without sacrifice and the mysteries of state that surround it, Maistre argues, every nation would topple. Because sacrifice makes sacred, it may be understood as a legitimation process. It confers the awe and veneration proper to power and sanctions the legitimacy of existing institutions by bringing them into contact with what society holds highest.

Sacrificial rituals first of all serve to establish an order of distinctions within society: distinctions between sacred and profane, high and low, pure and impure, inside and outside, norm and transgression. They thus set up a world of human culture, a habitus distinct at once from the order of gods, the order of animals, and the order of divine or bestial violence. Equally essential, they proceed to stage a representation of the proper relations between the terms thus distinguished.

As Lévi-Strauss has emphasized, the theory of sacrifice is a theory of social dynamics. Sacrifice is a moment of social metamorphosis that reestablishes the bonds between individuals by way of a periodic transgression. Maistre, we shall see, is far more attentive to this dynamic moment than to the stases that precede and follow it; this will be one significant mark that distinguishes him from his fellow conservatives. The sociology of the sacred introduces that disorderliness of historical dynamics into the overly neat categories of classical anthropology and political philosophy. The sacred is inextricably bound up with, because it serves to interpret, what is disorderly, transitional, and excessive in social experience, giving it meaning and form.[6]

This is the reason why the transition from nature to culture is so commonly described as a sacrificial purification, whether it is a matter of purifying a community by way of a scapegoat or of purifying meat or flour by fire. Vernant, in his account of Greek sacrificial techniques, thus informs us that "once roasted or boiled, a lump of raw, bloody meat is transformed into a civilized dish."[7] Sacrifice here appears as the primary form of acculturation, of humanization, of education as "flesh become spirit." It is precisely this transfiguration of raw violence into legitimate dominion that will be the primary theme of Maistre's history of constitutions.

Maistre's approach to these questions was veritably sociological. While his study of religious practices was by no means neutral or detached, its sociological thrust was to show that religious behavior is not strictly dependent upon overtly religious *contents* but is rather a universal *form* of social action. He pays surprisingly little attention to purely religious questions. His writings emphasize, on the one hand, the *religious forms of social life* found in sovereignty, punishment, war, and revolutions and, on the other, the *social forms of religion*, the public handling, staging, and managing of these socioreligious forces.

The sociological significance of a theory of sacrifice is confirmed by Durkheim in what is possibly his masterwork, *The Elementary Forms of the Religious Life*. Durkheim begins by defining the chief subject of his book as follows: "Rites are a manner of acting which take rise in the midst of assembled groups and which are destined to excite, maintain, or re-create certain mental states in these groups."[8] Like Maistre, he argues that all rituals are at least in some distant sense sacrificial: "there is no religious ceremony where blood does not have some part to play" (Durkheim 137).

For Durkheim the chief function of the rite is one of group cohesion, of centering individuals' attention upon their shared traditions, ideals, and beliefs and thus of fostering the intellectual unity on which society depends. While rites and ceremonials "strengthen the bonds attaching the believer to his god, they at the same time really strengthen the bonds attaching the individual to the society of which he is a member, since the god is only a figurative expression of the society" (Durkheim 226). Durkheim indeed argues that the sacred world is a displaced image of society itself. Yet this is not to treat religion simply as a delusion; as he and his followers never tired of remarking, sacred things are social and therefore real.

Religious practice thus expresses the truths of society. Durkheim admits that religion may err, but he adds that these errors could "never perpetuate themselves unless they were true practically," unless they served as reliable guides for proper social action (137). Durkheim closes his account by extending this argument to such a point that one cannot hesitate to call it traditionalist. Altogether in the manner of a Bonald, a Maistre, or a Lamennais, with only minor changes in vocabulary colored by the dominant neo-Kantianism of his epoch, Durkheim writes that "a collective representation presents guarantees of objectivity by the fact that it is collective: for it is not without sufficient reason that it has been able to generalize and maintain itself with persistence. If it were out of accord with the nature of things, it would never have been able to acquire an extended and prolonged empire over intellects" (437–38). This reappearance of a traditionalist defense of religion at the conclusion of one of the foundational texts of contemporary sociology serves to lead us, at long last, into the very heart of Maistre's philosophy.

Sacrifice is a subject that must trouble any defender of the truth of collective traditions, be he a Durkheim, a Maistre, or a multiculturalist. The traditionalist argument meets its limit in ritual slaughter, which anyone would hesitate to describe as good or useful. This dilemma that sacrifice thus poses for the traditionalist position is precisely what drove Maistre to the subject. His manner of confronting the question is worth the closest attention of anyone concerned with cultural traditions or human violence, namely, all of us.

The Laws of Violence

This chapter provides a close reading of an often neglected essay, "Eclaircissement sur les sacrifices" (Enlightenment on sacrifices), which provides a key to Maistre's philosophy as a whole. Written concurrently with *Les Soirées de Saint-Pétersbourg*, sometime between 1808 and 1810, this brief essay works out in a highly condensed manner some of the most problematic questions raised in his masterwork. It unites in a single knot the sum of Maistre's essential concerns. It engages the discourses of physiology and psychology, comparative anthropology and patristic theology. Among cited interlocutors, Homer, Plato, Hippocrates, Augustine, Origen, Pascal, Voltaire, and William Jones figure prominently. The issues addressed in the essay ramify outward to inform all the central themes of Maistre's thought: sovereignty, capital punishment, war, revolutions, the origins of civilization, political theology, myth, and the ways of Providence. Each of these subjects will be considered in subsequent chapters.

The logic that Maistre finds in sacrifice goes roughly as follows. Human existence is of its nature imbalanced, excessive, disproportionate, ambivalent. This is what it is to have a body, blood, life. Thus body, life, and blood are spent to redress imbalance, excess, and disproportion. This moment of expenditure, however, must have its measure if it is to restore good order, and that is the social role of ritual. Regardless of human intentions, however, the balancing continues. That human violence has its measure: this was Maistre's guiding idea on religion, law, history, and politics; more, it was his basic theoretical assumption that disorder has its logic and is thus capable of being understood.

For all its logic, however, there is no denying the equivocal nature of his essay. The very title is something scandalous. Its jarring juxtaposition of the seemingly opposed terms "enlightenment" and "sacrifice," of the progress of reason and ritual slaughter, seems an oxymoron meant to provoke. Yet, one must observe, it provokes both the "party of Enlightenment" and the "party of sacrifice." First, it plainly represents a challenge to "Enlightenment" to account for facts that must utterly appall it and seem to fly in the face of its most basic assumptions about human life. Second, however, it also represents a revealing of secrets, shedding light on the most carefully hidden "truths"; it is not what Nietzsche would call "priestly" writing but an audacious intellectual project.

The first chapter of the essay, "Of Sacrifice in General," begins with the deep problems raised by sacrifice for the traditionalist argument. The religious traditions of humanity, which must embody truth, give us a rather dim view of the religious life. The scandal is this: everywhere man has been terrified of the gods and done violence in their name. How could this tradition be true? Maistre's first words inform us that he rejects "the impious axiom" that it was fear that gave birth to

the gods. On the contrary, cultic ceremonies have always made use of
"all the agreeable arts," to a point that the word *festival* has become a
synonym of *happiness*. And yet, Maistre continues, "one must avow,
after having assured orthodoxy" (such necessary assurances commonly
mark the first sentences of Maistre's works), "that history shows us
man persuaded in all times of that frightening truth: that he lived under
the hand of an irritated power, and that this power could only be appeased by sacrifices."[9] From the very start, then, sacrifice is referred to
power (and not, say, to grace).

This belief in the efficacy of sacrifices "suffers no exception in time
or place. Ancient and modern nations, civilized or barbarous, epochs of
science or simplicity, true or false religions, there is not a single dissonance in the universe." With regard to an omnipresent practice such as
this, "the grand words *superstition* and *prejudice* explain nothing; for a
universal and constant error has never been able to exist" (Maistre, *Soirées*, OC 5:125–26). Sacrifice thus must have its truth.

Yet how can the horrific belief of "HEALTH THROUGH BLOOD" be
labeled true, what can it have to do with a beneficent deity? "These
doubts present themselves at first to all minds," Maistre observes.

> However, when one examines it more closely, something quite ex-
> traordinary happens, that is, the very absurdity of the thing, as it pre-
> sents itself at first, begins to render it likely: one cannot help asking
> oneself, "How could an opinion so revolting, at least at first glance,
> have become the belief of all men; perhaps it is supported by some
> reason of which we are not aware." And this initial doubt soon
> enough leads to reflections that turn the mind in a totally opposite di-
> rection.[10]

This opposite direction leads away from religion proper to reflections
on the nature of life in general and of human life in particular, but-
tressed as always by reference to ancient wisdom. If the belief in sacrifice "suffers" no "dissonance," its universality responds to the equally
universal discord we call life.

The truth of sacrifice is to have taken up and channeled "the general
law that weighs upon the universe," the law that subjects living beings
to violent death and is found "at the very frontiers of life": "How many
plants die, how many are killed! . . . A force, at once hidden and palpable, shows itself continually occupied with bringing to light the principle of life by violent means" (Maistre, *Soirées*, OC 5:22). Every genus of
life thus has its animals "charged with devouring others: insects of prey,

reptiles of prey, birds of prey, and quadrupeds of prey. There is not an instant of duration in which a living being is not devoured by another. Above all these numerous races of animals is placed man, whose destructive hand spares nothing that lives. . . . Supreme and terrible king, he needs everything and nothing resists him" (Maistre, *Soirées*, OC 5:22–23). Man "needs" butterflies on pins and embalmed animals for his museums, gut for harp strings, the bones of whales for virgins' corsets, elephants' tusks for children's toys: "his tables are covered with cadavers." Maistre here mercilessly reveals the violence, "at once hidden and palpable," upon which rest the most innocent of human occupations: knowledge, music, beauty, play, and nourishment (*Soirées*, OC 5:23).

Perhaps what is most startling in these remarks is Maistre's uncanny insight into the existence of suffering in nature, a pain that in no way corresponds to the common Catholic ascription of suffering to sin as its just amends. For what does the cow make amends? For man, for his community, Maistre answers: animals are, in this vision, innocent victims of man's will to power. Maistre's position, here as elsewhere, is very much influenced by his enthusiasm for Alexandrian Christianity, which, in its ascription of souls to plants, animals, and planets, emphasizes man's responsibility to nature for having occasioned a cosmic Fall (more on this below). Yet, here as elsewhere, Maistre brings what is most arcane into contact with what is most modern: an awareness of man's destructive nature that, we will see, leads him toward an ethic of the minimization of violence.

Does this law of violence stop at man? "No, without doubt. But who will exterminate he who exterminates everything? Him. It is man who is charged with slaughtering man" (Maistre, *Soirées*, OC 5:23). Applying this idea to European institutions, Maistre will be able to relate cultural types as apparently disparate as kings, priests, soldiers, and executioners. Maistre's "general law" truly is general in the sense that it provides a picture of the world that includes an economy of losses as well as gains, a law that finds an order within excess, a structure that includes both norm and transgression and that rests on no harmonious foundation.

Man has a special place within this general economy of violence, one that defines his very existence and makes of him the being who performs sacrifice. What then is man? As all the ancients attest, man is culpable, culpable for having fallen into duplicity: "upon this dogma were founded all the general institutions." Man's fallenness or "degradation" is above all found in his "thingness" (*réité*). The "root" of this thingness resides "in the sensible principle, in life, in the soul finally, so carefully distinguished by the ancients from the spirit or intelligence."

This talk of the *root* of *life* as a *thing* hints that what is at question is the Gnostic dualism of sacred mind and profane matter, a dualism that is here quickly bridged by the Catholic doctrine of the soul, which Maistre characteristically supports by reference to pagan authors: "Antiquity did not at all believe that there could be, *between the spirit and the body*," that is as much as to say, between the sacred and the profane elements of man, "any sort of bond or contact; in a manner that the *soul*, or the sensible principle, was for them a variety of proportional means, or intermediary power." Thus the mind according to Lucretius was "the soul of the soul," to Plato following Homer "the heart of the soul" (Maistre, "Eclaircissement," OC 5:285–86).

This double nature of mental life, Maistre argues in a manner redolent at once of traditional theology and of modern psychology, accounts for all of man's contradictions, all the ambivalence of his desire. To this effect he cites Plato's example of Leontius, who "absolutely wanted to see a cadaver he absolutely did not want to see" (Maistre, "Eclaircissement," OC 5:289n). Such remarks are evidence not of a mere taste for paradox on Maistre's part but of a stubborn attempt to understand the contradictions of human behavior. For having ignored how we are "continually agitated by two contrary forces," Maistre tells us elsewhere, "Locke was able to write fifty pages on liberty without even knowing what he was talking about" (*Soirées*, OC 4:303–4).

What is at stake is the nature and sway of human ambivalence. It is a matter of explaining not simply changefulness, how "a simple subject is capable of such sudden variations," but equivocality, "how a single simple subject can love both good and evil, love and hate the same object, desire and not desire, . . . in a word, how a simple subject can be not simple" (Maistre, "Eclaircissement," OC 5:289–90). Maistre's explanation starts with a citation of Origen, a not altogether canonical figure who holds a special place in his thought. In Origen's words, man incorporates "two souls, the one good and celestial, the other base and terrestrial," and "this soul of the flesh resides in the blood" (Maistre, "Eclaircissement," OC 5:290).

> What then is this "soul of the flesh," this "power" that contradicts man, or, better, his conscience? What is this power that is not *him* or not *all of him*? Is it material like stone or wood? In that case it neither thinks nor feels, and, by consequence, it cannot have the power to

trouble the mind in its operations. I listen with respect and terror to all the menaces made against the *flesh*; but I ask what it is. (Maistre, "Eclaircissement," OC 5:290–91)

Maistre notes in passing that Descartes, "who doubted nothing, is not at all embarrassed by this duplicity of man." For Descartes man has only one soul whose substance is at once "sensitive and reasonable"; what leads one astray is the agitation of the pineal gland by the vital spirits, an explanation Maistre finds "amusing" (Maistre, "Eclaircissement," OC 5:291). Here we begin to see that Maistre's discussion of the human body is not aimed at a biological explanation of violence. The argument from the body is less Darwinistic than Platonic: it does not so much naturalize violence as emphasize how unnatural the body is. The body is considered not as the cause of sacrifices but as what makes us subject to them, what makes the body capable of sacrifice, which is our constitutive duality.

Maistre now makes the following statement, remarkable for a purportedly obedient Catholic, in tacit reference to Origen's condemnation as a Gnostic: "I am not unaware that the doctrine of the two souls was condemned in ancient times; but I do not know if it was done by a competent tribunal" (Maistre, "Eclaircissement," OC 5:294). Maistre himself rejects the doctrine of "two intelligent principles of the same nature, of which one is good and the other bad"—such a claim would be Manichaean, a position he resolutely avoids (we shall later see why); "but that the intelligence is the same thing as the sensible principle, or that this principle, which one calls the *vital principle*, and which is *life*, could be something material, absolutely denuded of knowledge and consciousness, is what I will never believe" (Maistre, "Eclaircissement," OC 5:294–95). Or rather, he says with a bow to papal authority, he will not believe it unless he is contradicted by "the only power that has a legitimate authority over human belief," for while he now has "only the *certitude* of being right, I would then have the *faith* of being wrong" (Maistre, "Eclaircissement," OC 5:295). To have the faith of being wrong, however, is not to give up one's opinions.

Having thus reassured orthodoxy, Maistre returns to the wisdom of the ancients, where he finds the idea of a vital principle informing their sacrifices: "It is upon this *animal power*, upon *life*, upon *the soul* (for all these words signify the same thing in ancient language) that falls the malediction avowed by all the universe," for, as the irreproachable source of Deuteronomy informs us, the principle of life, life itself, is blood. "The life of the flesh is in the blood; that is why I have given it to you, that it may be shed on the altar for the expiation of your sins; for it is by the blood that the soul shall be purified." The effect of this biblical citation is hardly canonical, however, as Maistre treats the quotation as an example of hidden Eastern wisdom, which he sets beside modern medicine: "It is a most singular thing that these ancient oriental traditions to which one has paid no attention, have been resuscitated in our days, and upheld by the greatest physiologists" ("Eclaircissement," OC 5:297).[11]

What this ancient wisdom tells us is this: "heaven, irritated against the flesh and the blood, could only be appeased by blood . . . no nation has doubted that there was in the effusion of blood an expiatory virtue" (Maistre, "Eclaircissement," OC 5:300). To explain this belief in an "expiatory virtue," Maistre turns from the question of the human body to the "logic" at work in sacrificial ritual.

The doctrine of sacrifice, he argues, everywhere rests upon the two intertwined notions of substitution and reversibility, namely, that one life may be substituted for another and that innocence may compensate for guilt. "Men have never doubted that innocence could render satisfaction for crime; and they have believed, moreover, that there was an expiatory force in the blood; in a manner that *life*, which is blood, could pay for another life" (Maistre, *Soirées*, OC 5:125). Blood here appears as an abstract equivalent, as what men have in common among themselves and with animals (Maistre's treatment of the topic of blood thus differs from racist theories of national purity) and therefore what may serve as the principle of exchange within the sacred economy. As the terms "render satisfaction," "pay for," "compensate" make plain, the relation of man to God is understood as one of debtor to creditor. The gift of innocence compensates the debt of culpability. "The entire theory rested on the dogma of reversibility. One believed (as one has believed since, as one always will believe) that *the innocent could pay for the guilty*; from which one concluded that life being culpable, *a less precious life could be offered and accepted for another*. One thus offered the blood of animals" (Maistre, "Eclaircissement," OC 5:300–301).

Maistre is well aware that not just any animal will do as a sacrificial victim, that the choice of a victim always follows a clear rationale. The logic of substitution demands that, in order to render satisfaction for human culpability, the animal victim must itself be related to the community that seeks expiation. At the same time, this logic demands that the victim not be too closely identified with the social group so that it may fulfill its role of deflecting violence outside. The victim, then, must be at once alike to and different from man, within and without the sacrificial community, marginal in short, if it is to fulfill its role as a representative of the community. Thus one never immolated

> carniverous or stupid animals, or those foreign to man, like the wild beasts, the serpents, the fish, the birds of prey, etc. . . . One always chose those animals most precious for their utility, the most gentle, the most innocent, the most related to man by their instincts and habitudes. Not being able, in sum, to immolate man to save man, one chose among the animal species the most *human* victims. (Maistre, "Eclaircissement," OC 5:301–2)

Of the two terms, "reversibility" and "substitution," reversibility holds the primary place, both as a moral and a theoretical assumption. Absolutely fundamental to Maistre's argument is the symmetry of fall and redemption, curse and blessing, culpability and innocence. It is this symmetry or balance that for Maistre provides the ultimate measure of the human world, an order of legitimate norms, power, and authority. It is always upon this delicate balance of high and low, purity and impurity, glory and abjection that institutions are built. For norms and institutions would have no place in a world in which there were no measure between culpability and retribution, innocence and blessedness (even Job was tempted to deny the legitimacy of his situation!). The notion of reversibility counters the Gnostic apocalyptic that would deny any blessedness, any "good order," to this cursed world.

Yet the primacy Maistre gives reversibility is not merely misplaced moralizing. It is reversibility that allows the general law of violence to be a law, that gives violence its economy. Before the system of substitutions can be instituted, much less understood, the general order must have its coherence. The law of reversibility grants this coherence by making the general order self-compensating, as every excess is necessarily counterbalanced. Reversibility thus serves as a basic premise of Maistre's position, not so much argued as demonstrated, first in reference to religious traditions and then in its application to history.

Pushed to its limit, the idea of reversibility tends in Maistre's thought to encourage a "counterapocalyptic" vision, in which reversibility becomes reversion or even remedy. Thus the indefinitely repeated application of this principle will result in the "death of death," the reduction to a zero sum, to an ultimate balance or correspondence of debts and payments, faults and expiations (altogether analogous is Freud's idea of the death-drive's ultimate reduction to naught of all those tensions that are life). This is in the "last analysis" the telos of that "general law" of violence with which this discussion was begun.

> Thus is accomplished without cease, from maggots to man, the great law of the violent destruction of living beings. The entire earth, continually steeped in blood, is naught but an immense altar where all that lives must be immolated without end, without measure, without pause, until the consummation of things, the extinction of evil, unto the death of death. (Maistre, *Soirées*, OC 5:25)

Such immoderation and excess, such expenditure without reserve, constitute for Maistre the ultimate order of being, history, and society alike.

The second chapter of "Eclaircissement sur les sacrifices," entitled "Of Human Sacrifices," sets out to explain how the truths of substitution and reversibility were "corrupted" to give rise to this "horrible superstition" of killing people to save people. "One would like to be able to contradict history when it shows us this abominable custom practiced throughout the world; but, to the shame of the human species, there is nothing so incontestable" (Maistre, "Eclaircissement," OC 5:305–6). Here we are at the heart of the scandal: a universal tradition that is absolutely appalling. Maistre finds the habit of sacrificing children, wives, and strangers in Egypt, India, Greece, Rome, Carthage, Mexico, Peru, and Europe up to the eighth century "until it was put down by the divinely guided hand of immortal Charlemagne." "The immolation of human victims, the very idea of which makes us blanch, is natural, however, to natural man" (Maistre, "Sur les délais," OC 5:452). This "naturalness" of human sacrifice, it will soon be plain, is a matter not of instinct but of an "implacable logic" that misapplies the necessary axioms of substitution and reversibility.

As a thoroughgoing traditionalist, however, Maistre must argue that every religious tradition has its truth. Thus, while denouncing the spectacles of slaughter enacted by the Romans, "who watched men be killed to kill time" (Maistre, "Sur les délais," OC 5:455), he claims that human sacrifice is preferable to absolute impiety (ultimately because absolute impiety provides no bounds to bloodshed). Moreover, this degraded custom could only derive from a tradition and thus from a truth; it could never be an individual's invention. "In making abstraction of every antecedent idea, the man who would have proposed to immolate another, in order to render the gods propitious, would have been put to death as a response, or locked up as mad: one must thus al-

ways depart from a truth to teach an error" (Maistre, "Eclaircissement," OC 5:310). Human sacrifice, then, must be an example of the
general traditionalist claim that "strictly speaking, man never adopts an
error. He can only ignore the truth or abuse it; that is to say, extend it,
by a false induction, to a case to which it is foreign" (Maistre, "Eclaircissement," OC 5:306).

What truth then is it, the false induction from which accounts for the
"shocking error" of killing men to save men? It is the doctrine of reversibility itself. Because culpability is compensated by a proportionate
dose of innocence, the greater the innocence or "humanity" of the victim, it was thought, the greater the compensation. "In vain did reason
say to man that he had no right over his own kind, and even that he attested it every day in offering the blood of animals to buy back that of
man: in vain did gentle humanity and natural compassion lend new
force to the arguments of reason: before this stirring dogma, reason remained as powerless as sentiment" (Maistre, "Eclaircissement," OC
5:305–6). It is, however, precisely a process of rationalization, of *sophis-
try* before which reason has shown itself powerless. Two sophisms in
particular have been responsible. The first considered "the importance
of the subjects from whom it was a matter of diverting the anathema.
One said 'to save an army, a city, even a great sovereign, what is a
man?'" The second sophism extended the "particular case of the two
varieties of human victims already consecrated [or sacrificed: *devoué*]
by the political civil law; and one said *what is the life of a criminal or an enemy?*" (Maistre, "Eclaircissement," OC 5:306–7).

In Maistre's understanding, as I shall emphasize in the following
chapter, the enemy and above all the criminal are sacred beings for a society, marginal men at once within and without its confines who are
immolated to society's well-being by the executioner or the soldier in
his "priestly" function. They are sacred because they serve to bind the
community; the breaking of the social covenant by the criminal places
society in a position of default with regard to its gods, thereby incur-
ring a debt that must be satisfied, an imbalance that must be harmonized. The criminal thus instills social bonds by binding society to
compensation. "The first human victims were criminals condemned
by the laws. . . . The ancients believed that every capital crime committed in the state *bound* the nation, and that the culprit was *sacred* or devoted to the gods, until, by the effusion of his blood, he had *unbound*
both himself and the nation" (Maistre, "Eclaircissement," OC 5:307).

One hundred years before Durkheim, Mauss, or Freud, Maistre's meditations on capital punishment and human sacrifice led him to an understanding of the radical ambivalence of sacred forces:

> One sees here why the word "sacred" (*sacer*) was taken in the Latin language in good and bad part, why the same word in the Greek language signified equally what was holy and what was profaned; why the word "anathema" signified at the same time what is offered to God as a gift, and what is delivered to his vengeance. . . . "Sacred" signifies, in the ancient languages, what is surrendered to God, for whatever reason, and which thus finds itself *bound*; in a manner that the torment [the punishment] *desacralizes, expiates,* or *unbinds,* just like religious *ab-solution.* ("Eclaircissement," OC 5:307–8)

The religious in Maistre's usage is precisely what is thus bound (*rélié*); the immolation of the culprit as a gift to God transforms what is dangerous or poisonous to society into the source of its unity. It is thus that a society retains its health. For Maistre it is inevitable that the little violences that pervade society be deflected onto some culprit (*coupable*) or at the very least onto someone who is strikable (*coupable*).

Ideally, this sacrificial tendency should be rigorously channeled into duly constituted religious and penal rituals.

> Unfortunately, men being penetrated with the principle of "the efficacy of sacrifices proportionate to the importance of the victims," from the culprit to the enemy was but one step: every enemy was culpable [*coupable*], and, unhappily again, every stranger was an enemy when one had need of victims. This horrible public law is only too well known; thus "Hostis," in Latin, signified equally at the same time *enemy* and *stranger.* (Maistre, "Eclaircissement," OC 5:309–10)

In this brief description of the doubly unfortunate intellectual slippage from stranger to enemy and from enemy to culprit one finds a powerful analysis and critique of social victimization. The stranger, no longer simply outside the community but not yet an insider, combines (like the poor, the "parasite," the pariah) actual spatial proximity with the greatest figurative social distance—a relation that is a nonrelation. Lacking organic connections, he may be done violence without tearing at established social bonds, yet his proximity allows him to be blamed for social ills.

Maistre very much indicts this paranoiac form of social order, described again and again as "horrible" and "abominable." He shows that the foreigner's threat to the in-group's fundamental values is not a fact but a representation produced by an overly zealous social order: the transition from difference to antagonism is not the work of the stranger. Embedded in this analysis seems to be an inherent criticism of the identification of group unity with the good and of the newcomer with the bad or dangerous. Scapegoating, the victimization of difference, will be a primary object of Maistre's political criticism; it is always the result of a sacred economy gone haywire, whether it is a matter of the Aztecs or Marat. The sacred—what is fundamentally other or marginal to a society, at once within and without it, irreducible to society's rational categories and the object of radically ambivalent reactions, channeled by institutions that are thus necessarily quasi-religious or binding—appears in Maistre's work as an eminently political category.

Maistre, to continue our exposition, identifies the Latin *hostis* with the French *hôte* or visitor—the stranger who is victimized. "The *hostis* being thus an enemy or a stranger, and under this double regard subject to sacrifice, the man, and thus by analogy the immolated animal, was called *hostie*. One knows how much this word has been denatured and ennobled in our Christian languages [i.e., *hôte*, Eucharistic host]" (Maistre, "Eclaircissement," OC 5:310n). This will be the great contribution of Christianity to politics, its secular legacy: the denaturing and ennoblement of the unavoidable and unavoidably ambivalent relation to the other. The third and final chapter of Maistre's essay, "The Christian Theory of Sacrifice," is concerned precisely with how sacrifice is denatured and humanized by the "Christian graft."

Maistre's thoroughgoing traditionalism cannot but place the Christian belief in divine salvific crucifixion within the context of a comparative understanding of religions. "The Christian Theory of Sacrifice" indeed begins with the question, "What truth is not found in paganism?"; its first third is concerned with paganism alone (Maistre, "Eclaircissement," OC 5:335). Maistre insists that not only the crucifixion but all the sacraments were anticipated by non-Christian peoples: the comparative study of religious ritual reveals "the eternal forms of a positive religion that is found everywhere. The modern voyagers have found in America the vestals, the sacred fire, circumcision, baptism, confession, and, finally, the real presence under the species of bread and wine" (*Soirées*, OC 5:61). An accompanying note adds that "nothing is truer than this assertion" and specifies that "in Peru, the sacrifice consisted of the *Cancu* or consecrated bread, and in the *Aca* or sacred liquor, of which the Incas and their priests drank a portion after the ceremony"

(Maistre, *Soirées*, OC 5:73). What Maistre will call the Christian "graft-
ing" or domestication of sacrifice is already at work in other societies,
where he finds all the sacraments in place.

Christianity thus seems to have added little to the basic repertoire of
religious life. If anything, it represents a reduction of the traditional diversity of rites, a reduction that "disengages this universal sentiment
[religiosity] from the crimes that dishonored it" (Maistre, "Eclaircissement," OC 5:326). Maistre by no means argues that Christianity derives
from other cults—this would be to step out of the Catholic frame of
reference altogether—but rather that all religion shares a common origin and even that Christianity and the variety of pagan or primitive religions serve as mutual confirmations of one another's truth. Thus, as he
writes in the *Soirées*, Christianity "justifies" the general doctrine of antiquity, that is, "the prophetic cry of the human species, announcing
health through blood." "The innate and radical dogma did not cease to
announce the great sacrifice that is the basis of the new revelation. . . .
This revelation, shimmering with all the rays of truth, proves in its turn
the divine origin of the dogma we constantly perceive as a luminous
point in the midst of the shadows of paganism" (Maistre, *Soirées* OC
5:127). This prophecy, innate to the species, makes of man something
more than a passive recipient of divine lights. Here, one of the few other
places he mentions the Christian passion and one of the only places
where he does so in his own words rather than citations from Origen or
Paul, the religious is everywhere related to the human.

Maistre reiterates the essential role of sacrifice in establishing an order of values. The first service of religion is to show to man, "isolated in
the universe and unable to compare himself to anything," "how much
he cost." The sacrifice of the god himself demonstrates "the enormity
of the crime that demanded such an expiation; the inconceivable grandeur of the being that could have committed it; the infinite price of the
victim who said *here I am*" (Maistre, "Eclaircissement," OC 5:126). The
inconceivable grandeur of man that required to redeem it an infinite
price is emphasized all the more when Maistre cites Aeschylus's Prometheus, who cries out "Look at me, it is a God who has made a God
die"; the application of this pagan text as a gloss on Golgotha makes
man, not the Father, the god who had Christ be killed. Man, perhaps,
was what was revealed when the veil of the temple was torn and "the
great secret of the sanctuary was known, as much as it can be in the order of things of which we make up a part" (Maistre, "Eclaircissement,"
OC 5:126–27).

As the essay on sacrifices proceeds, Maistre argues that not only the beliefs but the practices and aims of traditional religion are retained and rectified by Christianity. Christian morality has thus certified sacrificial reversibility, the payment of innocence for guilt, but has corrected it by replacing the sacrifice of others with the sacrifice of oneself. "Under the empire of this divine law, the just (who never believes himself to be so) tries to approach his model from the painful side. He examines himself, he purifies himself, he makes over himself efforts that seem to pass humanity, to obtain finally the grace of *returning what he has not stolen*" (Maistre, "Eclaircissement," OC 5:349). Christianity makes of the willing victim, he who takes on himself the human share of violence, the exemplar of virtue. In thus "certifying" the universal dogma of reversibility, however, Christianity "does not at all explain it, at least not publicly; and we see that the secret roots of this theory much occupied the first initiates of Christianity. Origen above all should be listened to on this interesting subject, on which he much meditated" (Maistre, "Eclaircissement," OC 5:349). The passage clearly implies that early Christian theology itself sought its "secret roots" in ancient pagan traditions.

From the work of Origen, this heretic who above all should be listened to, Maistre borrows the "well-known opinion" of apocatastasis, which upholds the total redemption of all the universe, or, in Origen's words (cited by Maistre), that "the Blood spilled on Calvary was useful not only to men, but to the angels, and to all created beings" ("Eclaircissement," OC 5:349). Thoroughly in keeping with this Origenist thesis, Maistre himself writes of the Passion that "the great victim, raised to attract everything to him, cried on Calvary: All is Consummated" (*Soirées*, OC 5:126), for it was Origen's claim that Christ died off the ground in order to redeem the spirits of the air.

Characteristically progressing on dangerous ground by way of citations, Maistre next refers to Chrysostom, who "did not doubt that the same sacrifice, continued until the end of time, and celebrated every day by legitimate ministers, was performed for the whole universe" ("Eclaircissement," OC 5:351). This sacrificial interpretation of communion is further emphasized when Maistre describes the Eucharist as "divinized and perpetually immolated flesh" that perpetuates the redeeming sacrifice until the total accomplishment of its work. "Faster than lightening, the *theandric* blood penetrates the *culpable entrails* to devour their blemishes. It arrives at the unknown confines of those two irreconcilably united powers themselves, where the *élans of the heart* clash with the intelligence and trouble it" (Maistre, "Eclaircissement," OC

5:359). Again Maistre cites Origen, who asks us to "contemplate the expiation of all the world, that is, of celestial, terrestrial, and inferior regions, and see how many victims it required. . . . But the lamb alone could remove the sins of all the world" ("Eclaircissement," OC 5:352).

Origen's thesis of the redemption of the "inferior regions" was in large part responsible for his excommunication as a heretic two centuries after his death. Though this position served as an inspiration for his central ideas of the "death of death" and the autodestruction of the bad, Maistre was well aware that all these references to Origen—probably outnumbering those to any other theologian over the course of his life—could only appear questionable to the orthodoxy he was ostensibly defending. He thus qualifies yet defends his enthusiasm by citing first the upright Bossuet and then a most Origenist clause of the Catholic liturgy: "For the rest, while Origen was a 'great author' and a 'great man and one of the most sublime theologians' who have ever rendered the Church illustrious, I certainly do not intend to defend every line of his writings; it is enough for me to chant with the Roman Church: 'Both the earth and the sea, and the stars themselves, all beings are washed by this blood'" (Maistre, "Eclaircissement," OC 5:352). The question of whether this *was* enough will have to be addressed in a following chapter on Maistre's idea of Providence. Here it has only been a matter of Maistre's sacrificial reading of Christianity and his understanding of the transformation that sacrifice undergoes in its Christian appropriation.

This transformation works like a graft, making more fruitful and more human what was innate to man's social nature. "*Always and everywhere* man has immolated man; but *always and everywhere* too, from the moment when the human plant receives the divine graft, the wild stock [*le sauvageon*] lets escape its original bitterness" (Maistre, "Sur les délais," OC 5:452–53). The domesticated hybrid that Christianity makes of sacrifice, however, can only mitigate the dosage of sacred violence, not do away with it altogether, for without the sacred bonds that religion supplies society would founder into worse violence yet. Such, we shall see, are his readings of sovereignty, war, revolution, and, before all else, execution by the law.

Anthropology, Relativism, Critique
Rooted in the idea of sacrifice, Maistre's entire social theory is founded on a comparative treatment of religions that emphasizes the symbolic components of all human behavior. Undeniably, there is something in

Maistre's work of the tendency that Heine perceived in that of the Schlegels.

> These gentlemen regarded Hindustan as the cradle of the Catholic world order; they saw there the model for their hierarchy; they found there their trinity, their incarnation, their penance, their atonement, their mortification of the flesh, and all their other beloved manias. . . . In the *Mahabharata* and in the *Ramayana* they saw, as it were, an elephantine Middle Ages.[12]

This last phrase underlines the essential characteristic of Romantic Orientalism: first, a transferential misreading of cultural difference that seeks in the other the projection of one's own desires and, second, a politico-religious project of reaction. Heine finds the unity of these two tendencies in Friedrich Schlegel's dual conversion first to Calcutta and then to Rome.

It would be misleading, however, to attribute Maistre's interest in worldwide appearances of the sacred, as Heine does that of the Schlegels, to a hypocritical defense of theocracy that finds in the other only the mirror image of its own ideas. Indeed the effect of Maistre's analyses is more to place Europe itself within the global anthropological context of a comparative study of cultures than to universalize European ways of thinking to include all the world. Maistre is not an ethnographer, but he is more closely related to that contemporary phenomenon than were the supposedly more modern philosophes.

Two aspects of Maistre's anthropological argument are essential here. First, he insists on the proper creativity and truth of modes of thought that the Enlightenment considered only as evidence of backwardness, emphasizing as he does the socially productive function of cultic practices, be they Mayan or French. Here one finds the second and most significant of Maistre's contributions to anthropological thinking: his theory's claim to universality based on a comparative study of religious practices, a universality that includes Europe itself in its scope; he thus offers one of the first general theories of religion. "It was not only on the occasion of great calamities that sacrifice was offered: it was *always the basis of every variety of cult*, without distinction of place, time, opinions or circumstances" (Maistre, "Eclaircissement," OC 5:285n). In developing this line of reasoning Maistre became one of the earliest, almost a century before Nietzsche, to underline the barbaric side of the Greeks, their sacrifices and bacchanals.

There is certainly a limit to the progressiveness of Maistre's anthropology, however, and it is found in his denigration of what the Enlightenment celebrated as the noble savage. Maistre attributes this idea to precisely the sort of projection of illusions that Heine found in the Schlegels. He thus adduces two sources of the mirage: the charity of the Catholic priests' defense of local populations against the rapacious merchant armies, and the use in bad faith of savage existence by the philosophes for their own purposes of sapping the social order.

From the very start of his career as a writer Maistre took to task the picture of *natural man* painted by Rousseau, "one of the most dangerous sophists of his century, yet one of the most deprived of veritable science, sagacity, and above all depth. [Rousseau has] constantly mistaken the savage for primitive man, while he is and can be but the descendant of a man detached from the great tree of civilization" (Maistre, *Soirées*, OC 4:63). The "savage" is not the origin but the end result. Thus savage speech is to be understood not as the beginnings of a language but as "the debris of ruined ancient languages." There is surely some degree of insight in Maistre's refusal to see the isolated families encountered by Europeans in their conquered territories as universal prototypes of social existence as there is in his insistence that these people represent the vestiges of a once great and broadly based culture.

What the modern ear above all finds unforgivable, however, is Maistre's attribution of savage "degradation" to a fault committed by an indigenous leader.

> A people's chief having altered the moral principle by one of those prevarications that, following appearances, are no longer possible in the current state of things for we luckily no longer know enough to become culpable to such a point, this chief, I say, transmitted the anathema to his descendants; and every constant force being by nature accelerational because it continually adds to itself, this degradation weighing without interval upon the descendants, made them what we call savages. (Maistre, *Soirées*, OC 4:82–83)[13]

The violence of this claim of unique sinfulness is mitigated, however, by its accompanying assertion of a primitive science infinitely beyond our own that occasioned this fall: we do not know enough to be as guilty as they. Most importantly, this guilt of the savage is an extension of the process we moderns find ourselves in the midst of—the distancing from the sacred order of truth and power. Maistre agrees with de Pauw that the mound sites of the Ohio River valley point to a civilization "completely different from the current savages" but not with his claim that these monuments were thus the work of foreigners; either the first inhabitants brought their civilization with them from Asia, or these "Oriental traditions" are found at the origins of every society. In either case, we are faced with a high civilization that has drastically declined.[14]

Although such claims of a primitive fall from a previously advanced culture remain undoubtedly speculative and even mystified, they do have the merit of attributing to colonized peoples a history in scale with that of Maistre's own. In this there is some progress beyond the view, common even among anthropologists until recently, that traditional societies are somehow timelessly backward until the entrance of history alongside the colonizers. Further mitigation of the "degradation" thesis is found in the observation that Maistre was not unaware, as I shall point out below, of the depredations practiced by Europe on world cultures. While this does not wholly redeem Maistre's position, such mitigations and such an awareness were not, to put it gently, terribly common in the eighteenth century. A comparison with some of the dominant aspects of Enlightenment anthropology will help put both Maistre's contributions and his barbarities in context.

Throughout the French eighteenth century the figure of the "good savage" served either as the proof or as the refutation of Christianity, as evidence either of an innate predisposition to Catholicism or of the existence of an atheist society and a moral life free of hierarchies. In both cases, the native was taken as an image, a mythic figure that served as a stake in the game of European politics. The majority of the Enlighteners agreed that he was without history, without writing, without religion, without mores, without masters, without laws, without priests. Living prior to a social contract, savages for all their nobility could not possibly possess institutions on a par with our own. After the Jesuit Lafitau, Vico and Maistre were among the first to allow such men a society in the full sense of the term.[15]

In a controversial but powerful recent account of early anthropology, Michele Duchet has argued all too convincingly that for the Enlightenment the savage world was not an object of knowledge but the place of a practice oriented toward profit, whether material or spiritual: colonization. She argues that the alleged "humanitarianism" of the philosophes, their desire to conciliate humanity and interest through civilizing the savage and freeing him from superstition into enlightened self-interest, itself supposes the destruction of the native system and its replacement by European commerce and politics. The philosophes'

qualified criticism of colonialism, as an attempt to *remedy abuses*, served
to buttress an established order of "legitimate" and "humane" colonization. The picture of a violent savagery requisite to the needs of the
initial ethnocides was replaced by a kinder and gentler image more useful to businessmen and other assimilators who would like to *make use* of
the native populations, not destroy them. "All the texts on which one
grounds oneself in speaking of the philosophes' anticolonialism and an-
tislavery must in fact be considered as the expression of a neocolonial
politics, which serves the interests of the metropolitan bourgeoisie and
which finds in the "enlightened" fraction of opinion an immediate support."[16] It is in this spirit that Duchet reads Raynal's remark in *L'Histoire
des deux Indes* (1783) that, instead of murdering millions of Americans,
it would have been wiser "to civilize them, accustom them to work,
make them exploit the mines" (Duchet 160).

The philosophes' recourse to natural explanations of European superiority did not limit the sense of superiority itself. Thus Buffon has it
that human races "degenerate," their customs, bodies, and faces become "animalized" away from those Mediterranean climates where
one finds "the most beautiful, the most white, and the best made men
in the world" (Duchet 255). The suspicion that Western knowledge is
not omnicompetent and is capable of destruction seldom arose among
the Enlighteners.

Against this backdrop of Enlightenment anthropology, a discourse
commonly cited as the beginning of modern views of man, Maistre's
position comes to seem more open and even in some ways more reasonable. "The weakest part of French literature," he observes, "is, without
contradiction, that of travels; it is there that the most salient shortcomings of the French character reveal themselves—the furor to ridicule everything and the precipitancy of judgments" (Maistre, "Lettres," OC
7:141n). Maistre himself everywhere emphasizes the commonality of
culture and the fundamental continuity between the most exotic and
the most genteel of social rites. Indeed, the danger in his position is less
precipitancy of judgment than its contrary, a relativist respect for sacred
traditions whatever form they might take.

In a decisive passage emblematic of his ambivalent response to cultural difference, Maistre cites the Hindu practice of *pitrimedha-yaga*, or
suttee, the sacrifice of women, "martyrs to superstition," on the death
of their husbands. Typical of his traditionalist universalism, he insists
that this rite was once found among the Germanic tribes as well as
among those of Central America. After trying to account for this prac-

tice theoretically, he responds despairingly: "These horrors take place in a country where it is a horrible crime to kill a cow; where the superstitious Brahmin does not dare to kill the vermin that devour him" (Maistre, "Eclaircissement," OC 5:316–17). In this very passage, however, he shows himself highly critical of the alleged improvements brought about by the "humanitarian" aims of the English colonizers. After adding to the sacrifice of women the exposure of twins and of the decrepit, he asks,

> How could the Englishman, absolute master of these countries, see all these horrors without putting them to order? Perhaps he cries on the pyres, but why does he not put them out? Severe orders, rigorous measures, terrible executions have been employed by its government; but why? Always to augment or defend its power, never to stifle these horrible customs. . . . The despotism of free nations, the most terrible of all, too much despises its slaves to make them better. (Maistre, "Eclaircissement," OC 5:319)

Indeed, Maistre goes on to compare this forbearance of mass immolations "under the certainly very gentle and very human empire" to the relatively innocuous history of the Spanish Inquisition. The effect is to criticize the double standard operative in colonialist disdain for cultural differences by pointing out the violence underlying its "gentle" rule (Maistre, "Eclaircissement," OC 5:320n).

While these remarks do not impugn the aim of "improving" the colonized, the continuation of the passage clearly does. The result is equally ambiguous and revealing. Maistre's traditionalism leads him to question the perspective that would make of other cultures a blank slate for the inscription of Western culture; Hindu ritual practices, like all rites, play a role fundamental to local social structures, a role the modern European colonizers are in no position to understand. Yet, by the same token, the relativist or even "multicultural" thrust of his argument threatens to forfeit any rational criticism of social abuses that have become traditional. This danger is manifest in Maistre's assertion that "these atrocious sacrifices that so justly revolt us might be *good*, or at least necessary in India. . . . Would we believe that the ancient legislators, who were all prodigious men, did not have in these countries particular and powerful reasons to establish such usages?" (Maistre, "Eclaircissement," OC 5:320).[17] The equivocal nature this passage points to an ambivalence central to the anthropological encounter itself: the ethical conflict between a desire to correct the violence of traditional societies, those "horrible customs" that "so justly revolt us," and a hesitancy to judge these practices considered as integral parts of a cultural order with its own proper consistency to which the moral standards of the observer remain foreign.

The relativism inherent in Maistre's comparative study of religious ritual does not, however, lead to a nihilist result. While his generalization of sacrifice and the "law of violence" to include all social orders does indeed claim that the West and its others are fundamentally comparable, it disallows the tendency, common in functionalist anthropology, to view all traditions and all rituals as equally good forms of order or cultural integration. For the task of sacrifice is to reduce human bloodshed to its minimum, and by this it can be judged. Nor does he claim that all rites are reasonable when viewed within their proper context. Rather, he insists that social irrationality and violence may be reduced but not canceled and that this reduction is the work of symbolic action rather than reason, which must thus exercise extreme care in confronting seemingly illogical beliefs and practices whether foreign or domestic.

While I myself would argue that due respect to different cultures requires granting them the capacity to reason and to reform, a step Maistre does not take out of hostility to the project of Enlightenment, I would yet add that his awareness of the humanity of other peoples represents progress beyond the thinking of most of his more "enlightened" predecessors and contemporaries, among whom one finds colonialist ideologies but not yet the dilemmas proper to anthropology.

It is this commonality of basic elements of culture shared by all forms of society that Maistre everywhere emphasizes. Thus, in a remark salted with irony toward the antimonarchical uses of the "noble savage," he lays bare the similarity of indigenous and European cultures. The South American native "lives in society just as we do. His majesty the Cacique covers himself with a beaver skin, in place of a coat of Siberian fox; he royally eats his prisoner, instead of sending him back on his own recognizance as in our degraded Europe. But, finally, there is among the savages a society, a sovereignty, a government of laws of some sort." One would hunt in vain among many Enlighteners for such an awareness of the legitimacy or even existence of savage social structure.[18]

It is the basic commensurability of all forms of culture that motivates Maistre to write that "it would have been highly desirable for us to have a profound knowledge of savage languages," a knowledge that "would have been infinitely useful to philology and the history of man: the destructive fanaticism of the eighteenth century has made it disappear without return" (*Soirées*, OC 4:106). Or again, "the Discovery of the New World: That's the death sentence for three million Indians."[19] "We destroy these unfortunate beings with sword and alcohol. We gradually drive them into the middle of the wilderness until at last they wholly disappear, victims of our vices as of our callous superiority."[20] While Maistre's description of the "degradation" of savages devalues the ongoing development of indigenous cultures (and in this, one might add, he again anticipated modern anthropology in its nostalgia for the purity of origins as against a present fallen state), his complaint at the loss of savage languages means that there was something to be learned from them, beyond a sense of what they might be disabused, beyond the interests of enlightenment through empire.

A recent study on the sociologies of religion begins by observing that "a science of religions was the hope of the 19th century."[21] If Maistre does not quite offer us a science of religion, if he draws back from some ultimate consequences of what he began, it is due to his belief in a theology of politics, in an occult component of any political order, the ultimate possibilities of which he did not want to endanger. This theology of politics does not, however, take the direction of pointing out how men must act to accord with the teachings of religion (this is Bonald's position, which identifies social doctrine as a branch of moral theology where social truths are to be deduced directly from Scripture) but applies a sociology of the sacred to the political life of modern Europe. Moreover, this comparative treatment of the sacred dimensions of all societies brings Christianity into conceptual contact with other religious traditions, a tendency not fully developed until Renan. Finally, while obeying the taboos against revealing too much of the sacred bases of order, Maistre continually shows us the place of such forbidden territory in any sociopolitical organization.

The distance necessary to a critique of European institutions Maistre found in a detour through the comparative study of religions. The motivation for such a "return to a nearby exoticism by way of a detour through distant places," to use Certeau's phrase, may well be sought in the crisis of social and cultural representations that marked the revolutionary epoch as a moment of great indeterminacy in Western history. The language of bloodshed, horror, guilt, and devotion proliferated among both the Left and the Right from the fall of the Bastille to Thermidor and beyond. The preponderant place of violence in Maistre's writing, viewed in this context, was by no means unique or even unusual. What was unique was his effort to gain a theoretical perspective on that violence. Rather than simply reject the Revolution, Maistre treated it precisely as a sacrificial crisis that must be granted all the respect due sacred things. Before we consider his application of the theory of sacrifice to European institutions, a brief comparison with similar efforts in contemporary cultural criticism will once again underline Maistre's modern resonance.

Sacrifice Today: René Girard

The chief contemporary representative of the "sacrificial school" is without doubt René Girard, who in a series of books (notably *Violence and the Sacred*, *The Scapegoat*, and *Things Hidden since the Beginning of the World*) has argued that culture is universally founded on sacrifice and that sacrifice is above all a matter of violence.

In *Violence and the Sacred*, Girard follows Maistre in identifying substitution as the basic sacrificial procedure. He thus emphasizes how sacrifice works by a twofold substitution: first, within the community, of a "surrogate victim" for the community, and second, outside the community, of an animal or human victim for the surrogate victim; violence is thus dispelled by its condensation on the one and its displacement onto the other. Sacrifice is thus "primarily an act of violence without risk of vengeance."[22] This shunting off of violence onto a safe victim both founds society and maintains it.

While Girard cites Maistre as the one modern writer to theorize substitution, he insists that the "moral distinction" lurking in Maistre's idea of reversibility, that innocence pays the debt of guilt, "must be done away with."(!) Sacrifice is purely a matter of substitution, of the deflection of a violence that would otherwise destroy society onto a "relatively indifferent victim." As evidence of Maistre's misplaced moralizing, Girard cites his "bold and wholly unsubstantiated thesis" that one cannot kill a man to save a man (*Violence* 4). Girard takes this as meaning that substitution, for moral reasons, cannot apply to people and argues the rather plain fact that human sacrifices have occurred. He does not mention the second chapter, "Of Human Sacrifices," of Maistre's essay, where such sacrifices are indicted not as immoral but as abrogating the basic task of sacrifice to limit and delimit human violence.

Along with reversibility, Girard rejects any argument from cultural contexts. It is only through its essential violence, denuded of all symbolism and ritual trappings, that sacrifice may be understood: "Once one has made up one's mind that sacrifice is an institution essentially if not entirely symbolic, one can say anything whatsoever about it"; violence alone is independent of cultural variation. Girard thus begins his argument with a physiological stimulus and response model by way of a reference to a certain "species of fish" discussed by Lorenz that devour their own kind (*Violence* 1–2).

This functionalist model of sacrifice as a primitive means of stress reduction may provide it with a constant motive, but it ignores the tradition of consensual interpretations that make of a motivated rite a custom that is accepted as meaningful. The independence of violence from all cultural variables, its presence among men and fish, implies that it will have little to tell us about those variables themselves; questions of history and institutions tend to disappear in the return to origins and physiology. And yet, much like Ballanche, Girard claims to have discovered after an eon of ignorance a hidden unity of ancient knowledge, the most recent discoveries of science, and a superior Christian message, a discovery that initiates us into a new social gospel.[23]

The broad enthusiasm that has greeted Girard's argument testifies to the power of the sacrificial paradigm both to account for widely diverse social practices and to fascinate those who would understand it. The fascination exerted by ritual violence demands our closest attention, as it bears both upon Maistre's theory of sacrifice itself and upon how we read it. The precise nature of Maistre's response will be a primary concern from here on; for now, a few words on the problem will serve to conclude the chapter.

A fascination with sacrifice has marked the most archaic forms of human thought; it also marks the most chic trends in contemporary literature. Terry Eagleton has observed that "few literary texts are likely to make it nowadays into the new historicist canon unless they contain at least one mutilated body."[24] The observation is given added depth by Dominick LaCapra's remark that "the fascination with the image of violence may be ineradicable, especially in a society where spectacle, narcissism, and voyeurism," accompanied by a nostalgia for the sacred, "have assumed a pronounced role."[25] Thinking on sacrifice too readily slips into sacrificial thinking, finding in sacrifice an ultimate answer that puts an end to doubts, provides closure, by seemingly putting us in contact with ultimate things. What is called for then is a reflection on violence that will retain a critical distance rather than once again submit to its allure.

In this light, Maistre's own response is ambiguous, caught between a horror of what humans are capable of and a desire to defend those sacred traditions that alone, he believed, place a limit on human depravity. The danger here is that the theory may redeem sacrifice itself by revealing its logic, uses, and inevitability. Ultimately this would be to redeem its guiding idea of redemptive violence. Should violence ever be redeemed? Maistre argues that it must be, given the violence of which humans and human things are made. On a metaphysical plane, following Origen, he finds the redemption of violence in its autodestruction, as "evil does away with evil." On the social plane, ritualized violence is redeemed as the only alternative to violence run amok. This is perhaps to invite a bloodthirsty interpretation. Yet in both cases, sacrifice is only redeemed for the limits it places on human violence. In neither case, moreover, is the assertion that sacrifice must be redeemed mere moralizing. On the one hand, Maistre claims that violence *is*, always and inevitably, "redeemed": bought back, balanced out, compensated, reversed. On the other, he insists that society *requires* that violence be sublimated, delimited, domesticated, put in order.

In the following chapters Maistre will show us in great detail how social violence is mystified and legitimized in its ritual and mythical representations. He never recommends demystification, however, and this is what ultimately places him on the far side of Enlightenment. Yet this first step, an "Enlightenment on Sacrifices," remains deeply significant. Its significance may be measured by the immense questions it raises for social and political philosophy, questions to which we may now turn.

Chapter 3
Punishment and War

Thrones wilt when they are not fed with blood, their vitality grows with the mass of wrongs committed, with life-denials, with the crushing of all that is perpetually different and that has been ousted by them. We are disclosing here secret and forbidden things; we are touching upon state secrets hidden away with a thousand seals of silence. . . . Many things seem to point to the fact that Franz Joseph was in reality a powerful but sad Demiurge. – Bruno Schulz, *Sanatorium under the Sign of the Hourglass*

We now advance from one equivocality to another, from the law of violence found in sacrifice, to the violence of law found in executions, and from thence to the innocent slaughter of war. Maistre's reflections on capital punishment and warfare are indeed a direct application of the ideas of "Eclaircissement sur les sacrifices" to European institutions. For lack of attention to his theory of sacrifice, critics have been too quick, in light of his remarks on war and punishment, to dub Maistre a violent philosopher rather than a philosopher of violence. This is to blame the messenger for his bad tidings, as though Maistre occasioned the ills of which he speaks. There is no denying the dangerous allure of these dark subjects, dangers we will attend to closely. Of Maistre's writing, however, one must ask the same elementary question that he asked of the sacrifices of the Old Testament: "Does the Bible approve of everything it tells us?"[1]

In this chapter, then, we will see how Maistre applied his theory of sacrifice to European military and penal forms. The resonance of Maistre's ideas with major themes of modern European thought will lead us to reconsider the uses of the sacrificial paradigm for political philosophy, to spell out its potential abuses, and, finally, to trace the course of Maistre's influence on modern French sociology.

Before a word is said of Maistre's infamous discussions of war and capital punishment, however, an understanding of their textual setting is indispensable. This setting is precisely one of discussion, of the philosophical dialogues of *Les Soirées de Saint-Pétersbourg*. These dialogues take place among three characters, each of whom has his own highly distinctive intellectual traits: the Count, the Senator, and the Chevalier. The Count represents Catholic order and tradition, the Senator Masonic and Orientalist speculation, and the Chevalier the enthusiasm of the philosophical greenhorn.

Jean-Louis Darcel has argued that the *Soirées* reproduce actual discussions that took place in July 1809 at Maistre's Saint Petersburg lodgings among Maistre himself (the Count), Basil Tamara (the Senator), and Gabriel de Bray (the Chevalier).[2] Darcel's evidence is convincing, yet the claim requires qualification. While these actual discussions may well have provided the starting point for the text, Maistre so reworked the dialogues and put into them so much of his earlier thinking and experience that the interlocutors came to represent three tendencies or even three periods of his own thinking. Maistre himself had been not only a Catholic count but a senator ardently engaged in Masonry and, before that, on his own admission, a starry-eyed philosophical enthusiast. Tellingly, he puts in the Senator's mouth words that appear in his private notebooks and correspondence and that echo throughout his writing as a whole. In one scene he lends the Chevalier his own deeply cherished memory of having been read Racine on his mother's lap; moreover, it is the Chevalier who is said to have written the record of the conversations. The Count, finally, at one point cites the "anonymous" author of *Considerations on France* (Maistre), whose work he possesses only in extracts recorded in his notebooks. The biographical and autobiographical references, then, are highly mediated at the very least.

Short of a close formalist reading of the text, it is necessary simply to underline its thoroughly dialogical character: a dialogue between three philosophical positions, rooted in three individuals and representing three tendencies of Maistre's thinking, each of which challenges the others. The following passages on executions and warfare have always been read as the direct, unmediated, univocal expression of Maistre's personal view. Yet the most questionable assertions are actually presented in the voice of the Senator, who represents either another person altogether or at most one tendency of Maistre's thinking, and whose questionable views are continually challenged and thus limited by the other interlocutors. The *Soirées* thus highlight rather than hide or embrace the extremity of the positions advanced, while granting them a voice and a force to disrupt more comfortable points of view.

As an ongoing and ultimately unresolved dialogue, moreover, the *Soirées* contest the desire for final answers that commonly mars thinking on sacrifice. By the same token, they embody a way of responding to irreconcilable difference wholly different from the apocalyptic violence of sacrifice itself. The resulting open dialogical context, with its eschewal of closure and conflict, is anything but dogmatic.

The Violence of Law: The Executioner

Our reading of Maistre's theory of sacrifice allows us to perceive that his portrayal of the executioner as "the horror and bond of human association" (*Soirées*, OC 4:33) is no mere paradox or worse, as his commentators are too inclined to assume. Instead, it represents an effort to extend his theory of the logic and ritual practices of sacrifice to modern society, which, like any other, must manage the disorder and violence that Maistre believes define human existence and that he calls sacred.

Maistre finds the meaning of capital punishment precisely within the sacrificial economy of debts and satisfactions, of substitution and reversibility. Thus every torment (*supplice*) inflicted on the guilty serves at once to supplicate (*supplier*) and to compensate (*suppléer*) for man's faults: "Unhappy the nation that abandons torments! for the debt of each culprit not ceasing to fall back on the nation, this last will be forced to pay without sympathy, and even to the end could see itself treated as *insolvent* according to the full rigour of the law" (Maistre, *Soirées*, OC 4:159n), the general law of violence and the "death of death." The letting of the culprit's blood preserves the life of society. Seen in this light, the task of the executioner is to redeem a defiled and thus bound society through the killing of the reviled individual who occasioned the debt, the *coupable*, or culprit.

Without ritualized public punishment, the sacred relation between the criminal and the crowd would remain sterile, since the participants would remain distinct and separated and would thus forestall the redeeming effect of sacred substitution. Public executions, then, serve the same function as old-fashioned human sacrifices.

This sacred or socially excited character of ancien régime executions is evident in the ritualistic schema that underlies Maistre's infamous description of the executioner's performance. The *bourreau*, in the Count's words, "arrives on a public square covered with a pressed and palpitating crowd; he is thrown a poisoner, a parricide, a sacrilegist: he grasps him, spreads him, lays him on a horizontal cross, he raises his arm: then there occurs a horrible silence, and one hears nothing but the cry of the bones that burst under the bar" (Maistre, *Soirées*, OC 4:32–33). In these solemn gestures carried out in silence one finds a liturgical or even, if not divine, demiurgical activity.

For Maistre, all criminal punishment bears the double aspect that he attributes to sacrifice: the restraining of evil (violence against the violent) and its expiation. He thus describes capital punishment as the limit case of punishment taken as a form of correction as it passes into pure expiation: "every punishment (except the last) is inflicted by love as much as by justice" (Maistre, *Soirées*, OC 4:285). Faced with a limit of human badness, capital punishment is a case of justice with love left out (at least, we shall see, as far as humanly possible), of justice in its pure form that has become *inhuman*.

The sacred character of such an ultimate form of human justice is brought forward in Maistre's provocative rhetorical question whether "the priests of antiquity, who disgorged their own kind *with a sacred iron*, were they less *executioners* than the modern judges who send them to death in virtue of a law?" (Maistre, "Eclaircissement," OC 5:333). Such a comparison cuts both ways. If most moderns would wholeheartedly agree that the Aztec priest must be seen as an executioner, the identification of the executioner-priest with the judge would come as something of a shock, whether of revelation or disgust (two terms that demonstrate again the sacred context involved).

Another unexpected result of presenting punishment within a sacred setting is Maistre's identification of the culprit as a *victim*. The Count speaks of the "victim's bellowings" and, in a grisly vein that reveals a definite disgust with the workings of the law, describes how the victim is reduced to the status of a thing. The executioner "detaches the victim; he carries it onto the wheel: the shattered members are enlaced in the spokes, the head hangs, the hair bristles, and the mouth, open like a furnace, only sends out at intervals bloody words that call death" (Maistre, *Soirées*, OC 4:33). That the culprit is a sacred victim is confirmed by reference to Roman judicial practice. "When the laws of the twelve tables pronounce death, they say *sacer esto* (that it be sacred)! that is to say *devoted* [or sacrificed: *devoué*]; or, to express oneself more exactly, *consecrated* [*voué*]; for the culprit was only, rigorously speaking, *de-voted* [deconsecrated] by the execution" (Maistre, "Eclaircissement," OC 5:307). Execution absolves the criminal. This is not to say that the criminal is an *innocent* victim. Rather, the victim is *made* innocent, redeemed, by the social catharsis of public punishment. Maistre agrees with Hesiod that "crime is above all painful to its author," that the life of the guilty is itself a punishment, and that the death of the criminal is thus "less a punishment than the end and complement of punishment" (Maistre, "Sur les délais," OC 5:395, 397).

If the criminal is sacred as the victim of sacrificial ceremonial, this is all the more true of the executioner who plays the priest of this judicial sacrifice. As Maistre portrays him, the executioner neatly fits the sacred category that Victor Turner calls the "liminal persona" or "threshold person" who exists "betwixt and between the positions assigned by law, custom, convention, ceremonial." The executioner combines the attributes of lowliness and sacredness the unity of which Turner emphasizes: "the *liminal* and the *inferior* conditions are often associated with ritual powers and with the total community seen as undifferentiated."[3] This is precisely Maistre's picture of the executioner. Hedged around by prescriptions and prohibitions, he performs the specialized function of regenerating social structure through the sacred use of power. Whose work is more specialized? Society rests on the fact that only one, and not everyone, is the executioner (this will be the basis for Maistre's attack on the Revolution as a relapse into barbarism).

The sacred, marginal, and unique position of the executioner is emphasized in all of Maistre's remarks, as in the following words of the Count:

This head, this heart, are they made like ours? do they not contain something particular and foreign to our nature? For myself, I do not know how to doubt it. He is made like us on the exterior; he is born like us; but he is an extraordinary being, and in order that he may exist within the human family, a particular decree, a FIAT of the divine power is required. (*Soirées*, OC 4:32)

The Count thus asks himself whether such a figure can properly be described as human. He answers, "Yes: God receives him in his temples and permits him to pray"—again, the human is defined as a relation to the sacred. "He is not criminal; yet no tongue consents to say, for example, *that he is virtuous, that he's an honest man, that he is estimable, etc.* Not one moral praise is suitable for him; for all suppose relations with men, and he has none" (Maistre, *Soirées*, OC 4:33). This "inexplicable being" in some sense becomes a second victim or scapegoat, the living goat who is sent out into the desert bearing off the ritual impurities occasioned by the sacrifice.

The sacrificial dynamic of public torments as Maistre presents them may be outlined as follows. First, the culprit victim is made sacred by his transgression, which binds him with the community to expiation—a sacralization attested to by the ritual preparations leading up to his public punishment. Second, the victim is immolated—the high point of sacred intensity. Third, his impurity is transferred to the executioner, and, by that fact, the king's "body"—his sovereign dominion over his realm—is restored to purity.

In this sacrificial performance, the assembled community experiences both an *expiation* of the crime and a *communion* of sovereignty. Sovereignty and crime are the two poles of social violence, fully analogous to the pure and impure aspects of the sacred. Within this overarching dynamic, the executioner serves as the intermediary of these two realms, neither a criminal nor a member of society. He is a hybrid being sharing at once in the legitimate power of the sovereign and the infamy of the culprit who thus forces together the opposing poles of social purity and impurity. In bringing together in his person these social extremes, these excesses of the social order, these remains or remainders that exceed the measure of the social order's symmetries, the executioner becomes an excessive, impure, and yet necessary figure.

Maistre places special emphasis on this interplay of pure and impure at the moments of preparation and resolution of the executioner's performance. Ritual purity demands that the sovereign not come into contact with his impure counterpart, who carries out the violence of his law. The executioner is therefore only approached by an intermediary; pure and impure power are brought together gradually, by approximation, just as the executioner himself serves as an intermediary between sovereign and culprit. It is "an abject minister" who "comes to knock at his door" (Maistre, *Soirées*, OC 4:32). The abjection of the culprit, as a sacred force and thus contagious, passes from him to the executioner and to the minister in turn. Conversely, when the rite is accomplished, as the executioner "descends, he holds out his hand soiled with blood, and justice throws into it from afar a few pieces of gold, which he carries off between two rows of men separated by horror" (Maistre, *Soirées*, OC 4:33). This contact of blood and gold in the executioner's hands, brought on from a distance by authority, summarizes the relation between pure and impure violence that constitutes sovereign power. Sovereign power thus remains discrete, keeps its hands clean, in the midst of its excesses. Maistre's account shows us the inevitable tainting of power by blood (and the subsequent erasure of this taint), of which authority would rather hear nothing: the image of the king's gold in the executioner's hand demonstrates that despite appearances no power is clean.

It is precisely in this role as the impure operator of a pure sovereignty's power, indeed as that power's purifier, that the executioner is

the cornerstone of society, that "all grandeur, all power, all subordination rest upon the executioner. . . . God, who is the author of sovereignty, is also that of punishment; he has cast our earth upon these two
poles: for Jehovah is the master of the two poles, and upon them he
makes the world turn" (Maistre, *Soirées*, OC 4:33–34). From "that re-
doubtable prerogative" of the sovereign to punish crime "results the
necessary existence of a man destined to inflict upon crimes the punishments discerned by human justice." In order that the sovereign retain
the glory of his resplendent body while exercising his right over life, it
is necessary that there exist the abject body of the executioner. It is this
relation of glory to abjection that defines sovereignty. The *acentric* character of power, in which sovereignty is exercised by a being who remains outside of society and thus keeps sovereignty and society free
from the contagion of an impure violence, is emphasized in Maistre's
description of how the executioner "is created like a world." He lives
outside of the common order of things "in the midst of that solitude
and that type of vacuum formed around him" (Maistre, *Soirées*, OC
4:32).

Maistre's account of the executioner emphasizes not only his symbolic character but also, more troublingly, the very physicality of law
itself. The executioner is the figure of the law's enforcement, the force
necessarily found in every rule of law, the "rendering" of justice by
force. The executioner makes law real by bringing it to bear upon individuals, thus making it something more than a floating abstract imperative. His person lays bare the violence of judicial order itself, its un-
challengeable rights over lives and bodies, and thus exposes the
originary violence that is buried at the threshold of institutions. Maistre's close depiction of the confrontation of culprit and executioner reveals the transgression found within the law, the forces of destruction
within what preserves order.

This "return of the repressed" accounts for the uncanny quality of
the tableau. "Uncanny" is the right word. The irrational, traumatic
figure of the executioner at work stands for the acceptance *without sense
or reason* of the commands of law: that something within law that is beyond reason, consent, and question. If law were wholly rational, it
would not be internalized, believed in; if its enforcement were not traumatic, its authority would not be unconditional. The smooth, rational
functioning of law only maintains itself to the extent that somewhere
else (*an einem anderen Schauplatz*) there is some fundamental unaware-
ness, obscurity, excess, or lack.

It is precisely what thus escapes the sphere of rational consent that is the executioner's business. The king and the executioner are the "two poles" of the consensual, legal, and normative order, for, as the figures of ultimate power and force at the apex and nadir of the social hierarchy, they are at once within and without that order: their actions are not dependent upon but rather elicit consent. The person of the executioner symbolizes that fundamental imbalance of power, that fundamental inequality, upon which all other inequalities are founded and rely. This inhuman dimension of social power—the violence of authority—is socially mediated and made human in ritual, at the one "pole" in sacrificial punishment and at the other in royal ceremonial (see below). What is beyond and below the social order, violence, must be justified by what is beyond and above that order, the sacred (or by some equally irrational hypostasis of biology or will to power), for it cannot be justified on the basis of the social values it enforces.

One might then say that the executioner maintains the identity of Law and of Order through his violent expulsion of crime and disorder. If the Rule of Law is the state's monopoly of violence, then it is the obscene figure of the executioner who condenses upon himself all the repulsion that the Law's possession of ultimate violence would otherwise occasion. Order is thus split into peace and destruction, law into justice and torment. The executioner is the bearer of the nonidentity between order and peace, law and justice. Better, he is the alibi of this nonidentity who, by taking it all upon himself, erases the scandal it would otherwise provoke. By embodying all the destruction and torment it necessarily entails, the executioner allows the sovereign Rule of Law to appear as pure good order and public peace. The conclusion of such a train of logic would be that the difference between law and crime is to be found in this human aberration who stands at the threshold between them and who is thus "the cornerstone of society."

There will be much more to say later about sovereignty, legitimacy, and law; suffice it here to emphasize that Maistre's marked interest in the figure of the executioner by no means represents a celebration. Maistre's position must not be confused with the attitude typified by the remark of Canosa, chief minister to Ferdinand I, king of the Two Sicilies, that "the first servant of the crown should be the executioner."[4] It is essential to a proper understanding of Maistre's thought to distinguish his sociological "is" from the reactionaries' "ought": Maistre claims that order *is* reestablished at any price, whatever the regime, whereas the reactionary will argue that a particular order *ought* to be so restored.

Maistre, we shall see, consistently points to eighteenth-century absolutism as a primary cause of the Revolution, and, in one of his first works, the "Letters of a Savoyan Royalist" written during his first year of exile, argues that French absolutism was manifest in the absolute quality of its punishments. Savoy, where Maistre had been a magistrate, differed from France in his imagination above all by the moderation of its executions. After an even more explicit description of the agonies of the condemned than that found in the *Soirées*, Maistre continues,

> Never would we support that shocking spectacle. We would hardly want to ordain it for a parricide, if this crime were known to us. Strange thing! The French have given us the torture of the wheel; our tribunals still condemn the great criminals to it, and their condemnations contain horribly minute details of the torments destined for the culprit; but without knowing why and by the sole order of the public conscience these condemnations are not at all executed to the letter [the letter killeth, one might say]. The magistrate traces them without trembling: he knows that humanity will temper their rigor. This daughter of heaven accompanies the victim; she mounts up the scaffold, she permits the redoubtable apparatus that must frighten the eye of the multitude; but at the moment when the odious arm raises itself, she makes a sign to death, and the iron breaks only a cadaver. ("Lettres," OC 7:219)

Indeed, it was not only humanity, daughter of heaven, who took on the task of accompanying victims to the altar of punishment. It was assumed by the young Maistre himself (if only for a year before leaving Chambéry to attend law school in Turin) as a member of the Black Penitents. One of the chief activities of this order, founded by Saint Francis de Sales in 1594, the official title of which was "The Confraternity of Sympathy and the Holy Cross," was to keep vigil with condemned criminals awaiting execution. Descostes, one of Maistre's first biographers, describes this duty in typically lyrical fashion. "When a criminal had to be hung from the great trees of Verney, it was the penitents who went to pass next to him the night of the condemned, to assist him, support him, exhort him, and then to receive, from the hand of the executioner, the quivering cadaver, which they buried themselves."[5] One can only speculate on the effects this would have on a sixteen year old.

Yet the above contrast between the "great criminal" and the "odious arm" shows that Maistre's sympathies were at least somewhat mixed. The general effect of his interpretation is indeed less to naturalize capital punishment than it is to reveal the inhuman violence entailed by any rule of law. The unnatural character of judicial violence is emphasized in the *Soirées* when Maistre gives us both a dog's and an extraterrestrial's perspective on executions, a Hindu myth of "the genie of punishments," and a young Chevalier who becomes so enthusiastic in devising a code of punishments for the Russian military that he runs out of breath.

Maistre's project of laying bare the ritualized forms of power at work in the executions of the old regime has been taken up by one of the most influential texts of recent social theory, of which the above paragraphs inevitably incline the contemporary reader to think: Foucault's *Discipline and Punish*. A few words on the similarities and differences between their two analyses will help shed light on the historical significance of Maistre's thinking.

For Foucault, the executions of the ancien régime carried out two simultaneous and complementary functions. First, they *inscribed* the sovereign's power of reprisal upon the body of the criminal and upon the consciousness of the spectators. Second, through this spectacular manifestation of a superior power, they *restored* the sovereignty disrupted by the criminal's transgression. These two procedures closely approximate, respectively, Maistre's idea of the executioner as "horror and bond" of society and his evocation of the "dogma" of reversibility, of the compensation exacted by order for transgression. In the punishments of the classical age, according to Foucault, power was "exalted and strengthened by its visible manifestations," by its publicity, unlike the punitive practice of the nineteenth century that comes to mask the equivalence of crime and punishment by making the violence of authority invisible.

The atrocity of the older form of punishment responds to ("compensates for," "redeems," Maistre would say) that of the crime; it exacerbates the crime's violence, it masters, overwhelms, and annuls it in its own excessive deployment: "the atrocity of the expiation organized the ritual destruction of infamy by omnipotence"—a truly Maistrean theme. Foucault goes on to stress the social function of these dramatic performances. A certain identification on the part of the crowd with the criminal as victim, he argues, was necessary in order that sacrificial execution have its effect—in order that the people experience the over-

whelming character of power. It was the fear of too great an identification, however, of an identification with the criminal as a victim rather
than an enemy, that motivated the development of a "humane" and hidden punishment. Notoriously, Foucault concludes that this new form
of the "punishment-body relation," the modern prison, proved itself a
far more powerful means of social control than the open violence of the
punishments it replaced.[6]

Foucault's work on punishment has often been criticized for its nihilist implications, especially for how it downplays the role of humanitarianism in early modern penal reform.[7] Much of this criticism is
wide of the mark. One of Foucault's intentions was to show how the
discourse of humanity was able to serve purposes not altogether free of
inhumanity and, in particular, to underwrite a new "invisible" form of
domination. I would agree that the absence from his work of an account of the (at least occasional!) beneficent influence of institutions
hampers Foucault's account of modern European history by inclining it
at times toward an almost paranoiac vision of inescapable domination.
The tendency to view every institution as at bottom power over bodies
results not in the indifference of a nihilist, however, but in something
more resembling the passion of a Gnostic in revolt against the brute
reign of things.

All of this sheds important light on Maistre's own interpretation.
One of his contributions to modern political theory was to show how
the discourse of reason and humanity was all too compatible with practical barbarism (notably, of course, during the French Revolution).
Here he anticipates a basic feature of the Foucauldian critique, as he
does in emphasizing the violence of law. Yet, unlike Foucault, his
awareness of the dark underbelly of European institutions convinced
him that they must be defended at all costs as the sole limit on our potential for barbarity. The question of how Maistre himself represented
violent excess in his work, a question not simply of style but of the most
basic ethics, will be a guiding concern in what follows, starting with his
notorious reflections on war.

Other Sacred Killers: King and Soldier

After the executioner it is only proper to study the soldier. For these
two figures, whom Maistre as a rule discusses together, alone possess
the right to kill without crime and thus to fulfill the universal law of violence in a legitimate fashion. Yet these two figures occupy utterly opposed poles of the social imagination: one of these men is as glorious as

the other is abhorrent. Maistre's effort to answer why this is so leads him once again onto the doubtful terrain of human ambivalence.

In an almost humorous passage of the *Soirées*, Maistre has the Senator present the fiction of "an intelligence foreign to our globe" who comes to earth "for some sufficient reason." This foreign intelligence is informed that "corruption and the vices . . . demand that man, in certain circumstances, die by the hand of man" and that among men only the soldier and the executioner do the deed. The executioner kills only the condemned and does so rarely enough that "one of these ministers of death suffices in a province"; "as to the soldier, there is never enough of them, for they kill without measure and always innocent men." One of these "killers by profession" is highly honored, the other infamous. Asked to guess which, the foreign intelligence "would not hesitate an instant" (Maistre, *Soirées*, OC 5:4–5). Of the executioner he has nothing but praise. "He is a sublime being, the cornerstone of society: because crime has come to habitate your earth, take the executioner from the world, and all order will disappear with him. And what grandeur of soul, what noble disinterest!" The soldier, on the other hand, "is a minister of cruelties and injustices. How many evidently just wars are there? How many there are that are evidently unjust!" (Maistre, *Soirées*, OC 5:5).

It is significant yet always unremarked that Maistre puts this praise of the executioner into the mouth of an otherworldly visitor. Rather than directly expressing his own opinion, these words belong to an extraterrestrial who is in turn cited by one of Maistre's three interlocutors, the Senator, who is notable for his often dubious ideas. This very much qualifies the "inhumanity" and transcendental nihilism that have often been read into the passage: that the interlocutor is not of this world explains its *esprit de survol*. The general effect is to emphasize the bizarre nature of the claim, while allowing it to challenge our received opinions. The fictional welcome accorded this visitor and his strange ideas, moreover, differs markedly from the equation of the stranger with the enemy that Maistre outlines in his theory of sacrifice.

The interpretation of the foreign intelligence would be thoroughly mistaken, however. While the soldier and the executioner do "occupy the two ends of the social scale," the Senator continues, "there is nothing so noble as the first, nothing so abject as the second. . . . The soldier is so noble that he ennobles even that which is most ignoble in general opinion, for he can exercise the functions of the executioner without vilifying himself" (Maistre, *Soirées*, OC 5:6).

These shared functions are not merely a matter of the physical deed itself. In war and punishment alike, as in sacrifice, human ambivalence is both expressed and given form. The soldier directs outside the community the very same sacred violence that the executioner inflicts on those within who have become socially marginal by transgressing fundamental norms. It is the inadequate compensation of internal violence that requires it to be vented outward in war (thus the wars of the Revolution, which directed abroad the carnage that otherwise would have torn France asunder). "Domestic policy determines foreign policy," a contemporary political analyst might say, but that is not all that is at stake here.

The question Maistre asks is why the soldier's innocent murder is honorable; how it can be that "in the midst of the blood that he causes to flow the soldier is human, as the spouse is chaste in the transports of love"; or, most forcefully of all, how it is that "at the first signal, that lovable young man, raised in the horror of violence and blood, dashes from the paternal hearth, and runs, arms in hand, to seek upon the field of battle that which he calls an *enemy*, without yet knowing what an *enemy* is." If one proposed to this same young enthusiast that he "grasp a white dove with the sang-froid of a cook," however, he would be quite incapable (Maistre, *Soirées*, OC 5:17). Here we have one of Maistre's strongest statements of the constitutive ambivalence or duplicity of human life and of the relatively minor role of innocence within a broader economy of violence. We return, then, to the question of the sacred. Maistre's scandalous answer to the paradox of the soldier is that he remains unsoiled by his violence because war is divine.

This statement is more responsible than any other for Maistre's infamous reputation; "but war is not divine," his critics chime in chorus. This is to ignore, first, that for Maistre the sacred includes the impure as well as the pure, and, second, that these words are again put in the mouth of the somewhat unhinged Senator, who over several pages enumerates the sources of war's divinity.

Before all else, war is divine because it is humanly inexplicable or even mad and yet remains a law of the world. This is indeed Maistre's most general definition of the sacred, one that extends its relevance beyond the confines of strictly theological debate to all manner of symbolic practices unmastered by reason.

Second, war is divine "in the mysterious glory that environs it." This "mysterious glory" is evident in how war is triggered by minor circumstances, in the shocking imbalance between its causes and its ef-

fects, in its unforeseeable results, and in the undefinable force that determines success or failure (Maistre, *Soirées*, OC 5:26). Again, the sacred
appears to be involved above all in questions of order and the balance of
forces within a situation of chaos: the Senator's discourse on war is replete with references to relative equilibria and inclined planes. At age
twenty, Maistre had already written that war "slaughters men to rees-
tablish equilibrium, if the balance tilts too much to one side."[8]

Such meditations are not uncommon. What makes Maistre's account of unique interest is his claim that these orders and forces are
symbolic, a matter of consciences and imaginations, and it is this that
endows them not only with mystery but with what Maistre calls divine
glory. Battles, the Senator repeats in various modulations, are "neither
won nor lost physically." Rather, "it is opinion that loses battles, and it
is opinion that wins them," "it is imagination that loses battles"—victory is often a matter of interpretation, of taking the auspices of the battle's carnage. Glossing his metaphor of the victorious army's advance as
upon an inclined plane, the Senator cites Frederick II's remark that "to
vanquish is to advance," yet he asks, "Who is it that advances? It is he
whose conscience and countenance make the other retreat"—the inclined plane seems to be one of interpretations! Such interpretations are
imposed on materials recalcitrant to understanding in their extreme
amorphousness: the soldier "possessed in turn by fear, by hope, by
rage, by five or six different drunkennesses, what does the man become? what does he see? what does he know after several hours? what
power has he over himself or over others?" (Maistre, *Soirées*, OC 5:32–
36). War, it is emphasized, occurs outside the domain of conscious mastery, another way of saying it is divine.

Yet as in all sacred things, in the midst of unreason, chaos, and ambivalence there reigns an order of mores, limits, and bonds. The ritualized character of prerevolutionary warfare, the Senator emphasizes,
was evident in the mutual respect and courtesies of the combatants (this
affirmation of the other always marks the practices that Maistre calls
divine) and, above all, in the fact that these wars were never total: "the
nations," that is to say the peoples, "were never at war, and everything
that was weak was sacred throughout the lugubrious scenes of this devastating scourge." In short, "soldier only fought soldier": an indirect
yet clear indictment of emerging nationalist warfare (Maistre, *Soirées*,
OC 5:19–20).

This traditional order, these limits that made of the soldiery a veritable caste of sacrificial priests and victims by turns, alone makes war di-

vine. The soldier is only noble so long as he kills his own kind and with his own proper weapons. Otherwise, as the Chevalier remarks, one will fear him, "for any man who carries, in his ordinary capacity, a good pistol loaded with a good charge, merits great attention," but all the power he derives from honor or glory will disappear immediately. Fear does not make divine. The soldier indeed ceases to be a soldier when he "shoots a simple citizen or makes his own comrade [his enemy-comrade] die by fire or rope" (Maistre, *Soirées*, OC 5:7–8). In this case, Maistre seems to imply, the soldier would become an illegitimate executioner who breaks, not reestablishes, the bonds and limits that make up the social constitution. Perhaps he simply becomes a murderer. In either case, his actions necessitate further "compensations" and further bloodshed and disorder, not less, and this is always for Maistre the token of illegitimacy.

One can see that Maistre does not glorify force and carnage, as many readers are far too quick to affirm, but precisely the limits imposed on the use of power and violence. Indeed, Maistre's theory presents colonial and civil violence—the use of force against peoples—in a far worse light than do many liberal philosophies of the nineteenth century.

Democracy, we have seen the traditionalists argue, is maintained by war, patriotism by enmity toward other nations. Modern bureaucracies of war even still have their own proper mysteries; "national security" combines those characteristics of ineffability and infallibility that define sacred things—its demands cannot be brought into question. Nothing better demonstrates the sacrificial background of war than the awful logic that lay behind the "paradox" of Vietnam, a paradox that within the theory sketched above can only be a proof of that war's illegitimacy: "we must destroy that village in order to save it." This "sacrifice for democracy" relied on the murder not only of civilians but of civilians outside the democratic community; what was "sacrificed" was what men thought of as things, not as sacred, and what was "saved" was a village thought of as so many square feet of property. This surely is unholy, and Maistre helps us to see its full horror.

Finally, it bears repeating that because something is sacred it does not necessarily mean it is good. Although war is called divine in Maistre's published works, it appears in a rather dimmer light in his letters and journals. A letter of 1817, describing an army parade in Saint Petersburg to Maistre's predecessor as Russian ambassador, the count de Vallaise, confesses that "in all military spectacles, I am always besieged and afflicted by two melancholy ideas." First, "the art of war is the only one the perfection of which only serves to harm the human species in general. . . . Of what service are the perfections of weapons that soon become common?" New weapons thus aggravate "the ills of humanity without augmenting the power or security of any nation in particular. . . . Let the devil take every inventor of new means of murder!" The second sad reflection concerns "the frightening growth of the military state throughout Europe." Military expenditures "pass the bounds of reason and of politics" and "harass all governments, ruin them."[9] Here, surely, is a message not irrelevant to modern democracies.

This discussion of sacred social persons would not be complete without reference to the king, though detailed treatment of Maistre's royalism, his political theology and theory of sovereignty, must await another chapter. The sacredness of the king is closely associated in Maistre's work with the two social domains already spoken of as divine: war and punishment. For the monarch in his glory stands at the apex of these two economies of violence, on which he depends for his power without tarnishing his name with their horrors.

First, it is the king who leads society to war; he is the figure for whom and under whose banners one sheds one's blood. In one of his earliest writings, Maistre recommends that the young prince be led onto the field of battle to learn calm in the midst of carnage.[10] The sacredness of the king is to be a unifying symbol of order and calm in an otherwise unstructured, chaotic situation. The special affinity of the monarch with war is further emphasized by the Senator's remark that while Peter I of Russia could barely make men cut their beards, he easily commanded consent to follow him into battle even when he lost; such a situation exemplifies for Maistre the simultaneous grandeur and meagerness of monarchical power, always circumscribed by the ruling mores of a culture (Maistre, *Soirées*, OC 5:3).

It is in the name of the king that blood is shed, not only in war but in punishment. Glossing the saying of Thomas Aquinas that "God is the author of the evil that punishes but not of that which soils," Maistre's Senator comments that the sovereign, too, "is the author of the torments that are inflicted under his laws," just as he "authors" the bloodshed inflicted under his banners.

> In a distant and indirect sense, it is certainly he who hangs and works the wheel, because all authority and every legal execution derive from him; but in the direct and immediate sense, it is the thief, the counterfeiter, the assassin, etc., who are the veritable authors of this

"evil that punishes them"; it is they who build the prisons, who raise
the gibbets and scaffolds. (Maistre, *Soirées*, OC 4:23)

Here the culprit is presented as constructing the "theater of cruelty,"
the stage on which punishments are performed by the sovereign.
Above we saw how the sovereign delegates this function to the executioner, thereby remaining unsoiled by the impure side of violence. The
sovereign's impurity is always masked. The intimate relation of sovereignty to the inflicting of ultimate punishments, however, is everywhere marked in Maistre's work.

In an early work, the *Etude sur la souveraineté* (A study of sovereignty), Maistre notes that neither antiquity nor modern Asia "at all
disputed kings this right to condemn to death; all the pages of history
present judgments of this nature that the historians report without the
least sign of disapprobation." Domesticated by the graft of Christian
and Gallic traditions, Europe would consider such random condemnations a crime, though Maistre admits that in this regard "it would not
be surprising to find a little *Arabism* in Spain and Portugal" (Maistre,
Etude, OC 1:439–40). In Asia, however, the subject "does not at all seek
to penetrate this somber cloud that envelops or that forms the majesty
of the monarch." To simply note what will be the central theme of a
later chapter, this hesitation as to whether the sacred makes or masks
sovereignty ("envelops or forms" it) is essential: authority is the mask of
power, and it is the great crime of revolutionists to "want to see
within." Yet in some sense to see within is Maistre's aim as well.

In a passage that clearly shows the political tenor of his theological
speculations, Maistre claims that for the subject of an Asian ruler "his
master is a god, and he has with this superior being no relation other
than that of prayer. The laws of the monarch are oracles. His graces are
celestial gifts, and his anger is a calamity of invincible nature." Kingship in Europe, it is implied, has been "secularized" by the imposition
of institutions between ruler and ruled that lessen its absolute character,
counterbalancing and providing a measure for kingly authority. Even
Oriental despotism, however, is not without its own measuredness, for
according to Maistre any lasting institution must have its sacred symmetries of glory and abjection: imbalance of power requires compensation in blood—the blood of culprits, foreigners, soldiers, or the sovereign himself. "See how the supreme wisdom has balanced these terrible
elements of Oriental power. This absolute monarch can be deposed;
one by no means disputes him the right to ask the head that displeases
him, but often one asks him for his own" (Maistre, *Etude*, OC 1:442–

43). Again, divinity appears as the operator of necessary balances and symmetries; again, undiluted power is "terrible."

One begins to appreciate the distortion involved in calling Maistre a "theocrat," at least in the traditional acceptance of this word. Maistre, we shall see, was highly critical of the development of French absolutism in the eighteenth century (we have already seen him critical of the absolute character of its punishments): it installs an "Oriental" balance of power that accounts in large part for the revolutionary regicide and the other "Arabisms" of the Revolution. One of Maistre's greatest contributions to the study of the Revolution will be to approach it from the perspective of a comparative cultural anthropology sensitive to the sacred "envelope and form" of social power.

René Girard points out that the word "decision" derives from the Latin term meaning to divide by the sacrificial knife or to cut the victim's throat. One could depart from this observation to speculate that the sacredness of sovereignty resides in its power of decision—this indeed is the argument of Carl Schmitt, who mistakenly attributes the position to Maistre and Bonald. This is not Maistre's argument. Maistre's greatest praise is for the intermediary institutions that limit royal authority, that take the power of decision out of one man's hands. The king's grandeur is not at all a matter of talents, of personal mastery: quite the contrary. Maistre says of the monarchical constitution that "the greatest merit of the engine is that a mediocre man can put it into play"; while it is "a benefit without doubt if the king has great talents, and if his individual actions can immediately concur with the general movement; but, in place of his *person*, his *name* suffices." The sovereign *sanctions* decisions, above all decisions of war and judgment, he ordains or decrees them on the basis of a symbolic power. It is the king's very name that rules: "this word KING is a talisman, a magical power that gives to all forces and to all talents a central direction" (Maistre, *Etude*, OC 1:438).

This is the first sacred attribute of the king: he provides a symbolic unity and direction to social forces. The second attribute is found in the inevitability and ineffability of power: "People bend before sovereignty because they feel it is something sacred that they can neither create nor destroy" (Maistre, *Etude*, OC 1:354). Without a barrier between opinion and authority—the profane and the sacred in the realm of social ideas— no government is possible. The sacred, again, is found in an institutionalized symbolic order that provides a social unity and a balance for power, an order that inevitably resists and compensates the excesses of sovereign and subjects alike.

From Maistre to Bataille: The Lure of Sacred Violence

The abiding significance of Maistre's argument may be measured by setting it beside the work of one of the darlings of contemporary theory, Georges Bataille. The aim of this brief detour is not to do full justice to his work but merely to shed some light on Maistre's place in the history of modern thought. For Bataille and his circle returned, in the mid–twentieth century, to Maistre's fundamental project: the application of a theory of sacrifice, derived from a comparative study of religious traditions, to a critique of European institutions. To this end Bataille, with the help of Roger Caillois and Michel Leiris, founded the College of Sociology, a loosely knit forum for lectures and discussion on sacred sociology that existed from 1937 to 1939. The great positive project of the college was the analysis of irrational forces at work within the rationalized democracies of the West. This study was marked, however, by a strong tendency to affirm and identify with those forces.

Bataille himself emphasizes the immense amplitude of his meditations on sacrifice when he describes it as "the key of all human existence."[11] The ultimate basis for this large claim is Bataille's belief that excess energy is inevitable in any system of "living matter" and must somehow be expended, "voluntarily or not, gloriously or in catastrophic fashion," if that system is to maintain itself.[12] Such prodigal expenditure is the defining mark of sacred things and opposes them to the everyday world of accumulated labor, a world hypostatized as "real" yet which depends on the sacred for its maintenance and cohesion.

By departing from the realm of utility for that of "unconditional consumption," sacrifice replaces the thingly and neutral world of the everyday with a world of intimacy. It provides a contact with nature and with society that is denied by the workaday world of separated objects and individuals. The periodic transgressive expenditure of wealth and blood in sacrificial festivals thus serves social unity by temporarily undoing the limits and oppositions that otherwise define it.[13]

Sacrifice for Bataille is therefore an eminently political category. He defines sovereignty as that power of extravagant expenditure that devotes itself "in a privileged fashion to glorious activity, to useless consumption" (Bataille, La Part maudite, 73), to the shedding of wealth in potlatch or the shedding of blood in sacrifice or war.

In addition, sacrifice was central to Bataille's political vision for its thoroughgoing opposition to the guiding assumptions of modern life, a life he saw as wholly reified and profane that has reduced existence in its entirety to the status of a thing. In our world, denuded of the sacred, politics, economics, and science all conspire to tell us that this impoverished life is our only fate. Post-Reformation Christianity, what is more, has only furthered this tendency by making the sacred a wholly otherworldly affair.

In response to this utterly fallen situation Bataille called for a "counteroperation" that would return us from the reified world of productivist man to intimacy with the world; this entails a return to the unproductive expenditure of sacrifice. It is religion that will accomplish this return, for that is what religion always is: "a matter of suppressing that obstacle between the world and us that is created by labor." In its fundamental opposition to the reifying tendency of capitalism, religion "is more radical than the Marxist position," for Marxism operates altogether according to the dictates of productivity. Bataille thus calls for an extension of religious action to the profanized world: "the profane world must, in turn, be destroyed as such; that is to say, everything inside capitalism that is given as a thing that transcends man and dominates him must be reduced to the state of an immanent thing by a subordination to consumption by man."[14]

Against the "disconnected" world of modernity, Bataille thus calls for the affirmation of the "total world of myth, the world of *being*," a revolt to be carried out by "small numbers of men bound to each other by deep emotional bonds," in the words of Caillois a "virulent religious organization, new and uncouth from head to toe, one sustained by a spirit incapable of servitude."[15]

To pursue these ends, Bataille and Caillois formed Acéphale, a secret society closely linked to the College of Sociology. The central importance attached to this bizarre group is seen in Bataille's remark that the college "was somehow the external activity" of Acéphale rather than vice-versa. Aided by the "research" of the college, the conclusion was drawn that only a human sacrifice would answer current political needs. As Caillois explained it in hindsight, in order

> to bind energies as profoundly as it was necessary to complete a task that was immense and, besides,[!] had no definite object . . . the solemn execution of one of their members seemed sufficient to the new conspirators to consecrate their cause and guarantee their faithfulness forever. By making their efforts invincible, it was to put the universe

in their hands. . . . Who would believe it? It was easier to find a voluntary victim than a voluntary sacrificer. In the end, it was all unresolved. At least I imagine it was. (Hollier 381–82)

It is hard to decide which is more appalling in this project: its uncritical
embrace of archaic exoticism, its fervently puerile fantasies of power
and invincibility, or its assumption of the thoroughly romantic role of
the thinker as creator of new worlds. Perhaps the best commentary
comes from Bataille himself, who had written years before the
Acéphale episode that "the necessity of satisfying such a need," a need
"as inevitable as hunger" for sacrifice, "under the conditions of present-
day life, leads an isolated man to stupid behavior."[16]

As this incident all too clearly reveals, Bataille's otherwise impressive efforts toward a general theory of the sacred and a general criticism
of European institutions were often marred by a romantic nostalgia for
origins and even a Gnostic stance against the fallen world. Both these
tendencies encouraged the embrace of extreme solutions: "to the extent
that this world is destroyed, man will be able to return to his primitive
source. . . . He will return to the moment when he was confounded
with the universe, when he did not distinguish himself from either the
stars or the sunlight."[17] I suspect that it is sublime moments such as
these that account for the wilder varieties of enthusiasm shown to his
work today, while much of what is most powerful in his thought (specifically, the critique of reification, bureaucracy, and militarism from
the standpoint of the sacred) derives more from the tradition of French
cultural conservatism than from some self-proclaimed surradicalism.

The connections between Maistre and the College of Sociology
were underlined by Caillois himself in one of his most expansive lectures at the college, "The Sociology of the Executioner." Caillois emphasizes the complicity of sovereign and executioner within a framework of sacred purity and impurity: "Sovereign and executioner, one in
brilliance and splendor and the other in darkness and shame, fulfill cardinal and symmetric functions. . . . They are equally untouchable,"
one because of his holiness, the other his unholiness (Hollier 241). The
executioner fulfills the monarch's fundamental power, that over life,
while leaving him all his unsoiled glory:

Only the head of State has the right of life and death over the citizens
of a nation, and only the executioner enforces it. He leaves the sovereign the prestigious part and takes charge of the part that is infamous
[*la part maudite*]. The blood staining his hands does not sully the court

that produces sentence: the executioner takes on himself all the horror of the execution. (Hollier 244)

These claims, the theoretical kernel of Caillois's speech, could all have been drawn straight from Maistre, as could the imagery that informs them. As much is admitted when Caillois cites his name: "Joseph de Maistre, at the end of the impressive portrait he paints of the executioner . . . points out precisely that this living depth of abjection is simultaneously the condition and support of all grandeur, all power, and all subordination" (Hollier 244). Noteworthy here is the admiring tone, uncommon at the college, which spared no venom for its predecessors. Moreover, what Maistre "points out precisely" is precisely the college's fundamental thesis: the grounding of sovereignty in abjection. The last sentence of the last lecture given at the college asks the eminently Maistrean rhetorical question: "Could there be a society without a spiritual power, radically separate from temporal power?" (Hollier 341). Maistre's *Du pape*, we shall see, addresses precisely this question and answers it in the negative. Maistre and the College of Sociology could be called partners in extremity: at the heart of both of their works is a theory of transgression in which politics is understood as the interplay of limits and extremes, but where Maistre generally defends limits, the College affirms extremes.

The appearance of Maistre's name at the College of Sociology was no chance encounter; the relation between them may be traced historically as well as thematically. There are indeed two distinct historical lineages that link them, one sociological and the other literary. The latter goes by way of Baudelaire, whom Maistre "taught to think," feeding his obsession with victimization and human degradation while providing him with both a theory of symbolism and the model of a style that describes human evil with the utmost laconic elegance. Many of the strengths as well as the weaknesses of the figures surrounding the college may indeed be traced to their combined reading of Durkheim with Baudelaire, which too readily resulted in a lyricism of sacred violence. Our chief concern, however, is with sociology, where the lineage of Bataille and Caillois leads directly back through Durkheim and Comte to Maistre.

The most direct influence on Bataille's sociology, more so even than Marx and Nietzsche, was Durkheim. From him he borrowed his basic guiding ideas of the primacy of the social totality, as something more than the sum of its aggregate individual parts; religion as the guiding force of this social solidarity, generated in collective cultic performances; the heterogeneity of the sacred and the profane; the ambiguity of the sacred as both the low and violent as well as the high and noble; and finally the critique of the overrationalization and fragmentation of modern social life, based on the above principles. All of these Durkheimian ideas are already found in Maistre. Bataille parts company with Durkheim as with Maistre, however, when it comes to an application of the above principles, and he insists upon a sacrificial project for the present: "a virulent and devastating sacrifice, a rite that would end in an epidemic contagion, converting and exalting the person who had sown the first seed."[18] Such a project is marked by a Gnostic *politique du pire*, a search for catastrophic redemption, even the egomania of a heresiarch, tendencies that bore the brunt of Maistre's criticism as all too common in modernity.

Durkheim in turn claimed Comte as his master in sociology who inspired his effort to explain rationally the irrational forces of society. It was in Comte's work that he found the idea of the symbolic cohesion of society and thus of the decisive sociological importance of cultural norms and mores, of religion. It is likewise from Comte that he inherits the "organic" conception of the primacy of society relative to the individual. Durkheim himself restricts this claim to the theory of sociology while rejecting its practical application, embodied in the politics of Maurras, who also rightly claims descent from Comte, but from his programmatic authoritarianism and not his sociology. Durkheim thus takes up traditionalist theory while rejecting a retrograde politics; moreover, he took up a traditionalist-inspired critique of the excesses of classical liberal economics while maintaining a respect for liberal democratic values in the name of a likewise inspired corporatism.[19]

Comte himself praised Maistre in the highest terms as the greatest of modern historians who had invented the historical study of symbolic practices. Maistre represented for him the decisive counterattack on the Enlightenment's alleged ignorance and hatred of history and, as such, an antidote to its "social inanity."[20] Maistre's *Du pape* is put forward as the great example of a positivist history, "the most methodical, the most profound and the most exact exposition of the old spiritual organization" of Europe.[21] What Comte found most appealing in this work was its empirical treatment of the history of spiritual authority (significantly, he nowhere mentions the *Soirées*, which with their complex interplay of voices, fact and fiction, theory and mysticism could not possibly fit the positivist mold).

Comte sees Maistre's greatest contribution to sociology in his "very rational analysis of the necessary conditions of all spiritual power."[22] For Comte this meant above all the necessity of a moral force to restrain the egoistic, individualist, and materialist tendencies of the modern West. This idea of moral authority obviously converges with the concerns of the theory of ideology as it has been approached in France since the Revolution. One might indeed argue that it is the positive or negative evaluation of order per se, rather than a dispute over the structure of moral and symbolic authority, that has differentiated French theorists of ideology. The idea of the necessity of an order (whether old or new) created through authority over minds can thus be traced directly, though with variations of accent according to the political hopes of the theorists, from Maistre to Comte to Durkheim to Bataille and his contemporary acolytes.

Bataille and Caillois in many ways represent the opposite pole of interpretations of sacrifice from Girard. For the former, sacrifice is above all moral action, indeed *the* moral action; for the latter, it has nothing moral about it at all—it is at bottom a matter of biology, of stimulus and response. In both, however, one finds moments of uncritical enthusiasm for their topic. All these tendencies are found in Maistre himself, yet one also finds in his work a refusal to diffuse this tension between the moral and the amoral that indelibly marks sacred forms.

Every effort to understand sacrificial violence presents in an exacerbated and thus compelling form a general danger found in theories of irrationality and disorder. On the one hand, such a theory requires a certain detachment on the part of the interpreter, for to approach such a baneful subject with feeling leads inevitably to fascination or disgust rather than understanding. On the other hand, a stance of pure detachment would become inhuman, as the abominable is reduced to a purely formal question. These twin dangers are found at certain moments in the work of Bataille and Girard, respectively.

This transferential impasse is the double bind or double threat of a theory of sacrifice. Either its fascination or its inhumanity may itself give us the very irrationality or violence it would have us understand. Maistre's own response to this dilemma remains ambiguous. I have found and will emphasize in his work a general notion that the legitimacy of power is measured by its distance from sacrifice, violence, and bloodletting, yet one also finds, if much less often than is commonly believed, undeniable moments of fascination, of insufficient critical distance from the work of violence.

The deep lyricism of Maistre's depiction of the executioner at work would seem to connote just this sort of allurement by sacrifice. Yet this is a lyricism that challenges any identification with the work of degradation. The infamous scene does not erase or mask the violence of order beneath the glorious institutions of the State. On the contrary, the lyricism of the passage puts in relief the full monstrosity of domination: whatever the complex workings of Maistre's desire, the executioner does not at all emerge as an attractive, honorable, readily acceptable figure.

The shortcoming of Maistre's argument, like almost all interpretations of sacrifice, is not to consistently step outside the thought of sacred violence and, in particular, outside the perspective of the ritual community that seeks redemption in victimization. The way in which sacrifice reduces a living being to an object must be resisted without cease—to observe the fact of this reduction, as Maistre does, is an important beginning, but it is not enough. This shortcoming is by no means Maistre's alone. It is not the sign of his unique monstrosity but rather the paradigmatic ambiguity of those theories, those anthropologies, those day-to-day outlooks that treat sacrifice or punitive violence on its own terms.

Sacrificial violence thus raises essential questions of political responsibility. In this chapter Maistre has shown us that politics are not pure: the executioner is the figure of the brute domination found beneath the surface of every possible regime. He is the remnant that persists after the work of rational political analysis is done: an indecipherable presence, the monstrous adjunct of authority, what Benjamin calls that "something rotten in law." The question is, What is to be done with this insight? Modern European history has too often confirmed Conrad's observation that "it seems as if the discovery made by many men at various times that there is much evil in the world were a source of proud and unholy joy."[23] Awareness of the impurity of institutions too easily encourages not the demystification of violence but its contrary, what Derrida calls "archaeo-eschatological" thinking, a rash, apocalyptic response to a situation taken as degraded at its roots. Such indiscriminate calls for redeeming destruction are found at both ends of the political spectrum today as they were to a greater degree in the interwar period and in Maistre's time; they are especially seductive at moments of historical transition and uncertainty, moments that have traditionally called for sacrifices.

Maistre took up his pen in response to just such a situation of exacerbated change. Against the Revolution in which centuries-long transformations seemed telescoped into the space of months, he everywhere defended tradition and its sense of limits. This was his conservatism. Yet this same rejection of drastic measures led him to roundly criticize his fellow counterrevolutionaries' desire for war and retributional punishment against the Revolution. Because he read the Revolution as an apocalyptic sacrificial crisis, we shall see, he believed that it could only be resisted by nonapocalyptic means. He thus gives us the example of a theory of sacred violence that resists sacrificial politics so far as possible. While he believed that as long as there is life there will be violent death, this dark presentiment led him to defend existing institutions, compromised though they be, against the ever-present human potential for escalating barbarity. All this will be confirmed as we now turn to his ideas on sovereignty, legitimacy, and the divine origin of constitutions.

Chapter 4

Symbolic Power

It is really saddening to see the eccentricity of the Middle Ages repeatedly misused to teach men to boast of themselves, as if they were devilish fine fellows. – Kierkegaard, *Concluding Unscientific Postscript*

The idea of sovereignty has not received good press or even much attention in contemporary political theory, despite the prodigious efforts of a Bataille or a Carl Schmitt to revive it. Typical of the turn away from this venerable topic is Maritain's suggestion that "political philosophy must get rid of the word, as well as the concept, of sovereignty," not only because "it creates insuperable difficulties" but because "this concept is intrinsically wrong." Yet this "confusing" and "wrong" concept refers to a fact; a fact, wrong and confusing as it may be, is not done away with by doing away with its concept. While we may agree with Maritain that "there is no sovereignty, that is, no natural and inalienable right to transcendent or separate supreme power in political society," we must yet insist upon the reality of a *sovereignty effect*, a supremacy of power separated from the sphere of consensual self-government. Power does claim transcendence and must do so as long as its actions are not in fact just, that is, indefinitely.[1]

Political Anthropology: The Ritual Forms of Power
That this transcendence claimed by power is imaginary makes it no less consequent. President John Adams remarked of the sacred paraphernalia that make of power a sovereignty, "take away crowns and thrones from among men, and there will be an end of all dominion and justice."[2] Revolutionary and reactionary politicians alike have believed that power requires a sacred sanction if its de facto transcendence is to be translated into a de jure legitimacy. Maistre's position on sacred sovereignty pushes Adams's argument further: it is not only useful to power but necessary to the very idea of social order. Sovereignty and people are wholly complementary terms, the one necessary to the other: "the idea of a *people* reveals that of an aggregation around a common center, and without sovereignty there can be no ensemble or political unity" (Maistre, *Etude*, OC 1:324). This mention of a grouping

around a common center already points to sovereignty's ceremonial basis and to its place in the ordering of society, themes dwelt upon below. Unlike most other conservatives, Maistre does not so much simply call for a greater and more transcendent authority as provide a theory and a history of sovereignty as the ritualization of power, the respective subjects of this and the next chapters.

Maistre's mention of grouping about a common center points to where a theory of ritual may perhaps best contribute to modern sociology: social phenomenology. Such a phenomenology of ritual must attend to two complementary domains of political experience: first, what one may call its "horizontal" dimension, a constitution of center and margins, in which a sociopolitical space is ritually constructed within the group; second, a "vertical" dimension, a constitution of sovereignty and abjection, which manages social violence through the sacralization of power. As Maistre realized, these two dimensions always form a pair: no sovereignty without a foundation upon a cohesive social grouping, and no such grouping without a center around which to form. Maistre's constant attention to both of these dimensions of social experience is a fine token of his ambiguous place in the history of political philosophy. Whereas the majority of traditionalist and counter-Enlightenment thinkers sought to reduce all social and political considerations to questions of the vertical and above all to man's relation to the Christian god, the tendency of their opponents on the side of Enlightenment was to resolutely ignore all political questions irreducible to the horizontal. Let us start with the horizontal and work our way up.

In the terse formulation of Alfred Schutz, the "acceptance of a common system of relevances leads the members of the group to a homogeneous self-typification."[3] Schutz's insight applies directly to questions of political ritual. First of all, the gestures and movements of ritual articulate the spatiotemporal complex of the subject with that of society, they create an intersection of inner and outer meanings or intentions, and they make of this articulation, this unity of person and society, a vivid present. This gearing of the psychological into the social creates a habitus, a relatively stable and circumscribed symbolic sphere mapped out by the directedness of attention that defines ritual. Thus is constituted a densely meaningful nonprivate world, a meaningful sphere of everyday life. Ritual objectifies or projects before its audience the meaningfulness of social symbols, values, mores, and roles; it realizes these values by making them present to the senses of everyone involved as an actually shared objectification. Ritual thus makes of culture a given, of this particular possible institution one that is taken as real, taken for granted. Thus, in the broadest sense, ritual is socialization itself. Maistre hence observes of those latter-day minor rituals that "the principal effect of games, and that which places them in the rank of the most precious institutions, is that they *force men to look at one another.*"[4]

In this constitution of an everyday world taken for granted, ceremony is the great locus of legitimation conduct. As the establishment of dominant interpretations, of assumptions about meaning and power, and as an interiorization of institutions and roles accepted as endowed with meaning, ritual regularizes and makes accustomed a particular structure of status and prestige. The taking for granted of values that defines a culture here becomes a taking for granted of politics, which stabilizes or routinizes power. This is why Maistre always speaks of politics in relation to religion and its canonic symbolic practices.

Whether explicitly political or religious, the ceremonial staging of roles and hierarchies creates a horizon of shared expectations as to proper social conduct: this one behaves like a king, this one like a subject, that one like a magistrate. (This is the thesis of one of Maistre's most early and interesting texts, considered below: "the exterior character of the magistrate.") This ritual construction of hierarchies (the very word refers to the power of the sacred) is at stake in all the little ceremonies that make up daily life. Not that participation in such ceremonies allows one to understand social hierarchy, but one takes it for granted that it is meaningful, one accepts its inconsistency and incoherence as given. In ritual what is opaque to reason is presented in the clearest light to the imagination and thus becomes "true" (at least for the social imaginary—but that is all that is required) without proof.

An early Masonic text by Maistre shows his keen awareness of this unthinking sway of ritual power:

it is inconceivable to what point the forms and fittings of ceremonies strike the wisest of men, impose on them and serve to keep them in order. . . . Thirty or forty people silently ranged along the walls of a room hung in black or green, themselves distinguished by singular clothes, and only speaking by permission, will reason wisely on every topic proposed. Let the hangings or the costumes fall, extinguish one candle in nine, simply permit the seats to be moved: you will see these same men precipitate themselves on one another, no longer listen to each other, or talk women or talk shop.[5]

This passage neatly depicts the ritual construction and standardization of meanings, systems of relevance and typical conduct, *not at the discretion of any individual*. Ceremony induces an interindividual perception of social reality, induces form, and makes of an aggregate a society. Maistre concludes the above passage by remarking, "Again, form is a great thing."

Michael Walzer poses the problem as follows: "the state is invisible; it must be personified before it can be seen, symbolized before it can be loved, imagined before it can be conceived."[6] Political ceremonial may thus be defined, to borrow the Pauline phrase that dominates Maistrean cosmology, as a "system of invisible things manifested visibly," a manifestation of those invisible things, power, organization, order, hierarchy. This is not to say that all politics reduces to dupery or sleight of hand (pace Renan), but that all politics can only appear to participants or observers in symbolic guise.

Ritual makes meaningful the blunt factuality of social order. From this perspective, ritual is not merely (and perhaps not so much) the eruption of the irrational or unmasterable within daily life but also the surrounding of this unmasterable irrationality *by* the everyday, by discrete and manageable symbols. In turn, by way of this "surrounding" or bodying forth, society presents itself as carrying within it reference to ultimate values; reality is thus coupled with transcendence, though the latter remains invisible or may simply not exist apart from such ritual manifestations.

From another perspective (that of criticism rather than anthropology), ritual is understood as a socialization into irrational, or at least nonscientific, norms of belief and behavior; this is the use of a theory of ritual order for modern theories of ideology. Consent ultimately depends upon a common communicative environment, on a set of signs or symbols that may be meaningfully manipulated. The role of ritual in the construction of consent, in Victor Turner's words, is to convert "the obligatory into the desirable," in other words, to achieve an idealization of power as a value, as a transcendent constraint to which one consents.[7] Ceremonial presents compelling symbols and social meanings to the senses, in a situation of suspended judgment or sensory overload, as real, effective, and necessary. Enacting a common code of symbols, ritual allows social unification even in the absence of a unity of aims or beliefs and provides a regimen of social constancy against submission to conflicting social passions.

Maistre was among the first, after Spinoza and Vico, to thematize how power—the cohesive production and reproduction of asymmetric social relations—is based not merely on coercion but also, and even more fundamentally, on the symbolic, on custom, representation, and belief. "Government alone cannot govern. . . . All governments require, as an indispensable minister, either slavery, which diminishes the number of active wills within the state, or a Divine power, which, by a sort of spiritual *graft*, destroys the natural asperity of those wills, and enables them to act together without mutual injury."[8] This purely political "requirement" of a divine power points to the extent of Maistre's purely sociological interest in religion.

The ritual power that Maistre everywhere emphasizes has since become a central concern of political anthropologists. Thus Luc de Heusch has argued in wholly Maistrean terms that every sovereignty, every government, is "at once the depository of constraining physical force and priest of a cult of force." Ceremonial representation creates the mysteries of authority, the august character of the legitimate exercise of power. Power alone may be no mystery, but there is nothing more rare than power alone, without some admixture of symbolic authority. For Heusch, then, the sacrality of power "cannot in any fashion be considered as a typically archaic element."[9] Every sovereignty arouses the feeling of a "mysterium tremendum" that for Rudolph Otto defines the sacred.

Georges Balandier has thus insisted that "all legitimacy is a religion, a sacred consensus that cannot be put back into question. . . . It is the nature of power to maintain, either in a covert or a masked form, a political religion," a religion that sanctifies the political sphere and raises it a transcendent distance above daily social life. Thus the role of political ritual is to arouse "the feelings that bind the subject to the sovereign—a veneration or total submission that cannot be justified by reason, a fear of disobedience that has the character of sacrilegious transgression." This is the reverence of the social bond, of the bonding or binding that is the basis of social order and that makes the figure of the executioner, the binder par excellence and in more ways than one, such a compelling one in Maistre's texts. Because sovereignty requires legitimacy and legitimacy requires veneration, Balandier concludes, "every society links its own order to an order beyond itself, and, in the case of traditional societies, to the cosmos."[10] Whether this cosmos or meaningful order is one of nature, of political rights, or of social distinctions, its anchoring function remains fundamental; it is as a denunciation of all order as bad order that Gnosticism represents such a basic social threat and that Maistre will seek to combat it.

The urtext of political anthropology may well be Plato's *Laws*. It certainly was so for Maistre. His reading notebooks contain some hundred pages of notes on this work, "one of the most astonishing things written by any man before the age of Enlightenment" (B.C., that is), taken down in 1809, the period of the "Eclaircissement" and the *Soirées*.[11] Maistre found in the *Laws* confirmation of his belief in the conserving or constitutive role of ritualized behavior.

Even more than the *Republic*, the *Laws* emphasizes the civic role of the Muses—of festivals, drama, and music above all. Plato's guiding concern is the power of these public forms of representation to work for order or disorder within the polis through the shaping of social passions. This is plainly the motivation for his extended excurses, foreign to modern ears, on the propriety of the various musical modes, rhythms, and postures: respect for law begins in respect for form. The value of canonized genres for the social order is that "the child's soul may not learn the habit of feeling pleasure and pain in ways contrary to the law and those who have listened to its bidding, but keep them company, taking pleasure and pain in the very same things as the aged—that, I hold, proves to be the real purpose of our 'songs.' They are really spells for souls."[12] This figure of "listening to the bidding of the laws" nicely evokes the mysteries of authority and that "interpellation" that for Althusser defines the workings of ideology by leading the person to recognize and to form himself in the image of a subject of the State. This interpellation is achieved in ritual, which Althusser defines as "the material existence of an ideological apparatus."[13]

For Plato, social order is best maintained by the consecration of a canon of auspicious rituals, dances, and songs, fixed in a cycle of festivals, each with its respective guiding spirit or god (Robespierre seems to have come to the same conclusion). These festivals will "charm the young into virtue," and participation therein will achieve that "voluntary coercion" that is the foundation of ordered social conduct. Contravention of the canonic genres will be punished as blasphemy by the priests (Plato 671a, 799–800). Plato's insistence upon the mimetic bases of social order goes so far as to attribute the decline of Athenian authority to a blurring of musical genres, a "universal confusion of forms" and an attendant "contempt for musical law." Musical license precedes civil and religious license, and in Athens "sovereignty of the best" gave way to "sovereignty of the audience," the fear of every established authority (Plato 700–701).

Plato's masterwork raises in an exemplary manner the question of the political value of philosophies of order. Conservative thought at its best, whether in Plato, Durkheim, or Maistre, provides not only a call for social order but a theory of how that order comes about. Such a theory is by no means in the sole service of reactionary or repressive politics and may well serve the interests of their critique. Without Plato, one might say, Popper would lack half his theory of closed societies.

A critique of the ritual bases of politics must approach ritual from a dual perspective: first, as the moment of social irrationality (as shock, crisis, affect, imaging forth) and, second, as the moment of social routinization (as normalization, management of crisis, channelling of affect, image framing). Both of these aspects of ritual are capable of excess or abuse. The first, Dionysian side of ritual may degenerate to abandon, to an institutionalization of scapegoating, of violence and destruction, to ritual slaughter. The second, Apollonian side may rigidify to repression, to a stifling of difference and deformation by excessive formalization of personal roles. I have discussed this first danger at some length in the previous chapter; here I will briefly address the second before departing the paths of theory for the workshop of historical reconstruction.

To treat politics as nothing but ritual and symbol could only be mystifying. This approach, the greatest of all conservative ruses, often serves as a sleight of hand to conceal the real conflicts, contradictions, and injustices that must be the starting point for any democratic criticism of ideology and its social distortions. Such mystifications are none too rare in contemporary sociology. Emblematic is Peter Berger's widely read *Sacred Canopy*, which, due in part to its uncritical borrowings from Gehlen's anthropology, presents social order, control, and the "integration" performed by ritual as unqualified benefits for the resistance they offer to the "nightmare of anomic terror." (Berger's theses are supported by a disdain for the "man in the street," who is incapable of reason and is thus, for our good and his own, to be controlled.) Berger's work, like that of many conservative sociologists, is a celebration of what must be done if order is to prevail, and what must be done is ritualization. The clear danger here is that the necessary respect for social order engendered by the ritual sanctification of social norms may well degenerate into the passive apolitical sufferance of a coercive regime. This danger is not only found in traditional societies; indeed, one mark of these latter is that the powerful as well as the powerless are sub-

ject to the sacred norms of their religious ethic. (The self-interested rejection of such ethics is what Maistre called "practical atheism.")

There are, this implies, mechanisms internal to the ritual economy
that challenge the ceremonial celebration of brute domination and that
place ritual (and with it cultural traditionalism) beyond mere conservation. The ritual and symbolic tools of legitimation are always capable
of being turned against power, for, as Maistre everywhere emphasizes,
ritual traces the limits as much as the scope of its legitimate use. A society's ritual practices and the values they sanctify may either affirm or
deny the legitimacy of a particular power formation, which may well
diverge from the collective representations of the just relations of ruler
and ruled. This might be called the negative dialectics of the traditionalist (Adorno himself, of course, had more than a little of the traditionalist in him).

Ritualized symbols have a residual history and meaning independent
of the uses to which they are put: they must be used properly, "auspi-
ciously," within traditional limits. Ritual meaning cannot be created at
will. In particular, ritual legitimates the position of a given power
holder (the *sacre* of kings, the inauguration of presidents), but by that
very stroke it makes that position transferable, that is, no longer the
possession of any one individual. The result of all ritual investitures, in
the words of Evans-Pritchard, is that "kingship captures the king" and
binds him to its norms.[14] We shall soon discuss Maistre's emphasis on
the ritual checks upon the abuse of authority and above all the role of
the pope, that master of European ceremonies, as crowner and un-
crowner of kings. In the meantime, these remarks on ritual will help us
grasp the significance of Maistre's claim that constitutions are of their
nature "divine."

The Theory of Constitutions

What is a constitution? The broad outlines of an answer are already familiar from our opening discussion of traditionalism. Maistre pushes
traditionalist constitutional theory, with its emphasis on custom and
"prejudice," toward what is today called the theory of ideology.

First of all, Maistre insists the constitution is neither a set of legal prescriptions nor even exactly a form of government. It is, rather, a certain
consistency in what is done and how one thinks within a given society,
a cohesive cluster of norms, habits, and unexamined beliefs that one
might call a political habitus, the common background of a nation's
various *mentalités*. The constitution of France is thus "what you sense
when you are in France; it is that mixture of liberty and authority, law

and opinion that would lead the foreign traveler in France, himself the subject of a monarchy, to believe he lives while in France under a different government from his own" (Maistre, *Considérations*, OC 1:89). Constitutions are made not of statutes but of customs.

The idea that a constitution consists of the governing norms of behavior has a long history in French political thought. The sixteenth-century jurist Etienne Pasquier tells us that "well-ordered laws in any country form a habitude of manners and morals among those subject to them that over the long run appears to be imprinted on them by the disposition of their nature."[15] Maistre would accept this linkage of law and habitude but not its apportioning of cause and effect: he would argue to the contrary that it is the national ethic that forms the laws and *imprints* them on *nature* as *dispositions*.

Maistre emphasizes this secondary or derivative constitutional role of the actual laws themselves when he defines the constitution as "merely the solution" of the following conundrum: "given the population, the mores, the religion, the geographical situation, the political circumstances, the wealth, the good and bad qualities of a particular nation, to find the laws that suit it" (Maistre, *Considérations*, OC 1:75). This is exactly how Plato defined the constitutional problem in the *Laws*, with the significant exception that Maistre includes the mores in the list of givens prior to legislation. He extends Plato's emphasis on the power of customary forms to the point that he rejects Plato's belief that legislation can determine normative behavior. "Does one say that the government makes the mores? I deny it expressly. It is the mores, on the contrary, that make the governments."[16] The "true" constitution of England is thus no document or governmental structure but "that admirable, unique, and infallible public spirit that transcends all praise. It guides everything, conserves everything, and restores everything. What is written is nothing." This public spirit is "infallible" precisely because it both determines and outlasts all political vicissitudes—because it is constitutive, that is (Maistre, *Essai*, OC 1:241–42).

This is to argue that all political organization is founded in some absolutely basic manner upon what we call ideology. All power, Maistre argues, rests upon "beliefs," "prejudices," "superstitions," that is to say, upon "opinions of some kind adopted prior to all examination." These unexamined opinions are the "Palladium of empires" upon which the safety of nations depends: government "lives only by the national reason, that is to say by political faith, which is a *symbol*" (Maistre, *Etude*, OC 1:375). Elsewhere Maistre explains that "a symbol is by

no means an order addressed to the reason, it is a confession of love."[17]
Symbolic power is power over desire, which makes subjects *want* to
obey; the symbol, in politics as in religion, is what one consents to
without reason. "There is a point where faith must be blind, there is
likewise in politics a point where obedience must be blind," otherwise
it would not be obedience. This idea of a consensual order that is reproduced only on condition of oversight and misrecognition defines precisely the domain of ideology (Maistre, "Lettres," OC 7:39).[18]

Maistre always emphasized that power is power over opinion. Moral
order is "the only one possible for intelligent beings" (Maistre, *Soirées*,
OC 4:27); authority over man thus requires "sensible, material, palpable
ideas. You will never guide him by syllogisms" (Maistre, "Lettres," OC
7:166). Authority ultimately relies upon a religion of state, because rule
of law can only arise on the basis of a prior ethic of obedience. Maistre
thus cites Demosthenes: "to write a law is nothing. To make it wanted
is everything" (Maistre, *Essai*, OC 1:230n). Rule cannot support itself
by documents alone; it requires the consent of the nation "made palpable" or put into practice in its governing ethos.

It is this insight into the grounding of authority upon ideology, upon
the religious observance of governing symbolic and moral practices,
that guides Maistre's rejection of written constitutions or, rather, of the
claim that writing is the only stable foundation of social relations. What
holds society together is its prelogical order of symbolic practices, and
these cannot be written. "As there is something in music it is impossible
to annotate, there is something in all governments it is impossible to
write" (Maistre, "Lettres," OC 7:153). What cannot be written in constitutions as in music is the practical interpretation, which is presented
only in performance, and it is this practice that is basic to politics:
"There is the same difference between political theories and constitutional laws as there is between poetics and poetry" (Maistre, *Considérations*, OC 1:72). Just as poetics presupposes the existence of poetry,
Maistre would argue, social order cannot be the product of logical legislation, for logic and legislation alike presuppose an existing social order or constitution. As Maistre explains in the *Essai sur le principe générateur des constitutions politiques*, "Only when society finds itself already
constituted, not knowing how, can certain particular articles be made
known or put into writing" (OC 1:265). What is written in constitutions
finds its origin, its cohesion, and its sanction in what is unwritten.

Maistre condemns written law, however, not only for its insuffi-
ciency; he views it as a positive danger. Written law is "merely a neces-

sary evil, generated by human frailty or malice" (*Essai*, OC 1:258). These written declarations are as a rule either the cause or the effect of "great evils," and they "always cost the people more than they are worth" (*Essai*, OC 1:265): they either result from or lead to the usurpation of rights and privileges.

First of all, written laws may be the *result* of usurpations, of "frailty or malice." Laws are only put into writing "to declare forgotten or contested rights." Written laws are thus "only props, and an edifice only needs props when it has lost its equilibrium or when it is violently shaken from outside" (Maistre, *Etude*, OC 1:347, 370). The amount of written law is thus exactly proportionate to the weakness of the institutions and provides the very picture of constitutional decline. In *Considérations sur la France*, Maistre thus asserts that "laws are only declarations of rights, and rights are only declared when they are attacked, so that a multiplicity of written constitutional laws proves only a multiplicity of conflicts and the danger of destruction" (OC 1:69).

Maistre claims, however, that written law is not merely evidence of a danger of destruction but is dangerous in and of itself: what is truly fundamental and truly constitutional law only endangers the state by being written. "There are always some things in every constitution that cannot be written and that must be allowed to remain in dark and reverent obscurity" (Maistre, *Considérations*, OC 1:69). Maistre thus cites the "wise Hume" on the *parlements'* right of remonstrance against the sovereign, "which must be governed by certain delicate ideas of propriety and decency, rather than any exact rule or prescription" (*Considérations*, OC 1:69n). If this "intervention of the nation" is examined closely, Maistre clarifies, "it will be found to be *less* than a colegislative power and *more* than a simple consent. This is . . . the kind of thing that must be left in a certain obscurity, and cannot be submitted to human legislation. It is the *most divine part* of the constitution, if one may express it this way" (*Considérations*, OC 1:93n). Divine, that is, ritualized and "obscure." Indeed, this remark carefully leaves the very extent of necessary obscurity itself obscure. (Soon we shall have to see just why this "obscure obscurity" is the "most divine part.")

Writing threatens not only those whose rights are thus curtailed (the sovereign in the above example), however; it threatens even those whose rights are thus *expressed*. In one of his letters Maistre gives two examples of this threat, one "small" and the other "grave." A "small example" of the danger of expressed rights is that of the father who would ask if he had the right to open the correspondence of his son. In the ab-

stract, "I would respond: without doubt; I would believe to have
wounded paternal authority if I answered otherwise. But if you came to
ask me *in concreto* as one says in the schools: 'would you counsel me to
open this letter of my son that is suspect to me?' I would respond to
you: 'Papa, be very careful, for you have everything to lose, and little or
nothing to gain.'" That Maistre knew his letters were read by the czar's
police adds both piquancy and depth to this proviso. A "more grave"
example refers to sovereignty itself. Western sovereigns, in exchange
for forfeiting the right to condemn to death, have been vested with the
inviolability of their persons. "Is not inviolability good and sacred?
And yet, what people or what man has ever imagined to make a law
that permited the prince to do impuniously anything he pleased? The
Sovereign himself would repress this law, by which he would justly
consider himself offended."[19] Unwritten laws thus protect the sovereign by restraining him from the full exercise of his possible powers; to
write them would only be to encourage tyranny, the loss of power over
hearts and minds, and thus ultimately the "Orientalism" of regicide.

Finally, the chief failing of written law is that it bears no sanction,
which means it may be *un*written. Only what remains unwritten (custom, ritual, tradition) may not be erased. Whatever authority writes a
law has the right to annul it, so that "the law would not have that quality of divine immutability that characterizes truly constitutional laws.
The essence of a fundamental law is that no one has the right to abolish
it. For how could it stand above *all men*, if *some men* had made it?" Thus
one has the political necessity of elevating the "founding fathers" or the
"men of '89" above the status of "some men." The constitution must
not be subject to the mercy of *any* "some men." The sum of these reflections leads Maistre to bemoan "the profound idiocy, I repeat, the profound idiocy of those unfortunate souls who believe that legislators are
men, laws are paper, and nations may be constituted *with ink*" (*Essai*,
OC 1:236).

Much of Maistre's criticism of written constitutions is directed
against the theory of the social contract, which would propose that society is invented according to the canons of reason by contracting parties who thus have the right, as its creators, to annul and reinvent society: constitutions as human products may be "reproduced" at will. All
the above considerations—the ensuing lack of sanction, encouragement of excesses, and so on—militate against such a theory: "no mere
assembly of men can form a nation, and the very attempt exceeds in
folly the most absurd and extravagant things that all the Bedlams in the

world might put forth" (Maistre, *Considérations*, OC 1:72). In his notes Maistre thus speaks of Rousseau's *Social Contract* as "a novel."[20]

Because a constitution is that very something that exceeds the sum of its subjects, it cannot be the product of discrete individuals. It is indeed presupposed by the contract itself, as a common fund of shared experiences and expectations and as a sanction of the contract once it is made. In a powerful passage, Maistre directly confronts the argument of Locke, who

> sought the nature of law in the expression of aggregate wills. He must have been favored by chance to hit upon the very quality that excludes all idea of *law*. . . . Law is only sanctioned and properly *law* when assumed to emanate from a higher will, so that its essential quality is to be *not the will of all*. . . . This is the reason that primitive common sense, which, fortunately, is anterior to sophism, has always sought the sanction of laws in a superhuman power. (*Essai*, OC 1:236–38)

Law, Maistre argues, is by definition undemocratic, for in all societies it serves to normalize inequalities and to restrain the divergent wills of the people. The limit to freedom of choice cannot be freely chosen and requires a sanction to place it beyond the influence of political whim. It bears underlining that in this passage Maistre does not assert that this sanction derives from its divine origin but from the "assumption" of or "search" for a derivation from "superhuman power." If this is the case, it would seem to follow logically that if the "higher will" is a fiction, then the sanction would be a fiction, and then the compulsion of the law itself would be a fiction; and yet, it is argued, only on such fictions can society endure.

Maistre's theory of constitutions is everywhere guided by the desire to take power out of men's hands to vest it somewhere free from the direct intervention of human will. While men may take part in the growth of constitutions, they do so in unintentional ways, for institutions remain what is subtracted from the sphere of conscious decision. Every important institution is "formed of itself by the concurrence of a thousand agents, who are almost always ignorant of what they are doing; so that they often appear not to perceive the right they themselves are establishing. The institution thus vegetates insensibly over the course of ages" (Maistre, *Du pape*, OC 2:105). The multicausality or overdetermination of the history of cultures thus excludes the intentional transformation of basic institutions, which is precisely what is required.

All this is brought out forcefully in regard to the English constitution, which "was certainly not made a priori"; it is, rather, a complex unity of Roman, canon, and feudal laws, Saxon, Norman, and Danish customs, the privileges, prejudices, and pretensions of all social classes, wars and revolutions, and so on. English statesmen

> never assembled to say, "let us create three powers, balancing them in such a manner, etc." No one ever thought of such a thing. The constitution is the work of circumstances whose number is infinite . . . forming by their admixture and interdependent effects countless millions of combinations that have at last produced, after several centuries, the most complex unity and most beautiful equilibrium of political powers. (Maistre, *Essai*, OC 1:246–47)

This complex historical basis of institutions is adduced against those who would "brusquely transport" English institutions into France. Maistre compares this ambition to that of the "Roman general who had removed a sundial from Syracuse and placed it at Rome without worrying the least bit about the latitude"; he adds, of the would-be reformers, that "what renders the comparison inexact is that the good general did not pride himself on knowing astronomy" (Maistre, "Lettres," OC 7:214).

Maistre develops the traditionalist argument that constitutions are the work of history rather than individual intentions to such a point that he claims "the origin of the Church" must be sought in the fourth century: "it is from that time only that we see it acting externally as a publicly constituted society, having its hierarchy, its laws, its customs" (Maistre, *Du pape*, OC 2:47n). An institution only exists historically once it has, like the fourth-century Church, ceased to be an unstable grouping of allegiances and become constituted. The origin of the Church is not to be found in the Bible because religious constitutions, like political constitutions, are not found in books.

The Bible, Maistre thus writes in his private notes, is not a religious code.

> Dogma is always presupposed in it, never directly intimated: the form is historical, admonishing, never dogmatic. J. C. speaks of the Father, the son, the H. Spirit; he never says, "you will believe in the Holy Trinity, which is God in three equal and combined persons . . ." Not only is not everything written, but it was a dogma in the Church that not everything should be written. St. Ignatius was

praised in the first centuries for showing in the very society of the apostles what must be said and what must be hid.

True to his thesis that laws are written only in response to usurpations, Maistre observes that "the four evangels were only published to contradict others published by false zeal, ignorance, or heresy, and Instruction was already in full force when they were published. . . . Never does one find the tone or the form of a religious code."[21] Again we see that Maistre's traditionalism is less dogmatic than it is historicist.

Because constitutions are constituted by history, because they cannot be invented by any one man or group of men, Maistre concludes that every nation has the laws—that is, the fundamental laws integral to its history—it deserves. "All peoples have the government that suits them, and none has chosen its own. . . . For the rest, as every exaggerated statement is false, I do not at all intend to deny the possibility of political ameliorations" (Maistre, *Etude*, OC 1:351–52). Indeed, this potential for *ameliorations* is claimed to strengthen his thesis by showing that political *creation* is beyond human power.

Constitutions are thus the supreme instance of the general law that "man can modify everything within the sphere of his activity, but he creates nothing: such is the law in the physical world as in the moral world." Man has the power to "graft" but not to "germinate." "Germination" occurs only upon the ground of complex sociohistorical interactions and cross-purposes. Because, as we have seen, it is the mores thus generated that make the government, and because government cannot invent the mores, "no nation can give itself liberty unless it is already free. When a nation begins to reflect on its existence, its laws are already made. Human influence does not extend beyond the development of rights already existing but disregarded or disputed" (Maistre, *Considérations*, OC 1:67–70).[22] This was the error of the legislators of the French Revolution. Now we turn to their opposite number, the French monarchy and its constitution, leaving for the next chapter a close consideration of just how constitutions do "germinate" and why this process must never be meddled with.

Sacred Monarchy

For Maistre the monarch is above all the "visible sign" or "character" of social unity, a sign without which society would be impossible, the master signifier of the political imaginary.[23] The king marks the spot around which political ritual is organized. It would not be too much to describe him as a living totem: a sacred symbol that designates the place of authority at the center of social representation. Maistre so much defines kingship as a "national theater" of representations that representation is said to make the king: "every sovereignty that is not visible, exists not" (*Du pape*, OC 2:84n). Social unity requires a show of that unity, found in the symbolic or "talismanic" person of the king. It is by symbols and as a symbol that the king reigns.

Maistre argues for monarchy, then, not from divine right but from sacred sociology. This is confirmed when he emphasizes the idolatry of kingship, an idolatry he finds in every true, that is, traditional, religion. He thus cites Mirabeau, "the king is an idol that one sets up," adding only that "setting aside the reprehensible form of this idea" (reprehensible because of its denigration of traditional social belief), "it is certain that he is correct" (Maistre, *Etude*, OC 1:430). Maistre here hints at a certain artificiality of this "set-up" king. As a theorist of ideology, however, he realized that the artificial may have wholly real effects in society. Out of a conservative's respect for these real effects, he often veiled his remarks on ideology behind allegories.

Sometimes, however, his enthusiasm overcame his circumspection. Speaking of the devotion given to the monarch, Maistre asserts that the French "are perhaps the most monarchical people of Europe; its love for its kings . . . was carried even to idolatry, even to fanaticism, sometimes to ridiculousness." He goes on to cite a long passage from Young's travels describing the mawkish emotion to which the king's presence gave rise. That Maistre is theorizing rather than simply endorsing royal religion is manifest in this assertion that what is "most monarchic" is idolatrous, ridiculous ("Fragments," OC 1:205).

The symbolic nature of kingship, Maistre argues, defines both the powers of the king and the limits to that power. Within politics understood as ritual, the king becomes the dominant symbol of a world of symbolic practices. This dominant symbol allows for the concerted direction of the social imaginary: around the name of the king is organized the staging of representations that was power itself under the ancien régime. "Archimedes knew well that to lift the world, one requires a point of support outside the world" (Maistre, *Etude*, OC 1:525). The king is precisely this "point of support," one that was raised above the social world by the rites of coronation. "The Pontiff's finger has always touched the forehead of rising sovereignty," and "every sovereignty, on whose forehead the finger of the great Pontiff has not impressed its virtue, will always be inferior to the rest" (Maistre, *Du pape*, OC 2:428). Without this sanction, the king could not serve as the support of the symbolic empire—he must have been *lifted up* out of its network to be able to be the transcendent standard or measure of the cultural order.

The emphasis on the king's forehead points out that what is at stake is the *recognition* of power and the mysterious face that power presents: in the sovereign's brow or visage the subject will confront the person of the state and by this recognition participate in the social theater or simulacrum of ancien régime political culture. Maistre elaborates this metaphorics of faciality, recognition, and the marks of royal unction, characteristically employing allegory himself to describe political allegories: "Kings, heads of rising empires, are very often designated, almost branded, by Heaven in some extraordinary manner. How many frivolous people have mocked the Saint-Ampoule [the vial of holy balm with which French kings were anointed] without ever dreaming that it is a hieroglyph that one need only read to understand" (*Essai*, OC 1:267–68). It is thus his name and face, the hieroglyph that marks his image as an idol, that are the principles of royal power.

The king's symbolic position, however, also defines the limits of his power. Maistre thus remarks, "Unfortunate *Stylites*, kings are condemned to live their lives on top of a pillar, without ever being able to descend from it. They cannot, therefore, see so well what goes on immediately below; but, in return for this disadvantage, they see a greater distance" (*Du pape*, OC 2:421). The king here appears as society's head, seeing and seen from a distance; he is indeed almost a statue, a discrete role or position from which he cannot budge. This passivity foisted upon him by the ceremonial basis of his power is underlined when Maistre discounts the direct agency of the king in political culture (a problem we shall return to with the discussion of absolutism and decisionism below): "In fact, monarchy can only serve to centralize counsels and wisdom [*lumières*]." Beyond this rather passive role, the task of the sovereign is to "administer grandeur" (Maistre, *Etude*, OC 1:432).[24] He thus rules as a symbol over symbols, as the imaginary and yet actual prop of social representations.

This regime of social representation Maistre calls a "religion of state." "Government is a veritable religion: it has its dogmas, its mysteries, its ministers" (Maistre, *Etude*, OC 1:375, 366). Its dogmas are its laws, its mysteries its ideologies, and its ministers the aristocracy. It is these last who play the most active part in the direction of society and culture.

Maistre everywhere speaks of the aristocracy, both of sword and robe, as a ritual priesthood that guards and maintains the sacred attrib-

utes of power that the king requires if he is to be the transcendent image
of the nation. Maistre consistently defines nobility by this ideological
function, ignoring the claims of blood and descent. (This definition allows him to insist that every society has its aristocracy, differing only as
to means of recruitment: blood, talent, or wealth; the bourgeois aristocracy will be discussed in a following chapter.) The priestly role of
the nobility is no mere window-dressing. Thus he writes in *Du pape*
that "so long as a pure aristocracy (in other words, one professing to a
point of exaltation the national dogmas) surrounds the throne, it is unshakable, even if weakness or error come to sit upon it; but if the baron-
age becomes apostate, there is no longer any safety for the throne, even
if it were occupied by a St. Louis or a Charlemagne" (OC 2:xxxiii–iv).
Already here one sees how the king's power is qualified by his need for
the support of the bearers of the "national dogmas." Because Maistre
understood the sociopolitical as a ritualized symbolic space, the upkeep
of its mysteries becomes a paramount concern; because worship "viv-
ifies" sovereignty, the aristocracy must uphold its priestly role. "True
nobility is the natural guardian of religion; it is akin to the priesthood,
and never ceases to protect it" (Maistre, *Du pape*, OC 2:296). Maistre marshals to his support the sentence of Appius Claudius, "Religion is the
care of the patricians" [Auspicia sunt patrum], a sentence that, in a less
benign translation, Vico had made the basis of a critical history of symbolic practices: "The auspices belong to the fathers." (By way of clarification, Vico remarks of Appius that he, "by singing to the Roman
plebeians of the force of the gods in the auspices, of which the nobles
claimed to have the science, keeps them in obedience to the nobles.")[25]

   This priestly role of the political elite was the subject of Maistre's
first major text, one that overlaps Kant's "What Is Enlightenment?" and
Weber's "Politics as a Vocation" with its subtle treatment of the distinction between the private and public lives of the magistrate. This text,
"Le Caractère extérieur du magistrat" ("The exterior character of the
magistrate," often referred to as "Discours sur le caractère . . .") was
presented in 1784 on the ceremonial occasion of the Savoy *parlement*'s
appearance, at the opening of its session, before the city of Chambéry
("on this solemn day and on this solemn day alone it is given to our citizens to hear the voice of their magistrates"). It would not be too much,
adopting Derrida's expression, to call Maistre's harangue a social *mise-
en-abyme*. Maistre's essay is the public lecture of a magistrate on how
the magistrate must appear before the public, one indeed that publicly
announces the need for secrecy, simulation, and the maintenance of ap-

pearances. Starting from the claim that "integrity alone can obtain only an equivocal reputation," Maistre presents us with an "art of probity."[26]

Maistre begins with a problem essential to modern politics: the twilight of the political idols and the decline of respect for the allegories of the religion of state. In the eighteenth century, he writes in words that anticipate his reading of the Revolution:

> one has seen the universe become disgusted with those pompous ceremonies, with those imposing solemnities in which the ancient leaders of peoples spoke to the eyes to avoid being misunderstood: the present generation no longer knows how to see in objects anything but the objects themselves, and all the exterior pomp that aggrandized them in the eyes of our ancestors no longer makes an impression on men who calculate everything, even respect. (Maistre, "Discours," *OC* 7:9)

The remainder of the essay presents an apology of such solemnities.

To begin with, the opening discourse of *parlement* that Maistre is delivering is itself one of those political ceremonies that must be kept up. The ritual nature of the event and the symbolic character of its surroundings are emphasized: "Each of the mute beings that here surround us takes on a language if it is well questioned. . . . It would require a revolution to annihilate the physical titles of your origin and your rights; they are written on the stone of this building, on the clothes that decorate you, . . . on all the objects that environ you" (Maistre, "Discours," *OC* 7:10). Maistre turns to the mysteries housed in this temple of justice, closed except on this day to the eyes of the plebs, only to shift quickly to the public appearance of the political priesthood. Of all the attributes of the magistrature, "that with which the public is least familiar is the justice that you render them and the motives that determine you," for "all that passes within these walls is a secret for them." Given this secrecy, respect (or disrespect) for this institution begins outside its walls: "it is upon leaving the tribunal that censure awaits the magistrate" (Maistre, "Discours," *OC* 7:13).

The magistrate in his public life must therefore avoid any expression of prejudices or even too great a sociability, for it is his reputation that is his chief support. "If it is our first duty to be just, our second is to appear such; and whatever the rigor of our principles may be, inasmuch as the public has the right not to believe in them it has the right to condemn them" (Maistre, "Discours," *OC* 7:11). Legitimacy is here a matter of public belief, something one believes in and obeys; the keeping up of appearances and reputations is thus a duty, because it alone maintains belief in the legitimacy of institutions. While it is the probity of the magistrate's conscience that turns away illegitimate influence on his decisions, it is the *reputation* of probity that turns away *attempts* at illegitimate influence, and it is upon these attempts that belief in his reputation rests. When it comes to appearances, "the public pardons us nothing because it has a need to esteem us" ("Discours," OC 7:22). The public (before whom, one recalls, Maistre is speaking) thus judges the legitimacy of its judges according to their ability to dissimulate their private lives behind the mask of an official reputation.

Toward the end of the speech, Maistre emphasizes the broader sociopolitical significance of the probity of the magistrate's "exterior character." In doing so, he underscores his belief in the representational basis of social order, founded on appearances and the public imagination. He wishes to present us with "one fundamental law . . . the extreme importance of which one has never exalted enough," namely, that "every time minds become heated in public, that of the magistrate must be cold or appear so. . . . A thousand causes produce this fermentation, which must never be contagious for us" ("Discours," OC 7:27). The public appearance of coldness is thus to counteract a social "fermentation" of minds (one of Maistre's favorite metaphors). The mimetic nature of both this contagious fermentation and its magisterial antidote is confirmed and emphasized as Maistre continues:

> How many opposed pretensions come to cross one another, to collide on the stage of the world, and cause to be born through their impact the fire of discord and the furor of parties? On all these occasions, may the most penetrating eye not be able to read what passes in our souls! . . . In these moments of effervescence and delirium let us redouble our calm and circumspection; we will even please passion in making it blush at its own excesses. ("Discours," OC 7:27–28)

Here the role of dissimulation is brought subtly to center stage: the maintenance of magisterial authority depends on keeping its feelings hidden, and its victory entails bringing its opponents to the surface in a mortifying "blush" at their extravagant conduct.

All this manipulation of appearances in a regime of justice conceived as a public moral theater, Maistre insists, serves not only to protect the magistrature from the public but also to protect the public from the magistrate. Would a magistrate conscious of the political value of his reputation "descend in the swamp, prostitute a respected name, and sell his glory to the vilest temptations? Ah, without doubt the prospect of the ultimate punishment would frighten him less than that humiliation" (Maistre, "Discours," OC 7:32). In all this Maistre addresses himself particularly to the eighteenth century, in which the above guidelines for magisterial conduct acquire a far greater significance: "Laws, customs, received systems, ancient institutions, it has attacked everything, shaken everything, and the ravage will extend to limits one does not yet perceive" ("Discours," OC 7:30). Implied but left unspoken is the claim that what is not perceived is what above all else must not be shaken. Indeed, one has the foreboding from the tenor of the entire essay that this "shaking" is precisely an extension of "enlightenment," of what is "perceived"—to begin with, the noncoincidence of political theater and political actuality.

With these sorts of considerations in mind Maistre would later speak of "the great tribunals" as a "veritable priesthood" (*Essai*, OC 1:285). The consistent use of this metaphor to describe the workings of politics (the law as "political dogma," the elite as "natural guardians of religion," the king as an "idol," etc.) demands that its conceptual background be brought forward.

What for Maistre is a priesthood? It is before all else the guardian of the sacred allegories. But what is political about that?

The most eloquent ancient writer on allegory and a major source for Maistre was Clement of Alexandria, whose remarks may serve as a useful introduction to the question of allegorical politics. Clement tells us that at the shrines of Egypt and Judea alike "only the consecrated . . . were allowed access. For Plato also thought it not lawful for *the impure to touch the pure*." Those who are without "understanding, or the undazzled and keen vision of the contemplative soul, . . . like the uninitiated at the mysteries, or the unmusical at dances, not being yet pure and worthy of the pure truth, but still discordant and disordered and material, must stand outside."[27] In this fragment one finds the peculiarly Hellenistic synthesis of Greek, Egyptian, and Judaic discourses that so fascinated Maistre and, more significant for present purposes, the sacrificial background of purity and impurity that governs the social revelation or concealment of the "pure" truth (whether at the mysteries, at a dance, or at the bar).

Like the magistrature, the priesthood's concealed knowledge allows it to "dazzle" the impure and uninitiated. This is the political role of allegory: to separate insiders and outsiders within the symbolic community. In the words of Alfred Schutz, "only the members of the in-group, having a definite status in its hierarchy and aware of it, can use its cultural pattern as a natural and trustworthy scheme of orientation."[28] In this manner allegory answers to the dual need of a political elite: to maintain social unity, the precondition of power, through shared ritual performances, but at the same time to separate rulers and ruled through mastery of those performances.

Maistre's understanding of such mysteries was not a purely religious one. To begin with, he believed *all* knowledge, and not merely theology, to have been kept from the uninitiated plebs: "in primitive times we see science closed up in the temples and covered with the veils of allegory." All knowledge was thus safeguarded with a religious zeal, he tells us, citing that most political of historians of religion, Vico: "in ancient Italy, an illiterate was called a *laic.*"[29]

Decisive testimony concerning Maistre's understanding of the mysteries of daily life, whether religious or political, is found in his remark that traditionally the word "mystery" "signified in principle only a *truth hidden under types by those who possessed it.* It was only by extension, and so to speak by corruption, that one has applied this expression since to *everything that is hidden*, to everything difficult to understand." Two usages of the term "mystery" are thus distinguished. On the one hand, mystery is that which is unmastered by reason; this is the "corrupt," one might say secularized, usage (and, by extension, "impure," for the use of those not initiated into the mysteries of truth). On the other hand, mystery means what is *kept* from reason. In the latter, more proper definition of the term, Maistre reveals to us that the mysterious is something consciously constructed to veil the meaning of a performance and to carefully restrict it to an elite set of performers and knowing spectators. Allegory thus appears to be the principle of political domination in and by language, assuring communication among the included or elect while refusing it to the impure or uninitiated, even in their very presence. Perhaps mystery is nothing but a restricted language.

All of this is at once emphasized and broadened when Maistre asserts that "the words *mystery, sacrament, sign* and *figure* are rigorously synonymous" ("Mémoire," 110). Language itself in its privileged signs and figures is a form of knowledge the mastery and truth of which is kept hidden. These remarks do nothing if not present the allegorical coding of signs and figures (and, a fortiori, their interpretation) as a political act, perhaps indeed *the* political act.

In this elucidation of the shadowy sphere of symbolic politics, mys-

tery, sign, and figure, by defining membership in a guarded community of knowledge, are presented as problems of power. In a fashion
typical of his appropriation of mystical language to social theory, Maistre thus applies to politics the claim of Clement that "all things that
shine through a veil show the truth grander and more imposing"
(Clement of Alexandria 255). Not to give away secrets—*last* secrets—is
the principle of all authority as theorized by Maistre (yet once more, as
with the magistrature, he himself reveals what must be hidden and
why).

What we now call ideology thus appears as what one might call the
"allegorical imperative": political truths must be veiled by power; at the
same time, the understanding of politics must go by way of the interpretation of veiled forms. Power, as the distinction between an elite and
its outsiders, becomes a question of language: hegemony as possession
of the means of symbolic production. This means that the voice of authority must never be taken at face value but that political interpretation
must be hermeneutic—not literal but symbolic and indirect, according
to the principles of allegory.

Maistre concludes the passage just discussed by citing Anastasius,
Moses Bar Cepha, and Maimonides to back up what in the context
concerned is a heavily laden claim: that heresy derives from the literal
interpretation of allegories. True knowledge is thus presented as the allegorical interpretation of allegories. (Later we shall apply this schema
to Maistre's own mystical writings, which behind their talk of plural
worlds, spiritual hierarchies, and incorporeal substances, reveal to the
initiated deep political concerns.)

The above reflections on the symbolic nature of power led Maistre to
write that "all civilization commences with the priesthood, by religious
ceremonies, by miracles, even, whether true or false. There never has
been, there never will be, there never can be any exception to this rule"
(*Du pape*, OC 2:428). But this implies, and the mention of necessary
though false miracles confirms it, that some kind of deception or at
least dissimulation lies at the basis, at the beginning, of civilization; indeed it is claimed that it not only has been but must be so. What is it that
the political priesthood found in every society must hide? As the above
chapter on sacrifice would seem to imply, what must be veiled is sacred
violence.

Chapter 5

Legitimacy and the
Origins of Sovereignty

Any statement of authority has no other guarantee than its very
enunciation. . . . And when the Legislator (he who claims to lay
down the Law) presents himself to fill the gap, he does so as an im-
poster. But there is nothing false about the Law itself, or about him
who assumes its authority. – Lacan, "The Subversion of the Subject
and the Dialectic of Desire in the Freudian Unconscious"

The previous chapter focused attention on what constitutions are, the
peaceful order and stability they provide, and how they must accordingly be approached (or not approached, that is) in the present. If we
now address the history of what constitutions have been and the question of how a nation becomes what it is, however, the result is quite different. Here it is intervention and conflict that dominate, not good order. How these two apparently conflicting treatments of constitutions,
the one theoretical and the other historical, are reconciled in Maistre's
work shall be our central concern, one that will lead us to the foundation of power—its basis and its beginning—in myth. This question of
how present political order arises out of past conflicts is the question of
legitimacy, a word that itself refers at once to existing rights and historical origins.

Beginnings, Violence, Myth

Maistre's teaching on legitimacy, on the history of institutions, sovereignty, and constitutions, begins with "an axiom as important as it is
universal," reiterated throughout his works and that for its ubiquity he
does not hesitate to label "divine." "NOTHING GREAT HAS GREAT BE-
GINNINGS: all of history yields no exception to this law. . . . Imperceptible growth is the true promise of durability in all things. . . . The idea
of an institution full grown at birth is a prime absurdity and a true logical contradiction" (Maistre, *Essai*, OC 1:259–60). Here again, the metaphor of organic growth is employed against the invention of society according to the norms of written law, which can only be a prosthetic, not
a principle of growth. The non sequitur involved in the idea of an
ahistorical constitution, without need of gradual maturation, is likened
to imagining that a man may be born an adult: "Caesar the victor at

Pharsalia is not the same as Caesar wetting his pants fifty years earlier" (Maistre, "Réflexions," OC 8:409).

This "axiom," however, is the basis of positive claims as well as negative and refers to how constitutions *do* arise. Three examples of this historical dynamic will show the intricacies to be untangled. First, of the history of the papacy we are told that "from the scaffold of the martyrs" (note the sacrificial background of originary lowliness), the pope "ascended a throne that at first escaped observation but that, like all great things, was imperceptibly consolidated and became known from its earliest existence through an indescribable atmosphere of greatness, which surrounded it without any assignable human cause" (Maistre, *Du pape*, OC 2:204). This statement would seem to beg the question whether it is only because the process of constitution is imperceptible that no "assignable" human intervention is to be found. For reasons that will soon be clear, Maistre's treatment of the beginnings of legitimate institutions seems rife with inconsistencies; this should not dissuade us, however, since intellectual inconsistency is often the sign that something elementary and decisive is involved. A second such inconsistency is to be found in Maistre's response to the idea that "liberty is born amid storms: never, never. She *defends* herself, she *consolidates* herself during storms, but she is *born* in silence, in peace, in obscurity" (*Etude*, OC 1:357). The term "consolidation" has so far consistently been used as a metaphor of constitution; what, then, is the difference between the "birth" and the consolidation of constitutions, and why the insistent emphasis upon this distinction? Finally, the puzzle posed by the beginnings of sovereignty is completed by a remark that hardly seems to fit the "universal axiom" of humble beginnings: "there has never been a royal family that could be assigned a plebeian origin" (Maistre, *Essai*, OC 1:231). Perhaps, one suspects, such a plebeian origin cannot be "assigned," again because it is somehow "imperceptible."

In line with the reasoning of the previous chapter, Maistre insists that the constitutive and basic rights and institutions upon which national power is founded bear neither date nor author and are thus not subject to historical verification (*Considérations*, OC 1:68). This would simply follow from the nature of institutions: because the constitution of a nation is a "firming up" or coalescence of social relations and historical circumstances, its beginnings cannot but be invisible. To ask about sovereignty's action prior to its legitimation in the constitution would be equivalent to asking what God did before creation: any possible answer could only deny the premise of the question that God creates and the sovereign rules.

Other comments, however, imply that this invisibility of origins not only logically follows from the process of constitution but instead is something actively pursued. Sovereignty "resembles the Nile; it *conceals* its head" (Maistre, *Du pape*, OC 2:204, my emphasis). Above, it was said that the head of the sovereign is marked by the finger of the pontiff with the sign of legitimacy for all to see; here his head is hidden. Either this is a different head, or it is the same one seen from a different perspective: the back of the head, as it were, not the forehead.

The above doubts about the origin of sovereignty begin to be confirmed when one hears that legitimacy does not derive from "birth" but from simple longevity: "Everyone knows that there are fortunate revolutions and usurpations very criminal in their beginnings, to which however it pleases Providence to affix the seal of legitimacy by a long possession."[1] Maistre indeed expresses the suspicion that no great power has origins as "humble" as they might appear: "At the present day, with all our philosophy, all our civilization, all our fine books, there is not, perhaps, one European power in a position to justify all its possessions in the face of God and reason" (*Du pape*, OC 2:191, 193). (To the papacy alone, he claims, belongs the honor of "possessing no more than it did ten centuries ago.")

This last quotation invites comparison with the remarks of Maistre's contemporary Tom Paine on the origins of the great landed estates of England, remarks that Maistre will generalize to hold for the origins of all power. The great estates, Paine tells us, could only have been "plundered from the quiet inhabitants at the conquest. The possibility did not exist of acquiring such estates honestly . . . They were not acquired by trade, by commerce, by manufactures, by agriculture, or by any other reputable employment . . . Blush aristocracy to hear your origins for your progenitors were thieves. They were the Robespierres and Jacobins of their day."[2] Maistre, were he to speak openly, might well respond that every nation has its aristocracy, the beginnings of which are always veiled: Paine ignores that the country whose cause he championed itself acquired its initial riches and began its reputable "trade, commerce, manufactures, and agriculture" amid slavery and the theft of land; it is the invisibility, conferred by time, of this founding violence that allows for the image of legitimacy to prevail. As Hume expressed it, "Time and custom give authority to all forms of government, and all successions of princes; and that power which at first was founded only on injustice and violence, becomes in time legal and obligatory."[3] It was perhaps with Hume in mind that Maistre noted the "embarrassment" that eighteenth-century British royalists found themselves in "to maintain at one and the same time their principles on Revolt and the legitimacy of their Revolution. Perhaps it would be better to say that the Deposition of James II was a crime but that this crime produced an order of things that has since become legal" ("Mélanges A," 85).

Maistre presents this same general claim in an even more provocative form. In the early history of constitutions, "everything reduces to what I have called *legitimate usurpation*; the sovereign acts, obedience is general, tranquil, and constant; the opposition, if there is one, is particular, turbulent, and temporary; finally, the sovereign sits down, and on his throne is written: *I possess because I possess*."[4] This is legitimacy!

For Maistre the beginnings of sovereignty, its "birth" if not its acquired name, are always illegitimate: hybrid, puny, inglorious, vague, and bloody. First of all, they are hybrid: as we have seen, "no political amalgamation could ever be brought about except by the intermingling of different elements, which, having clashed at first, ended by combining and settling down into tranquility" (Maistre, *Du pape*, OC 2:233). In words that evoke nothing if not sacrificial crisis, Maistre describes the "clash" that always precedes this "amalgamation" as a civil war. In the illegitimate (or not yet legitimated) form of political violence that is civil war, one finds "a frightening reciprocity of outrages and proscriptions. If one confiscates, if one puts to death on the one side, it is certain that one will do as much on the other; and from severity to severity, one finally will come to make a war of savages."

This mimetic escalation of violence is clearly not the place to look for legitimacy. And yet, Maistre says, "even in a civil war, good faith and innocence can be found on one side and the other." The measure of such "good faith," however, seems to have little to do with the establishment of legitimate rule:

> When finally one of the parties has taken a decided superiority, when it shows all the characters of a peaceable organization, when its internal enemies quiet themselves out of fear, lassitude, or conviction, and finally when the consent of foreign nations fully gives to the victorious power all the characters of legitimacy, only then is all opposition rebellion. (Maistre, "Lettres," OC 7:68–69, 74)

Georges Dumézil, in *Mitra-Varuna*, has shown how these two forms of rule, the violent and the legitimate, are met in a philosophy of sovereignty common among Indo-European peoples that everywhere establishes a conceptual opposition between the following pairs of the attributes of power: Celeritas and Gravitas, violence and law, transgression and norm, creation and conservation, force and consent, chthonic and humane, Dionysian and Apollonian, *pouvoir* and *puissance*. These terms, of course, are complementary and not incompatible; every authority exercises dominion, and every dominion has some authority. The question here is how one gets from the one to the other, from violence to legitimacy. Maistre finds this transformation in a passage through sacrificial violence, from which authority emerges as sacred.

The sacrificial background to constitutional beginnings and changes is emphasized again and again in Maistre's work. "When one uproots a royal house from its place," he claims, re-echoing the metaphor of organic growth and the sacrificial thesis that life is blood, "the vacuum it leaves behind is filled immediately with human blood."[5] "Every new dynasty" is thus "a plant that grows only in human blood." Because of this impure origin of sovereignty in violence, contempt for kings "exposes Europe anew, and consequently the world, to interminable carnage" (Maistre, *Du pape*, OC 2:222). Maistre's reading notes illustrate this argument with a citation from Machiavelli (*Discourses* 3:3): "One cannot consolidate a republic without some memorable execution of the enemies of the new order of things" ("Mélanges A," 193).

This relation to violence, we know, does not end at the origin: the sovereign is he in whose name one dies, he whose maintenance of power at the expense of others is legitimate and whose judgments are just and, we shall see, "infallible." That he who is thus above violence himself emerged out of violence: this is the illegitimate origin of all legitimacy, the reason why the sources of sovereignty are hidden or veiled under allegories. Maistre here seems wholly at one with the political ethic upheld by Pascal: "The truth about the usurpation must not be made apparent; it came about without reason and has become reasonable. We must see that it is regarded as authentic and eternal, and its origins must be hidden if we do not want it soon to end."[6] The difference would be this: where Pascal underscores the illegitimacy of every earthly institution, Maistre defends their legitimacy. Yet that legitimacy, by the time Maistre is done with it, becomes something wholly artificial. Its artificiality, however, makes it all the more precious.

The legitimacy of power (or at least of its birth) must always be feigned. Indeed, the legitimacy of a given constitution *is* the invisibility of the crisis that precipitated it, and the forming of constitutions *is* the de-forming of origins. What Maistre calls "legitimate usurpation" refers to that originary violence that establishes legal authority and which thus *cannot* be justified or authorized by any existing legitimacy. The originary usurpation is therefore neither just nor unjust, legal nor illegal, founded nor unfounded, but rather an unfounded foundation. Strictly speaking, it is an uninterpretable moment that escapes all the categories and criteria of legitimacy: neither legitimate nor illegitimate but alegitimate. This founding violence, one might say, is constitutively repressed (Freud's *Urverdrängung*) from the start, dissimulated and buried under the history of institutions and ideologies. It *is* the start, that is, it is constitutive. Order establishes itself as a distance and a difference from its polymorphously perverse beginnings.

While no constitution has a pure origin because all arise out of violence, each one relies upon a myth of the purity of its origins or, more modestly, upon the invisibility of their impurity, an invisibility that must be constructed by means of myth. The defining feature of the history of a given constitution, then, is that it sutures its own past, erases its scandalous contingency, gentrifies its initial transgression, and finally emerges as an unquestionable norm.

Power's passage from violence to institution is for Maistre one of those "political mysteries" that are better not seen, so that another crisis, a new illegitimacy, and a new masking of violence may be avoided. This is why, though he may come ever so close, he never directly speaks of the illegitimacy of origins. This same reason is why he never, unlike his romantic readers, advocated a return to medieval political forms: for him, every legitimacy is won at great cost and is thus never to be rejected out of hand. Finally, as we shall see, the awareness of the illegitimate birth of sovereignties led him to seek other measures of legitimacy than that of birth.

It is obvious that Maistre's reflections on "legitimate usurpation" present a conservative argument against rebellion. Less obvious but perhaps more important, they argue equally against what one might call the revolutionary character of reaction and the reactionary character of revolution: against the tendency, found across the political spectrum and across the modern age from Rousseau to Heidegger, to seek a return to what had been a pure origin from out of this time of degeneracy. Maistre insists that there are no pure origins. Because all beginnings are low and violent, politics cannot be a matter of purity but only of a gradual purification through a distancing from origins.

The history of institutions is thus not one of decline and decay but of germination *out of* degradation. History gradually replaces violence with the orders of language and symbolic forms, order enforced through consent rather than coercion. Institutions thus must be safeguarded at all costs: any institution is "worthy" of its origin. Here one can perceive Maistre's distance from decisionism, from attacks on parliamentary institutions, from the celebration of irrational and sovereign interventions in the course of history. If there is a danger here it is not of irrational activism but of irrational quietism, the acceptance of what is bad in the name of avoiding the worst, of given violence to avoid greater violence, that is, not the *demand* for blood, violence, sacrifice but rather the *acceptance* of it without necessary demur.

Bearing this in mind, we are now in a position to address the significance of Maistre's "religion of state." Again, sovereignty is legitimate "if nothing is known of its origin." Unknown origins are the mark of legitimacy, or, rather, they are the invisibility of a mark of illegitimacy. Sovereignty is legitimate, that is, "if it has commenced, so to speak [another *so to speak*!], of itself, without violence on the one hand as without acceptance or deliberation on the other" (Maistre, *Du pape*, OC 2:422n). Legitimacy thus requires that there be no violence and no assent; it must be neither imposed nor accepted. It can only then be one of two things: either "what is" (the "I possess because I possess") or a *fiction*. In fact, legitimacy is both: it is ritualized. The "gathering together" or "rapid formation" of constitutions "is only accomplished in the name of the Divinity. The polity and the religion are founded together; the legislator is scarcely distinguishable from the priest, and his public institutions consist principally of ceremonies and religious holidays" (Maistre, *Considérations*, OC 1:71). Ritual thus gives rise to polity and organized religion at once by bringing about the passage from mimetic violence to social order. Maistre's theory of sacrifice as a passage from violence to order thus forms the background to his talk of the "divine origin" of sovereignty.

These sacred origins appear in the political mythology of every people, which cloaks the originary usurpation in the garb of religion. The annals of all nations thus show us

> the cradle of sovereignty environed by miracles; always divinity intervenes in the foundation of empires; always the sovereign, at least, is favored by heaven: he receives the scepter from the hands of the divinity. It communicates to him, inspires him, it engraves on his forehead the sign of its power; and the laws that he dictates to his kind are

naught but the fruit of these communications. . . . These are fables,
one will say; I know nothing about that, in truth; but the fables of all
peoples, even of the modern peoples, cover many a reality.

The reality "covered" here is plainly that of the origins of power. It is
also this underlying reality to which all Maistre's talk of the political
priesthood, of the political mysteries hidden in the temples, likewise refers. He concludes the above remarks from the *Etude sur la souveraineté*
by revealing that the ancient legislators spoke of the deity so often because "they felt that they did not have the right to speak in their own
name." This will be the basis of all political theology: power's reference
to ultimate values in the name of which it may "speak" (Maistre, *Etude*,
OC 1:331–32).[7]

Maistre does not limit this divinization of politics to the ancients: *all*
true legislators "have interlaced, if it is permitted to express oneself
thus, politics and religion, in order that human weakness, fortified by a
superhuman support, may thereby uphold itself. . . . Human reason,
flattened by religious ascendancy, cannot insinuate its insolent and cor-
rosive poison into the fundaments of government." All of Solon's laws
"were, so to speak, religious precepts" (Maistre, *Etude*, OC 1:361–62).

Every law thus becomes a political dogma, for legitimacy rests upon
belief. Politics of any form includes a religious dimension, for without
an insurmountable barrier between the voice of opinion and the voice
of authority, government is impossible. This difference is government
itself. "People bend before sovereignty because they feel there is something sacred in it that they can neither create nor destroy" (Maistre,
Etude, OC 1:354–55). This something sacred is the difference between
ruler and ruled. That is why Maistre may speak in all seriousness of
"the bishops, successors to the Druids," as the "veritable Orpheuses of
France who tamed the tigers and made them follow in chains" (*Considérations*, OC 1:90).

We are now at last in a position to understand why Maistre says of
Proverbs 8:16, "BY ME PRINCES RULE," that this is "not a church
phrase," not a "metaphor," but a "literal truth, simple and palpable," a
"law of the political world." "God literally makes kings [by] maturing
them under a cloud that conceals their origin. At length they appear,
crowned with glory and honor; they take their places; and this is the
most certain sign of their legitimacy" (Maistre, *Essai*, OC 1:232). Once
one is aware of what is behind Maistre's own allegories, nothing could
more clearly express that legitimacy is simply a power whose sacred
character conceals a founding impurity. Before addressing Maistre's

political theology itself, however, we must first, before leaving the history of constitutions, examine that essential component of a religion of state: its believers.

Everything above refers tacitly or indirectly to the question of consent and the encouragement of obedience. Even leaving aside all the talk of divine maskings and veiling fables, the very historicity of constitutions—their gradual coalescence and legitimation by time—implies that there is no legal title to sovereignty. Legitimate sovereignty is rather a dominant force that gradually comes to be *accepted*. It must not, however, *appear* to be either forced or accepted. Legitimacy, we have seen, relies on the difference between what is perceived and what is—relies for its acceptance on the appearance that it is above all questions of acceptability. That is to emphasize rather than elide the basis of legitimacy upon consent.

Sovereignty is always founded for Maistre on the structures of consent, not the exercise of will. For Maistre the sovereign's will is indeed binding, but only by means of the bonds of consent. Where Bodin claims that "the principal point of sovereign majesty" consists of "giving laws to subjects in general, without their consent,"[8] Maistre asserts the diametrically opposed thesis that "sovereigns only command efficaciously and in a durable manner within the circle of things avowed by opinion; and this circle, it is not they who trace it" (*Soirées*, OC 5:2–3). This "circle" is that of "political faith": the norms, mores, and customs consolidated in the constitution. The essential character of sovereignty is therefore not physical force; Maistre affirms instead "the ancient, universal, invariable maxim that always asked each prince *Who are you?* and not *What can you do?*"[9] Sovereignty is thus a matter of *recognition*. This is why "the exterior character of magistrates" is so important: the expectations generated by the myths of power must be respected by and recognized in the magistrature, because belief in these myths maintains the order on which politics is built.

Even the originary usurper himself depends upon this ideological dimension of authority. This is implied even where Maistre emphasizes the usurper's freedom of action: "there appears a man invested with an indefinable power: he speaks and makes himself obeyed"; that this charismatic authority goes by way of speech means that it entails consent. The usurper's power is defined as one over wills, as moral persuasion to obey: "usurpers . . . have no other means of acting than a certain moral force that bends men's wills like grain before a wind." The power of even this moral force is highly qualified by its need to fit into the established popular traditions: despite their "extraordinary power," usurpers can "only combine elements preexisting in the customs and characters of a people" (Maistre, *Considérations*, OC 1:70–72).

In a metaphor that recalls and complements the mark of legitimacy made by the pontiff's finger upon the sovereign's brow, the *Etude sur la souveraineté* describes the obedience etched into the subject's heart: allegiance to the state is founded upon a sentiment of respect "engraved in the people's heart with deep marks." If this sentiment be "effaced, . . . all is lost." Evoking sacrifice by the violence of its terms, this remark points to an originary writing, upon faces and hearts, that must precede the formation of institutions that may only then, though only at the risk of precipitating crisis, be put into the form of a "written constitution" as we moderns understand the term (Maistre, *Etude*, OC 1:355). This "archi-trace," to use Derrida's word, is to be sought behind all Maistre's mystical discourse of incarnations, signatures, and incorporeal substances, themes we shall pause over below.

What must be emphasized here is the wholly fundamental role of ideology in Maistre's understanding of political power. In a powerful sentence that describes politics as a process of edification, Maistre informs us that "if one wants, in the political order, to build on a grand scale and build for the centuries, one must support oneself upon an opinion, upon a belief that is wide and deep: for if the opinion does not dominate the majority of minds and if it is not profoundly rooted, it will furnish only a narrow and fleeting base" (Maistre, *Etude*, OC 1:408). Nothing could state more forcefully that in the formation of power ruling ideas are not "superstructural" elements but the very basis of all authority. The extent of an institution depends upon the dominion of its ruling idea; its historical fixity depends upon the fixity of its idea.

Indeed, given that the constitution is defined as a coalescence of mores, norms of behavior, and customary practices, it follows that ideology makes up not only the foundation but the very house of power. "The insensible and powerful sanction of opinion" makes institutions "what they are" (Maistre, *Etude*, OC 1:353). All government is not only "the result of the tacit convention of united men" but the "real expression of their assent, founded on their character, and on circumstances without number that are impossible to detail" (Maistre, "Lettres," OC 7:154, 152). Although necessarily limited by "numberless circumstances" and more fundamentally by the fact that man is not free to choose his social nature, it remains true that in a basic sense "sovereignty is founded upon human consent, for if any people agreed on the spot not to obey, sovereignty would disappear, and it is impossible to imagine the establishment of a sovereignty without imagining a people who consents to obey" (Maistre, *Etude*, OC 1:313–14).

Before we investigate how the people must be made to choose to consent to obey and, in consequence, how sovereigns must rule, it is essential to emphasize the following. That the rule of law represents a usurpation, that its origins are illegitimate, that it rests on tautology *(law is what is done with authority)*: these assertions are at the farthest remove from the obscurantism habitually ascribed to Maistre's political philosophy. On the contrary, Maistre here voices those truths the disavowal of which forms the basis of all classical political philosophy. Classical political thought, that is, conceals the concealment, dissimulates the dissimulation, upon which rests the normal functioning of the law. Thus the social contract, as it appears in Hobbes and Locke, simply presents us with what we must assume to have been the case if we are to grant to a given order a legitimacy free of pathological sources or remainders. To reveal this originary trauma (the lawlessness upon which law rests) and its constitutive repression is the very opposite of obscurantism. This revelation, rather, belongs to the sphere of the "uncanny": the return of a repressed past that horrifies us not in its foreignness but in its very centrality to the reign of law. Maistre's unveiling of the founding myths and usurpations of legitimate sovereignty confirms my fundamental thesis: that Maistre was not a violent political theorist but rather a theorist of political violence.

Political Theology

We have seen that Maistre understands legitimacy as a wholly religious category, a matter of bonds and belief, a "religion of state" or political theology. Legitimate order necessarily requires that "religious and political dogmas, blended and confounded, form together a universal or national reason strong enough to repress the aberrations of individual reason" (Maistre, *Etude*, OC 1:375). This claim that order rests on religion was a commonplace of the traditionalist argument. Rivarol, for example, tells us that "every state, if I dare say so, is a mysterious vessel that has its anchors in heaven."[10]

Maistre's sociological approach to religion and his theory of sacrifice in particular, however, give good grounds for the suspicion that he will offer something quite different from such traditional pieties. To properly grasp his idea of the religious origins of legitimacy as not merely another romantic medievalism in bad faith, something must be said of why we should still concern ourselves with political theology, a discourse modern political reflection would seem to have put well behind it.

Political theology remains a contemporary concern insofar as legitimacy in the modern age remains irreducible to the reasoned assent to wholly rational norms but instead still involves unreasoned consent to reigning values. It remains relevant, that is, to the extent that what is "right" extends beyond the aggregate of laws and legal procedures into the sphere of ultimate value choices, to the extent that political loyalty still rests upon belief and not reflection. Political theology refers to just this sanctioning of political order beyond the bounds of reason.

One recent writer who has argued that political legitimacy requires this theological supplement is Hans Barth, whose position reveals both the importance and the dangers of religious sanction. "Religious sanction," he informs us, "lends the political and social struggle an absolute quality. Through religious sanction, an historically changeable, essentially transitory structure is consecrated and thus removed from the realm of debate."[11] This sounds very much like Maistre's argument, with one significant difference. For Barth, as for many German conservatives, life means struggle, and order thus requires some degree of constant repression. Within such a model, political religion only functions as a set of allegedly necessary chains: what is given is a "real" world, violently profane, onto which is slapped a sacred world as seductive window dressing. This variety of conservatism thus repeats the vulgar Marxist image of the cultural superstructure as nothing but an *excuse*, a politically expedient afterthought.

Barth's account is useful, however, for underlining how religious sanction places existing social structures in an inviolable zone beyond human discretion. It provides them with that "mysteriously impelling power" of the sacred that Rudolf Otto calls the "mysterium tremendum," an experience that "occupies the mind with a well-nigh bewildering strength" and thus grants sovereignty a majestic unapproachability, a "blind wonder that strikes us dumb."[12] The mysteries of state, like those of religion, may thus be upheld against objections without requiring justification. "That it is thus" suffices; this constitutes the theological dimension of state apologetics.

Yet religious sanction serves not only this negative or masking role but also a positive and directive one. It makes of society a moral order, something beyond need and compulsion alone. The fundamental nature of this "something extra" was most forcefully stated by Lamennais (for whom, indeed, it was a bare essential): "never was a state founded for the satisfaction of physical needs. The increase of riches and the accumulation of possessions create no real bonds among men, and a bazaar is not at all the same thing as a society."[13] Lamennais's insistence upon the necessity of moral order to political order, a moral order that finds its unity and its binding character in religion, was by no means a monopoly of the traditionalist camp.

The claims of political theology to be the basis of all social relations irreducible to force were asserted by the father of French liberalism, Montesquieu. Montesquieu insists in the most forceful terms that the reality of an eternal moral order must be believed in at all costs:

> If there were not a God, we would still have to continue to love Justice. . . . Free as we may be from the yoke of religion, we should not be free of that of Equity. This is what has made me think that Justice is eternal and depends not at all on human conventions; and if it did depend upon them, that would be a terrible truth which one would have to hide from oneself.[14]

Whether we call it God or Equity, Montesquieu implies, some such vertical reference or theological a priori is necessary to any society to give it a higher meaning and purpose. Here it might well be objected that the defining feature of modern politics and the great achievement of the French Revolution is to have replaced a law justified by divine fiat with one grounded on rational consensus. Yet this undeniable and epoch-making shift from a single divine law to a plurality of natural laws still poses the basic problem of those laws' coherence, their ruling principle, that "spirit of the laws" that provides them with an eternal, universal, and legitimate binding force.

The danger of such sacred legitimation, of course, is its ability to sanction any given order and to brand any resistance as defilement. This theocratic vision of order and the seeds of its dangers are found in the great champion of divine-right monarchy, Bossuet: "In resisting legitimate power the seditious resist the order established by God; they render themselves enemies of God: in reversing the old form of government they are rebels against God who ordained that they respect it."[15] In a more vulgar form, the sacred may become a mere political tool and thus be reduced to simple hypocrisy. Emblematic in this regard are the words of Necker: "the more the burden of taxes keeps the people in a state of prostration and poverty, the more indispensable it is to give them a religious education."[16] Faced with such talk, many members of the Enlightenment came to see the sacred as an opiate, a veil of illusions that could be stripped off politics and replaced with a rational organization of society. It is not without reason that post-Enlightenment thought has tended to insist upon the separation of the political and the theological and to denounce all "denaturing" or "contamination" of politics by theology. These very words, however, belong to the vocabulary of the sacred, and a certain uneasiness thus enters into this familiar tale.

Moreover, the refusal of all such transcendental reference bears its own dangers. Positivist and historicist schools of legal philosophy alike can thus in principle make no allowance for legal crimes or unjust laws. Each leaves aside the question of what laws ought to be in considering only what they are. Their answer, "law is law," identifies the mere existence of a legal/penal apparatus with the legitimate "rule of law." Indeed, in the jurisprudence of Carl Schmitt, "the rule of law" becomes a tautology, because rule *is* law. The specter raised here is that of legal absolutism, of the infallible sovereign whose will is law. This topic is Maistre's own. We have seen him argue that laws are dogmas that refer to mysteries, not facts. How is this compatible with the thesis of sovereign infallibility? In answering this question, we shall have to rectify some influential misunderstandings.

Decisionism: Maistre, Critic of Carl Schmitt

On the face of it, Carl Schmitt's political philosophy seems to have much in common with Maistre's. Schmitt indeed cites Maistre as one of his primary theoretical forebears in asserting the sovereign's absolute power to make normative decisions without resistance. Because a recent vogue for Schmitt has brought Maistre's name to the attention of many otherwise unfamiliar with it and because Schmitt's endorsement only seems to confirm the received image of Maistre at its worst (i.e., as a reactionary absolutist and founding father of fascism), Schmitt's interpretation demands the closest attention.

Schmitt's theory of sovereignty, elaborated in his *Political Theology*, is quite simple in its main outlines. First, he defines sovereignty itself as the power to decide what is to be done in that "state of exception" in which "the entire existing order" is suspended.[17] Because "there exists no norm that is applicable to chaos," the state of exception reveals "the decision in absolute purity." Within such a situation of complete political disorder, "looked at normatively, the decision emanates from nothingness." Every order, arising out of chaos, thus "rests on a decision, not a norm." He who makes this decision is the sovereign, and sovereignty is the "monopoly to decide" (Schmitt, *Political Theology* 13, 32, 10, 13). Schmitt claims to find just this argument in Maistre's idea of the sovereign's infallibility.

Second, Schmitt says of political theology that a given society's understanding of proper government is structured identically to that society's metaphysical or theological image of the world, each providing in its own sphere an equivalent model of legitimate order. From this presupposition Schmitt sets out to systematically distinguish and oppose the political theologies of the Enlightenment and the counterrevolution. The Enlightenment rejected the ideas of state of exception and decision, just as Deism did their theological equivalents of miracle and divine intervention. Against this, Schmitt argues, early conservatives like Maistre attempted "to support the personal sovereignty of the monarch ideologically, with the aid of analogies drawn from theistic theology" (*Political Theology* 37).

Maistre's theology is indeed relevant to his politics, but its relevance is to show the anything but absolutist background of his ideas. Schmitt portrays Maistre as an extreme Augustinian, urging the absolute and unmotivated divine decisions of creation and salvation, and not the Origenist that he was, defending both an infinite plurality of spiritual powers and apocatastasis, that is, the complete but gradual solution of cosmic conflict by the reformation of wills, *not* by an apocalyptic absolutist intervention. Moreover, Maistre's masterwork, the *Soirées*, takes precisely that form of an open and unresolved discussion that Schmitt so abhors on the political level. Maistrean theology and textuality alike thus provide analogies for legitimate order that are by no means decisionist, absolutist, or dictatorial. Schmitt's claim that no norm governs chaos, moreover, is implicitly denied by the very nature of Maistre's intellectual project: to find in a sociology of the sacred and a providential history an order within social and political disorder.

Precisely where Schmitt's reading of Maistre might seem most convincing (his equation of Maistre's infallibility thesis with his own decisionism), he repeats the most hackneyed readings of Maistre's work, but in celebratory rather than admonishing tones. "To him the relevance of the state rested on the fact that it provided decision, the relevance of the Church on its rendering of the last decision that could not be appealed, and the infallibility of the spiritual order was of the same nature as the sovereignty of the state order. . . . To him every government was absolute" (Schmitt, *Political Theology* 55). Schmitt then cites

Maistre once more: "every government is good once it is established." In the context of Maistre's ideas on constitutions as we have been following them, this sentence simply means that legitimacy and consent are complementary, mutually necessary ideas: a government can only be established if it is perceived as legitimate, and thus all established governments are legitimate. Schmitt instead glosses the citation as follows: "a decision is inherent in the mere existence of a governmental authority, and the decision . . . is valuable precisely because . . . making a decision is more important than how a decision is made. . . . In practice, not to be subject to error and not to be accused of error were for him the same" (*Political Theology* 55–56). This last remark may be accurate, but only from the perspective of legitimacy and consent, not authoritarian command. Infallibility for Maistre, we shall see, is necessary because legitimacy is necessary, not despotism, because of the need for consent, not command. As I will later emphasize, Maistre nowhere calls for decisive intervention in the political sphere; he always speaks with great force against the extreme measures of the counterrevolution, insisting that the royalist program must go by way of consent, not coercion. Indeed, it was the Revolution's absolutist decisions "out of nowhere," its disregard for the political and juridical norms of what he called the constitution of France, that more than anything else turned him against it.

There are indeed, as Schmitt asserts, occasional decisionist moments in Maistre's thought, but they are very rare, and they are not to be found in the late texts where Schmitt looks for them. It is in the early texts, emotive responses to the Revolution, that one finds them. As crisis came to be no exception but a norm, on the one hand, and as his own authorship came to be "constituted," on the other, Maistre came to emphasize more and more the ordering force of constitution and consent.

The most clearly decisionist of his remarks is this one, from the 1793 "Lettres d'un royaliste savoisien." After detailing the various restraints on monarchical power, he adds that it is nonetheless "always necessary to leave something to the arbitrary; it is necessary that there be, independent of legal force, an administrative force freed from formalities and that could act brusquely in a host of occasions" (Maistre, "Lettres," OC 7:147–48). He adds that if this force exists "under the name of lieutenant-general of police, or of military commandant, or of committee of investigation, of public security, etc., etc., what does it matter? It is always the same power, under different names" (Maistre, "Lettres," OC

7:148). In this most Schmittian of Maistre's texts, it is worth noting that decision is described as inevitable, not invoked; nowhere are strong-arm tactics upheld against parliamentary dilettantism as in Schmitt. In the same early piece, it is argued that one "should not love one's sovereign because he is infallible, because he is not." Instead, one should love him "as one loves *order*: with all the force of one's intelligence" (Maistre, "Lettres," OC 7:156–57). It is only when Maistre defines sovereignty in terms of consent that it is granted the attribute of infallibility.

This is already hinted in the other most decisionist of his moments, found in the speech before the magistrature already discussed. Notably, however, Maistre here attributes the power of decision to the *parlement*. "It will always be necessary that there be a power that judges and is not judged: this power (which will always reside somewhere) resides in you: alone among your own you *study the law*; united in the Tribunal, you *discuss the law*; but in the eyes of the people *you are the law* . . . The Oracle does not dispute, it pronounces."[18] Here it is argued that in the magistrate's activities the instituted law has precedence, and only in the public reception of its judgments ("in the eyes of the people") *is* the magistracy the law. Also significant is the inevitably ironic reference to the Oracle: for all his ambiguous interest in pagan mysteries, Maistre does not expect the Savoy *parlement* to identify itself with the Delphian Sybil. Rather, he plainly has in mind the truth effect, the sovereignty effect perhaps, of the juridical pronouncement as something believed in, accepted on faith.

One cannot dispute Schmitt's claim that no code of law can legislate what happens beyond its sphere of competency, that is, the state of exception. However, his position very much threatens to gainsay the everyday sublunary sphere in which legislation *is* competent in the name of some jack-in-the-box hidden Gnostic sovereign. To subordinate the everyday to the crisis is not helpful for any politics that would seek to manage apocalyptic situations with as little violence as possible (this indeed may define politics in general as Maistre understood it and his conservatism in particular).

Schmitt argues convincingly and in a wholly Maistrean fashion that law is founded on sovereignty and sovereignty cannot be founded on law (the law does not govern the origin or enactment of law); but then, most simplistically, he identifies power with the power to command, to *decide*, and altogether elides the problems of eliciting consent and obedience to the sovereign's decisions. The "uncaused beginning," the unprecedented decision, would be for Maistre one of those laws that refer to the ultimate grounds of legitimacy and that must be left unwritten, discussion and legislation of which would only provoke ruler or ruled to excess and thus to illegitimacy. Indeed, in light of Schmitt's example, one is tempted to say that it has been not so much the absence of decisions as the felt need for them that has led to the overthrow of constitutional regimes by modern dictators.

We have seen Maistre argue that the place and scope of decision itself must be decided by tradition, must be sketched out and filled in by history, by the train of circumstances in which the powers of decision are ritualized and thus delimited. We have seen him argue that the state of exception must be resolved by tradition or constitution (which are here wholly equivalent terms), not by intervention from above or without and not by decision. Constitution is indeed an *immunity* to decisions.

Maistre's work always emphasizes the limitation on sovereign decision by religion, culture, and the fundamental social bonds expressed in the constitution, which the sovereign only tampers with to meet his doom. Next to Maistre's brand of philosophical conservatism it is Schmitt himself, and not the defenders of parliamentary democracy to whom he applied the term, who appears as the political romantic, ignoring necessary limits while building his fortress in the clouds. We must now turn to just what Maistre did mean by his defense of infallibility.

Infallibility

It is one of the cornerstones of Maistre's politics that political *sovereignty* and religious *infallibility* are "perfectly synonymous words." Each word denotes in its respective sphere "that high power that rules over all other powers from which they derive their authority, which governs and is not governed, which judges and is not judged" (Maistre, *Du pape*, OC 2:2). Maistre further underlines this symmetry between sovereignty and infallibility when he explains that "the pope is the king in the Church and the king is the pope in the State."[19] Reciprocally, rebellion in Church and State become functionally equivalent: "in civil society a *rebel* is nothing but a *political heretic*; and in Christian society, a *heretic* is nothing but a *rebel* against the authority of the Church" (Maistre, "Réflexions," OC 8:410–11). The question is whether such statements represent a theocratic politics or a political theology.

Maistre's equation of sovereignty and infallibility, forcefully asserted in *Du pape*, carries two implications that deserve close attention. First, power is spiritualized (as it were) by gaining the attribute of infallibility. Second, infallibility thus becomes a thoroughly practical matter. An emphasis on practice and reality pervades all Maistre's remarks on infallibility. Infallibility, he tells us in words that ought to make us squirm, is "exactly the same thing" as supremacy, or supremacy "under a different name. . . . It is, in reality, absolutely the same thing in practice not to be liable to error, and to be above being accused of it" (Maistre, *Du pape*, OC 2:6). Sovereignty, whether democratic, aristocratic, or monarchic, is defined as precisely this "being above accusation" and is, in this sense, by definition "absolute." All governments act "as if infallible" whether or not they make real mistakes. "For every government is absolute, and from the moment it can be resisted, under pretext of error or injustice, it no longer exists" (Maistre, *Du pape*, OC 2:2). A suspect authority is no authority at all.

It is useful here to distinguish two aspects of Maistre's doctrine of absolute sovereignty, one based on the human condition and the other on logic. The first argument starts from that constitutive ambivalence of being human, elaborated in the theory of sacrifice, which requires that we be subject to authority. "Man, as a being at once moral and corrupt, of right understanding and perverse will, must necessarily be governed; otherwise he would be social and antisocial at the same time, and society would be alike necessary and impossible" (Maistre, *Du pape*, OC 2:167). Infallibility, this practical argument runs, follows from the necessity of society: man requires society, society government, government sovereignty, and sovereignty infallibility. This last link of the chain of requirements is "so absolutely necessary that we are obliged to suppose infallibility, even in temporal sovereignties (where it is not), on pain of beholding society dissolved" (Maistre, *Du pape*, OC 2:157). There is thus an infallible need for infallibility, even where it is a fiction. As so often in Maistre's work, the legitimacy of state authority is reduced to a matter of "as ifs" and necessary fictions.

The second argument avoids the anthropological contingencies of human will and refers solely to the necessary structure of political order per se. Political order requires political unity, and political unity requires a unity of government that is incompatible with fundamental dissension: government entails that order outweigh disorder. There can be no corporate unity "without a supreme chief, nor supreme chief, if a part of the body he commands has the right to raise itself against him"; authority thus "cannot cease to be *one* without ceasing to exist" (Maistre, "Réflexions," OC 8:411). This means that, whatever its outward form, sovereignty is necessarily absolute, in other words, one and inviolable. Democracy is no exception. In republican Rome, for exam-

ple, "sovereignty was in the *Forum*; and the subject countries—that is
to say, about two thirds of the known world—were a monarchy, of
which the *Forum* was the absolute and merciless sovereign" (Maistre,
Du pape, OC 2:4–5). The general thesis is that every variety of government, when all is said and done, is reducible to "an absolute power that
can do evil with impunity, that will thus be *despotic . . .* in all the force
of the term, and against which there will be no rampart but that of insurrection. . . . The will of every sovereign is always invincible"
(Maistre, *Etude*, OC 1:417–18).

Here as elsewhere Maistre does not so much celebrate as theorize political domination. He was indeed none too sanguine about the despotic tendency of authority, whether democratic or monarchic. His
very defense of absolute sovereignty, always as something necessary if
not altogether desirable, points to its excesses: "In order to conserve the
force that is necessary to it, each government needs to be a little exaggerated, and to maintain itself a little beyond the theoretically just limits
of its power" (Maistre, "Lettres," OC 7:205). Every power is at least
somewhat unjust. Maistre ultimately prefers monarchy to democracy
as a less unjust form of power in this sense, that is, less exaggerated, less
unlimited, less absolute. That every government by its sovereign
power "can violate with impunity the moral laws" is "a truth, sad no
doubt, but incontestable." For the sovereign judges but is not judged—
not by fiat but by definition (Maistre, *Etude*, OC 1:422).

In *Du pape* itself, his strongest assertion of the claims of authority,
Maistre elaborates at quite some length the "inconveniences" of sovereignty. Not one power in the world is above all criticism, he tells us,
"and if they are judged by what they can do (without allusion to what
they have done), they must all be abolished" (Maistre, *Du pape*, OC
2:154). There is "scarcely any" means of justifying the conduct of sovereigns other than comparing its inconveniences with "those that would
arise if the sovereign did not exist" (Maistre, *Du pape*, OC 2:169–70).
This is a purely negative defense of sovereignty as the lesser of evils, as
bad but preferable to its alternative. In a particularly pathos-laden letter, Maistre presents absolute power as simply an equal and equally dis-
heartening alternative: "I do not dream of extenuating its evils; I only
say we are placed between two abysses," the abysses of absolutism and
civil war. The question Maistre poses is how to remain between these
abysses, how to avoid both authoritarianism and unending conflict:
"the greatest problem Europe has to solve is, *How is sovereign power to be
restrained without being destroyed?*" (Maistre, *Du pape*, OC 2:175).

The first answer he provides to this question, surprising given the received idea of his argument but in keeping with his role in the Savoy *parlement*, is the constitution, understood in the sense outlined above as tradition. "Religion, the laws, custom, opinion, the privileges of the orders and corporations contain the sovereign and keep him from abusing his power." Twenty years later, he wrote that "whether it be a law, a custom, conscience, a tiara, or a poniard," there is always something that checks the will of the sovereign (Maistre, *Etude*, OC 1:432). Indeed, resistance to sovereignty is defended in exactly the same terms as sovereignty itself, namely, as a necessary evil the advantages of which outweigh its abuses: "should this resistance cause blood to be shed, the inconvenience thus attending it is like that arising from inundations and conflagrations, which by no means prove that water and fire ought to be suppressed" (Maistre, *Du pape*, OC 2:262–63).

Maistre defends the limits on sovereign power in a yet stronger and more far-reaching form, going so far as to argue that it is unflagging resistance to its decrees that vests sovereignty with its legitimate authority. Rejecting out of hand the identification of authority and authoritarianism, he argues that authority is judged by its stability and not its ability to impose its will. Against another counterrevolutionary's claim that Europe stands in need of strong governments, he responds,

> What do you mean by that? If monarchy seems *strong* to you to the extent that it is *absolute*, in that case, Naples, Madrid, Lisbon, and so on, must seem to you to be vigorous governments. You are aware, however, and all the world knows, that these monsters of weakness exist only by their aplomb. Be persuaded that, to *fortify* monarchy, it is necessary to seat it upon the laws, to avoid the arbitrary.[20]

These are forceful words for an exile in 1794, and they sharply contradict Schmitt's interpretation, but they follow directly from Maistre's theory of constitutions. Power may have its roots in the arbitrary, its scandalous origins in usurpation and the right over life, but legitimacy is measured by its *distance* from these sacred sources.

Only within the parameters established by constitutional laws does the sovereign hold absolute sway: sovereignty is unlimited only insofar as it is legitimate. In a very significant passage from *Du pape* Maistre thus concludes that it is equally true

> that *every sovereignty is limited*, and that *no sovereignty is limited*—limited, inasmuch as no sovereignty can do everything; not so, inasmuch as, within its legitimate circle, traced by the fundamental laws

of each country, it is always and everywhere absolute, in that no person may say it is unjust or mistaken. Its legitimacy consists not, therefore, in conducting itself in such and such a way within its sphere, but in not stepping beyond that sphere. (OC 2:178)

Here what defines the sovereign's legitimate authority is not the powers with which the constitution invests him but rather those that it grants to the institutions that resist him and thus keep him within his proper sphere. Maistre thus says of the *parlements* that "in containing a power within its proper bounds, the tribunal contests neither its legitimacy, its character, nor its legal extent; on the contrary, it acknowledges them" (Maistre, *Du pape*, OC 2:179).[21]

Again, it was democracy's lack of such limits on sovereign decisions that turned him against it. As we shall see, what he most opposed in the French Revolution was the absolutism of *democracies*, without any restraint upon the directive will of the people. He pointed to the danger that in a democracy the sovereign will (of the people) is always legitimate because it is always consented to (by the people): without some undemocratic institution like the United States Supreme Court, there is no institutional position from which to contest power or its extension. If the liberally minded would here demur and cite the system of checks and balances, one must recall Maistre's insistence that all powers must be considered in sum: if executive, legislative, and judicial branches all concur in tyranny, there is no one to decide upon their illegitimacy, and government remains infallible, its word remains law, as much as ever.

This argument, forceful as it is, does not yet provide for cases where the legitimate bounds of sovereignty *are* violated, that is, when sovereignty becomes illegitimate. In such cases "the point is by no means *whether*, but *when* and *how* it is permitted to resist. The problem is wholly practical, and so considered, it makes us tremble." What is required is a solution that "admits resistance without revolution, and without any violation of sovereignty" (Maistre, *Du pape*, OC 2:182). Neither the sovereign's subjects nor other monarchs may fulfill this role. The people can only offer fundamental resistance by way of insurrection, which, besides subjecting the nation to civil war, would deny the principles of sovereignty, which rules but is not ruled. This would be to redouble rather than resolve the problem of legitimacy. No more may one sovereign judge another. "If kings have the right to judge kings, this right belongs with greater reason to the peoples. Why not?" Monarchic sovereignty cannot be invoked to violate another monarch's sovereignty. This is not simply a logical difficulty. The conflict of kings, like that between ruler and ruled, can only inaugurate the reign of violence that Maistre's politics aims to contain: "because *every* legitimate judge can *always* be invoked by *every* wronged party, if kings are the legitimate judges of another king, every people has the right to invoke every sovereign against he whom the people have something to complain about. Then we would see some pretty things!"[22]

We thus remain at the same impasse. No power within the state is entitled to decide that a case for resistance has occurred, neither the people nor other kings, and plainly sovereignty cannot indict itself. Yet this is an impasse for Maistre, not the dream solution of an alleged devotee of absolute power. Would one then "unmuzzle the tiger, and reduce men to passive obedience? Well, behold what the king will do!" (There follows a long passage from 1 Kings 8:11–17 on despotic rulers.) Again, "unfathomable gulfs present themselves on every side" (Maistre, *Du pape*, OC 2:175).

What confronts us here is precisely the state of exception, with all the dilemmas entailed by dispensing with law. "It is not in the power of men to create a law that shall require no exception whatsoever. . . . Hence arises in all legislation the necessity of a dispensing power, for wherever there is not dispensation, violation must ensue" (Maistre, *Du pape*, OC 2:176). This remark is deceptively reminiscent of Schmitt's argument, detailed above. Unlike Schmitt, however, on the one hand, Maistre is concerned to find in this dispensation a means of acknowledging and not abrogating the rule of law. On the other, the legal exception he refers to concerns subjects' obedience, not sovereigns' responsibility, to the law. The problem is to find a *resistance* that does not *violate*.

Maistre's answer is unambiguous if not untroubling. The sacred bonds of power can only be transgressed by a sacred being. Because sovereignty is something "essentially sacred," the right to release from the oath of allegiance belongs to the supreme representative of the sacred, to "the high spiritual power that stands above the world," the pope (Maistre, *Du pape*, OC 2:177). Papal dispensation from obedience, Maistre claims, avoids the dilemma of despotism or revolt. First, the papacy is an already established authority and yet a power of a different order outside the state, whose jurisdiction, as purely spiritual, cannot conflict with that of the temporal sovereign. Second, because the papacy is eminently divine, its authority is neither belittling nor desacralizing. "The people who beheld a king excommunicated reflected thus: *That power must be very high, very sublime, far above all human judg-*

ment, since it can only be controlled by the vicar of Christ" (Maistre, *Du pape*, OC 2:186). The popes, Maistre concludes, have only contested particular sovereigns, while leaving the principle of sovereignty intact. They thereby "consecrate" sovereignty by leveling their attacks upon the person, not the institution, of the prince. This would be in complete contrast to those other spiritual guides, the philosophes of the Enlightenment, who, while ridiculing the institutions of sovereignty, "flattered, servilely enough, too, the person who gives employments and pensions" (Maistre, *Du pape*, OC 2:187–88).

The existence of an independent spiritual authority thus allows for an equilibrium between servitude and revolt, despotism and anarchy. We have already seen how for Maistre the authority of power derives from its religious attributes; here we see that spiritual authority must be kept separate from the state apparatus as an ultimate recourse, as a primary and universal authority that remains during the decay of local secondary authorities. And as we have also seen, when another "legitimate usurper" arises, the spiritual power will again restrain the development of temporal sovereignty without effacing its newfound legitimacy and august character.

Finally, Maistre argued that infallibility makes the pope no more omnipotent than it does kings. Were he asked what will restrain papal power, he tells us that he would answer "EVERYTHING; the canons, the laws, the customs of nations, sovereignties, the great tribunals, national assemblies, prescription, representations, negotiations, duty, fear, prudence, and above all opinion, *queen of the world*" (Maistre, *Du pape*, OC 2:153). These limits on the papacy are precisely those that circumscribe royal authority: constitutions and consent.

All in all, this is less theocracy than a separation of Church and state, or in broader terms, of power and authority, force and belief. This should serve as a warning to those who would bemoan the alleged lost spiritual unity of the old regime: for Maistre one of the greatest dangers of the Revolution was to conflate in the most dangerous manner the object of obedience and the object of belief, to attribute to the state that allegiance that belongs only to the sacred.

Let us conclude this section by considering a remark that, while summarizing the theory of papal authority, brings us full circle back to the founding of empires and the sacralization of power, a sacralization, however, now subject to erasure.

The excommunications of the Popes by no means injured sovereignty in the minds of the people; on the contrary, in repressing it at

certain points, in rendering it less ferocious and less crushing, . . .
they caused it to be more venerated; they made the ancient mark of
brute power to disappear from its brow and placed there in its stead
the character of regeneration; they rendered it holy, and thus it became inviolable. (Maistre, *Du pape*, OC 2:187)

Papal infallibility, and Catholic politics in general, have not of course
always shown this benign character or fulfilled this critical role. Thus
the pope could not have been more indifferent to Lamennais's call, influenced by a reading of Maistre, for intervention against the restored
monarchy's renewed absolutist tendencies. Maistre himself did not always meekly defer to papal authority. Nothing would seem to militate
so much against the claim of infallibility as his assertion that, although
"everything is miraculously bad in the French Revolution," the pope's
coronation of Napoleon the usurper

> is the *nec plus ultra* . . . I have no words to describe the chagrin the
> pope's project causes me. . . . When once a man of his rank and char-
> acter forgets to this degree the one and the other, what one must then
> hope for is that he will succeed in degrading himself until he be only a
> pulchinello without consequence. When I see the role that he plays
> and that which he has lost, I am truly furious.[23]

Even in the act of pointing to this "hideous apostasy," however,
Maistre confirms the services that papal endorsement renders to authority: the pope's apostasy could only be one from the religion of
kings. Maistre indeed asserts the fundamental principle of Catholic
politics to be that "against our legitimate sovereign, be he even a Nero,
we have no other right than that of letting our heads fall in respectfully
telling him the truth."[24] Though this remark manifests a certain irony,
an irony informed by the fact that Maistre often found himself in the
position of obedience to the royal will against his better judgment, it is
an irony that clothes an unpleasant truth: just this sort of demurring obedience must have been among the all too ardent hopes of many an advocate of a restored throne and altar. Nowhere is the potential of Catholic politics for passivity before violent authority more glaring than in
Maistre's defense of the Inquisition in the name of unity—the worst
travesty of the principles of his thought, produced by Maistre himself.

   In conclusion, one can say in the most general terms that the thought
of the impurity of all origins, the denial of any originary unity and simplicity in history, tends in Maistre to lead in two opposed directions,
both in his philosophy and his politics. On the one hand, it encourages

a more realistic and responsible idea of the beginnings and ends of historical change, informed by an understanding of the growth of culture through hybridization and a nonapocalyptic historical project of gradual amelioration. On the other hand, this complex of ideas tends also toward highly philosophical speculations on order before and after the rule of blood: primitive Eastern knowledges lost to corruption and Origenist apocatastatic final unities (neither of these notions, I would argue, however, is utterly devoid of critical/utopian value). The same equivocality is repeated on the level of historical action. On the one hand, Maistre's thinking tends away from the all-encompassing solutions urged by both Revolution and counter-Revolution alike in favor of an idea of politics as an inescapable interplay of differential forces incorporated in institutions. On the other hand, one sometimes finds in his work the fantasy of an escape from endless interplay, difference, and discussion in the pope's sovereign fiat and the sovereign's equally infallible will.

For those of us, unlike Maistre, whose allegiance to democratization seeks to be unequivocal, the remembrance of the unfounded foundation, of violence legitimated by time and possession, must be a goad to steady amelioration, to an awareness of the disproportion of myth and fact, and to the unceasing questioning of power that justice implies, rather than to a simple alternative of passivity or destruction. I have sought to argue, however, that though an unfailing if sometimes hesitant supporter of the monarchy, Maistre provides us with conceptual tools that may serve critique as well as apologetics. In Pascal's words, "The art of subversion, of revolution," and, one might add, of democracy "is to dislodge established customs by probing down to their origins to show they lack authority and justice."[25] Probing origins and justifications was neither Maistre's project nor Pascal's. Yet that is precisely the result of Maistre's philosophical conservatism, which is driven to uncover those very things it says must be veiled if it is to justify them.

From a democratic perspective, the sovereign failure of conservative and counter-Enlightenment philosophy is that its thoroughgoing historicism provides no basis for any notion of universal human rights to which the local "constitution" would have to defer in order to maintain its legitimacy. The idea of universal rights natural to the person as a person is the essential kernel of those achievements of the Enlightenment and the French Revolution that it would be foolhardy and altogether retrograde to reject. Yet where early conservatism and Maistre in particular remain useful is to demonstrate how the proclamation of these natural and universal rights was itself in practice compatible with tyranny and injustice, with a "usurpation" that still demands religious adherence. Perhaps then their greatest service to political theory was to reveal unflinchingly the aporias and possible abuses within the discourse of the Enlightenment. This task remains necessary to any understanding of modern politics that would not treat the sources of democratic discourse as sacred texts to be accepted on faith and without question.

It is to this task that we now turn—to Maistre's critique of the theological, cosmological, and anthropological underpinnings of the Enlightenment world picture. By this point, it should not surprise us that he here again anticipates major trends of modern and postmodern historical reflection. While his critique seems sometimes to take a most retrograde mystical form, Maistre's remarks on the veils of sacred allegory should encourage us to believe that beneath that religious envelope something fundamentally political is concealed.

Chapter 6
Science and Society

It is no different with the faith with which so many materialistic natural scientists rest content nowadays, the faith in . . . *a world of truth* that can be mastered completely and forever with the aid of our square little reason. What? Do we really want to permit existence to be degraded for us like this? – Nietzsche, *The Gay Science*

This chapter addresses Maistre's critique of the Enlightenment's way of knowing and, more specifically, of eighteenth-century naturalism, a mechanical philosophy of nature derived from Descartes. Such issues might seem far from the social and political questions with which we are concerned. Yet, as Maistre shows us, how one defines the order of nature and the nature of man has everything to do with the question of legitimacy. First of all, legitimacy is at stake because of how the norms of public discourse are shaped by physical and metaphysical assumptions. In naturalism's replacement of the traditional religious and symbolic world order with a mechanical one, Maistre sees a dangerous disenchantment of the natural world, a desacralization that is carried over into politics. While wholly retrograde on the surface, his attack on the excesses of technical rationality raises the essentially modern question of the sociopolitical consequences of the scientific organization of thought and life.

Maistre's ire is directed not at science in general, however, but at the radical dualism he finds in the naturalist school, which, following Descartes, assumed a complete disjunction between matter and mind, the physical and the metaphysical, science and religion. Naturalism reduces nature to a mechanism, to clockwork, and when the Enlightenment takes this as the paradigm for a science of society the result is not only misguided, Maistre believes, but disastrous. Wholly denuded of the sacred, this world comes to seem fundamentally unsound, subjected to the powers of illegitimacy, compulsion, and deceit; against it the Enlightenment posited a future heavenly city, attainable through knowledge, that will have nothing in common with the old dispensation. Maistre treats the resulting worldview not as the triumph of reason but as a Gnostic revolt against the legitimacy of the world. Because nature was understood as a mechanical order and because this mechanical nature was taken as the exemplar of all good order, mechanical organization became the norm for society in turn. To Maistre's mind this not only ignored the symbolic, ritual, and religious dimension of society he considered fundamental, but, with equally disastrous results, it encouraged revolt against an order now denuded of all sanction and the desire to replace it with a clockwork constitution.

Finally, legitimacy is at stake in the Enlightenment's understanding of the scientific revolution as a radical break with past illusions and superstitions, carried out by pure reasoning alone. Against this history of science as revolution, Maistre offers a traditionalist account of the origins of early scientific thinking that anticipates the work of recent historians in emphasizing how science was shaped by its cultural settings and traditions. Maistre insists that the founders of modern science—Kepler, Galileo, Descartes, Newton—came out of a tradition: a tradition of reasoning about the world, of experimental techniques, but also of mystical nature speculation, of alchemy, Neoplatonism, and Cabala.

Gnostic Enlightenment

Any treatment of mechanical thought must begin with Descartes. Descartes's mechanical view of nature rests upon a fundamental cosmic dualism that divides reality into the wholly distinct realms of extended substance and thinking substance, *Res extensa* and *Res cogitans*, the first governed entirely by mechanism and the second the province of man alone. By using the passive principle *extensa* in contrast to the active participle *cogitans*, Descartes emphasized that physical nature has no activity of its own. Nothing could be further from the Renaissance view of nature in which every body had its active principle and the universe as a whole retained an active, spiritual, and occult character. Cartesian dualism thoroughly severed the active realm of the mind from a purely inert nature, which the mind could now survey in complete autonomy.

In this way, Descartes allowed natural philosophy to proceed free of the claims of religious controversy. Since nature was wholly conceived as extended substance, there could be no religious prohibition against human curiosity toward the natural world, for nothing religious was at stake. Cosmic dualism thus provided Descartes with a compromise between the rival claims of theology and the new philosophy of nature. By sundering nature from theology, Descartes was able to treat the former as a pure sphere of mechanical determination and physical fact, matter and motion, to which all questions of final causes, of meaning, value, and intelligence were utterly foreign.[1]

Starting from this theoretical divide, Cartesian thought developed in two wholly distinct directions: first, a metaphysics starting from his analysis of the subject that was allied with theological authority and was perfected by Malebranche, and, second, a physics starting from his ideas on automata taken up by the naturalist materialism of the philosophes. Significantly, both of these traditions separated man from nature. The doctrine of animal automatism, allied with the distinction between universal extension and the capacity for thought found only in man, maintained the doctrine of the soul's immortality within a mechanical world and thus supported a Christian and metaphysical anthropocentrism. At the same time, this doctrine legitimated any and all human domination over the inferior realm of nature, thereby encouraging a technological anthropocentrism in which men could "walk with assurance in this world" as "the masters and possessors of nature."

While this assured mastery over the natural world would seem a wholly secular and wholly modern project, its sources in medieval theology have been underlined by Hans Blumenberg, for whom modernity represents a victory over continually reawakened Gnostic challenges to the legitimacy of this world. As Blumenberg points out, at the end of the first of the meditations, before he introduces the *cogito* as the source of future certainty, Descartes presents us with an avatar of the Gnostic demiurge who serves to raise doubt to the highest possible degree. He imagines the possibility that the world is governed not by "that deity who is supremely good" but by a "most powerful deceiver," a "malignant genie of the utmost power and cunning," who is intent on misleading men by appealing to their defining credulity and who has "employed all his artifice to deceive me." Here, Blumenberg argues, the nominalists' doubts about divine goodness and human certainty are brought to a Gnostic fever pitch. Against the possibility of this "deceiver God" who may have thoroughly duped us with his power and cunning, we can do only one thing: withhold our judgment. To withhold assent is the one freedom we cannot be denied, whatever power of deception may dominate us, "whatever be the power and artifice" of an all-powerful deceiver. The *Meditations* thus take the form of a spiritual exercise in which doubt serves as an artifice to arrive, beyond every possible deception, at an authentic philosophy.[2]

This complex interplay between authenticity and artifice is essential to the structure of Descartes's thinking and, unlike later Cartesianism, served as a background to his thinking on automata as *imitations* of life forms. In one of the more highly charged moments of the *Meditations*, he remarks, "If I look out the window and see men crossing the square, as I just happen to have done [a fiction of authenticity—the *Meditations* are written as if simultaneous with the meditations themselves], I normally say that I see the men themselves. . . . Yet do I see any more than hats and coats which could conceal automatons? I *judge* that they are men."[3] Here, it is concealment and masking, artifice and authenticity that are at stake, and not anatomy. This impression is reinforced by Descartes's recourse to judgment, not reason, to decide that these are humans rather than robots.

Descartes's early private notebook is replete with references to illusions with mirrors, masks, shows of devotion, and recognition of dissimulated inner states. Thus the first entry: "Actors, taught not to let any embarrassment show on their faces, put on a mask. I shall do the same. So far I have been a spectator in this theater which is the world, but I am now about to mount the stage, and I come forward masked" (Descartes 1:2). These are questions of representation and distortion; indeed, representation here is distortion. The world theater does not show, it hides, and action thus must be disingenuous, inauthentic, for to act is to enter the sphere of what, from the perspective of the authentic ego, could be automata. This is a rather Gnostic outlook.

How does it compare with Maistre's "exterior character of the magistrate"? For Maistre, social representations, as the symbolic basis of cultural order, must be interiorized by the magistrate himself. The theatrical aspect of the law must become a social truth that holds for magistrate and public alike—it is, indeed, precisely what holds them together as the shared language of their constitution. For Descartes, knowledge of representations, which are always false, separates the philosopher from the people: representations are ciphers, not symbols. In his philosophical autobiography, unlike in Maistre, the mask never becomes a face: it is always a principle of concealment, not revelation.

Descartes's anatomical excursus, the "Treatise on Man," begins and ends by reference to automata. He proposes that an artificial mechanical man may serve to understand actual people. After describing how an automaton may replicate all the natural functions of man, including memory and imagination, he concludes that the artificial man may "imitate perfectly the movements of a real man." All these perfectly imitative functions "follow directly from the mere arrangement of the machine's organs every bit as naturally as the movements of a clock or other automaton follow from the arrangement of its counterweights and wheels" (Descartes 1:108). Descartes does, however, grant man a soul that sets him apart from automata and from animals, of which the latter really might be automata. There is no way of distinguishing the two. The only things that ultimately distinguish men from automata are the very same things that distinguish men from animals: meaning- · ful language and intelligence are as lacking in animals as in machines (Descartes 1:139–41). This difference from animals points to man's autonomy from nature or, rather, that of man's soul, which, in contrast to animals, is entirely independent from the body.

Marx claimed from this evidence that "Descartes, in defining animals as mere machines, saw with the eyes of the manufacturing period" when the factory was to be "a productive mechanism whose parts are human beings."[4] As Elster has pointed out, however, Descartes's model derived from mechanical "marvels" that display and expend wealth, not produce it.[5] In fact, the early public clocks that served as Descartes's models were items of *display* that commonly moved a variety of subsidiary automata with, in Mayr's words, "a wide variety of capabilities but no concretely definable practical function." The linkage of technological thinking to the productive investment characteristic of capitalism, Elster argues, was first found in Leibniz.[6]

Until the industrial revolution the clock, understood as a variety of automaton, remained Europe's most intellectually demanding technology and was thus "good to think"—it became ubiquitous in the seventeenth and eighteenth centuries as a metaphor for processes of nature and society alike. It was the great metaphor of the emergent mechanical world picture, above all in its Cartesian strain of thoroughgoing rationalist determinism.

This tendency culminated in the Enlightenment naturalism of La Mettrie and D'Holbach, who extended the scope of mechanical materialism to describe every life process. At the same time, they replaced Descartes's image of the machine as a form of display with one of purely functional efficiency. Not only did Enlightenment naturalism argue that organic life and its evolution obey natural laws (in Cartesian terms, the laws of matter in motion). To this it added two more dubious claims: first, that all such laws are mechanical and, second, that not only animals' organic functions but their sensibility or intelligence may be reduced to purely mechanical processes. The first added claim did contribute to the history of *physiology*, to an understanding of man as a natural being, by excluding all teleology, and with it theology, from the biological sciences. The second claim, however, contributed to the emerging *ideology* of man as the engineering master of nature by excluding all nonmechanical motivation from the conduct of animal (and sometimes human) societies. In all this the clock-automaton served as an overriding symbol, but as the symbol of a nonsymbolic universe—of a world denuded of metaphors and meanings.

La Mettrie extends this way of thinking to men, whom he describes as "only animals and perpendicularly crawling machines."[7] Man simply has "a few more wheels, a few more springs" than other animals, for "the soul is clearly an enlightened machine."[8] For La Mettrie psychology is either physiology or theology, with no intermediate possibilities. One finds a complete absence of hermeneutic perspectives on thinking, which has become purely a function of organs. Everything human, in man and animals, is relegated to a now illegitimate theology. While quite properly defending the boundaries of science against religious incursions, La Mettrie thus anticipates the unedifying spectacle of neurophysiology's attempt to explain all inner life.

This physiology/theology opposition derives in large part from Descartes's separation of domains of knowledge competence according to the separation of extended and thinking substances, but here there is nothing that extended substance cannot do. It may even produce language. "If Vaucanson had to employ more art to produce his flutist than his duck, if he had employed still more energy he might have produced a being with the power of speech. . . . The human body is a clock." Hence follows La Mettrie's explanation of education: "As a violin string or a harpsichord key [?] vibrates and gives off sound, so the cerebral fibres, struck by the waves of sound, are stimulated to render or repeat the words that strike them."[9]

The attempt to reduce language, education, and ethics—those interhuman things most bound up with transference and interpretation—to mechanical physiology was a recurrent feature of Enlightenment naturalism. One finds it in Condillac's hypothetical statue brought to life by the mere impingement of the proper sensations in the proper sequence. One finds it in the reduction of morality, in Maupertuis's "Essay on Moral Philosophy" and Bentham's "felecific calculus," to the quantitative measurement of amounts of pleasure and pain. What one nowhere finds among the naturalists is reflection on the cultural sphere that, defined as it is by the imaginary and symbolic, is not amenable to wholly mechanical explanations. While mechanical metaphors may apply to questions of "social engineering," of "technologies" or "systems" of power, they cannot wholly account for cultural processes or for symbolic cohesion.

This did not stop them from trying. In *Authority, Liberty, and Automatic Machinery in Early Modern Europe*, Otto Mayr argues that the mechanical imagery of automated clockwork "insinuated values into politics that had no basis in the requirements of statecraft and that were recommended only by their efficacy in machinery."[10] Most generally, this tendency is manifest in the Enlightenment ideal of a programmatic political constitution that would "run of itself," an ideal embodied in the remark of that proud son of a clockmaker, Rousseau: "the great lawgiver . . . is the mechanic who invents the machine," whereas the prince "is merely the workman who winds it up to make it run." Mayr emphasizes the absolutist connotations of this metaphor, which places the source of all movement in one single and central origin, the "mainspring." Whether this is found in an absolute sovereign or absolute deity, a clockwork order can only describe a centralized hierarchy of functions ultimately directed from a single center. The *Encyclopedia*, in the entry for "system," thus claims that "just as there is one main spring in a clock upon which all others depend, there is also in all systems one first principle to which the different parts are subordinated" (cited in Mayr 79). Rousseau's political system thus requires the unchallenged sovereign unity of the general will if society is not to come unsprung.

The clockwork metaphor provided Enlightenment philosophy with a metaphor to describe the social order as a harmonized, tempered, predictable, and regular unity; taken as a norm, however, it also upheld a conception of political order as something homogenized, repetitive, and oppressive. Clockwork here points toward regimentation: a society that "goes like clockwork" requires unflagging regularity of action and thought. This ideal of regimentation is found in Holbach's call for the "simplification" of the French machine of state, which had become too delicate in its complication, by the removal of all "unnecessary, useless or counteracting springs" (cited in Mayr 109).

These mechanical fantasies of eighteenth-century political theory were subjected to scathing irony by no less an ally of the forces of the Revolution than Michelet:

> And again they made administrative machines. . . . The machines had the advantage of employing man as a regular power, of employing life—minus its whims and inequalities. . . . The marvel of Machinism would be to do without men. So let us seek powers which may act without us, like clockwork, once they are set in motion. . . .

> The Thinking Machine, being enmeshed in the Political Machine, will roll on triumphantly and will be termed Political Science.[11]

This "naturalism" that reduces life to a machine, this "rationalism" that sees political subjects as cogs and wheels, was by no means necessarily egalitarian; La Mettrie describes himself as one of those who "dare to express the truth for the benefit of the few who are willing and able to think. As for the rest, who are voluntary slaves of prejudice, they can no more attain the truth than frogs can fly" (85).

This tendency might best be described as Enlightenment Antihumanism. Automata are the very image of those docile bodies, punched out by the power factories of institutions, that many social scientists, inspired by this side of the Enlightenment, have taken as the proper model of the person in society. In more contemporary terms, one might point to a certain complementarity of Taylorism and Parsonian sociology, as the practice and theory of life as an assemblage of functions, governed by mechanical structures of constraints and steered by elites, in which all action is centrally coordinated according to strict guidelines of conduct. This is the way of thinking of all those social "planners," whether capitalist or communist, who treat norms and language as incidental tools of social production and not its very basis.

Against Mechanism

It is against such seductions of technique, against the "machinist politics" of the bureaucratic state administration emergent between Louis XIV and Louis Napoleon, that traditionalism offers in riposte some of its most compelling social critique, insisting that technical measures alone can neither maintain sovereignty nor forestall violence. What makes Maistre particularly significant in this regard is his deep fascination with Enlightenment mechanical imagery, which is at once taken up into and contested by his work.

It is to this imagery that he turns to describe the mutual dependence and formative influence of sovereign and nation in a passage that significantly challenges the sovereign role of the "political mainspring." "The mainspring of the watch is not made for the balance, nor the latter for the former, but each of them for the other, and both the one and the other to tell the hour. No nation without a sovereign and no sovereign without a nation" (Maistre, *Du pape*, OC 2:169). Here the clock metaphor is displaced toward an image of cohesion rather than aggregate parts. In another relatively straightforward use of the metaphor, it is the mystery rather than the rational self-evidence of clockwork that he emphasizes, claiming that it is on this mystery that social cohesion depends:

> When one gives to a child one of those toys that perform movements inexplicable to him by means of an interior mechanism, after he has amused himself with it for a moment he breaks it in order to *see inside*—it is thus that the French have treated government. *They wanted to see inside*: they have uncovered the principles of politics . . . without reflecting that there are things that one destroys by opening.[12]

In a powerful passage that again underlines the mysterious cohesion of society, Maistre altogether explodes the clockwork image of social order. Society is "a watch all of whose springs vary continually in strength, weight, dimension, form, and position that nevertheless keeps perfect time," in which, that is, "the irregularities introduced by the operation of free agents fit into the general order" (Maistre, *Considérations*, OC 1:2). It is just this general order, an elastic equilibrium that includes elements of disorder, that Enlightenment social theory cannot grasp with its machinist models. It is one of the cardinal errors of the Enlightenment that "one can make a constitution the way a clockmaker makes a watch" (Maistre, *Etude*, OC 1:344). Society cannot be known in the way an engineer knows a machine, by taking it apart into its constituent pieces and reassembling them, for society is and can only properly be understood as constituted, not as simply aggregated.

For Maistre as for E. T. A. Hoffmann, automata were anything but conducive to "walking with assurance in this life" but were rather something most uncanny. They serve as the emblem less of man's power to create than of his weakness. In Maistre's work, society is described as behaving like a machine only in anomic situations of crisis when symbolic bonds are broken, notably in the French Revolution. There is thus nothing more indicative of the fragility of the revolutionary Republic than the fact that

> it does not *live*. What an enormous machine! What a multiplicity of springs and clockwork! What a fracas of pieces clanging away! What an immense number of men employed to repair the damage! Everything tells us there is nothing natural in these movements, for the primary characteristic of the creations of nature is power accompanied by an economy of means. Everything is in its place, there are no jerks or bumps, friction is low, and there is no noise, only majestic silence. So it is that in the mechanism of nature, perfect balance, equilibrium, and exact symmetry of parts give even rapid movement the satisfying

appearance of repose. Therefore there is no sovereignty in France. Everything is artificial and violent, and it all announces that such an order of things cannot last.

As opposed to this cohesive equilibrium that defines nature and legitimate government alike, the French Republic "is only an automaton possessing merely the exterior appearance of life. Man, by his own powers, is at most a Vaucanson; to be a Prometheus, he must aspire to heaven, *for the legislator cannot obtain obedience either by force or by reason*" (Maistre, *Considérations*, OC 1:80).[13] Here again, society is held to be irreducible to force; mechanical models cannot account for the cohesiveness provided by consent, which Maistre characteristically refers to political theology.

Maistre is much closer to another facet of Enlightenment naturalism: transformationism and its talk of germinations, fermentations, and palingeneses. He sometimes endorses a version of vitalism, leaning on the ideas upheld by Bonnet, Needham, and Haller of a creatively active nature. As a rule, we shall see however, this is qualified by his Neoplatonic vision of nature, with its emphasis on allegorical interpretation and ideal causes. Maistre's vitalism is most plainly marked in his identification of life with blood, which serves as the metaphysical ground of sacrifice. Even here, though, the vitality of blood serves not as a physiological explanation (physiology merely confirming ancient tradition) but to pose the problem of life's bloodiness, a social dilemma answered by means of custom, belief, and ritual.

Most often, Maistre makes allegorical use of transformist language, employing its words as figures for psychological and sociological processes (his autobiographical remarks are strewn with talk of intellectual "fermentations"), above all to describe the changes wrought by ideas upon practices. This is clearest in a passage that emphasizes the political force of opinion. Just as the water that fills a young girl's thimble could, if reduced to a vapor, make a bomb burst, "the same phenomenon happens in the spiritual world; a thought, an opinion, a simple affirmation are only what they are; but if a sufficient degree of heat makes them pass into a vapor, then these tranquil principles become enthusiasm, fanaticism, passion in a word (whether good or bad), and under this new form, they can move mountains."[14] Noteworthy in this passage is the secular emphasis of this purely terrestrial spiritual moving of mountains.

It is to transformist discourse that Maistre appeals when he discusses the *vital force* of societies: "there is, generally speaking, a secret force that carries each individual to his place: otherwise the State could not subsist." This "moral mechanism of empires" is hardly a mechanism. Likening it to the life force of plants and animals, he asks in the language of Christian Neoplatonism, "How can we believe that the political body does not have its law, its soul, its plastic force, and that everything fluctuates according to the bursts of human ignorance?" (Maistre, *Etude*, OC 1:480–81).

Maistre's split allegiances between transformist and religious discourses are neatly demonstrated in an exchange between the mystical Senator and the Catholic Count of the *Soirées*. Typical of the differences between them, the Senator is concerned to unearth the hidden secrets of nature, while the Count emphasizes the social role of religion. The Senator thus argues that "the existence and activity of governments cannot be explained by human means, any more than the movement of bodies can be explained by mechanical means. *Mens agitat molem.* There is thus in each empire a directive spirit (allow me to steal this word from chemistry in denaturing it) that animates it as the soul animates the body and that produces death when it withdraws." The Count "agrees," claiming that only the "intervention of a supernatural power" could explain the creation and duration of governments, "the multiplicity of wills that concur upon the same end without knowing what they do, that which shows they are simply *employed*." The chastened Senator is only able to respond, "I do not know if you have perfectly grasped my meaning" (Maistre, *Soirées*, OC 4:179–80).

What both these "chemical" and "supernatural" perspectives have in common is a concern with ideology—both agree that what makes a society more than the sum of its individuals and what makes for both its historical and functional unity is something not physical but ideal. Maistre employs organic metaphors to describe the historical process of social cohesion, of the mutual adjustment of component roles.

We have seen Maistre argue that constitutions are not constructed but generated. The model is organic rather than technological. Yet we have also seen Maistre insist that constitutions are generated in symbolic practices and in language, as a step beyond the physical domain of force and violence. The vitalist metaphor thus entails no biological reduction to organic urges. Society is ultimately "organized" neither as an organism or a machine but as a ritual order. In Maistre's historical account, moreover, we saw how this "organization" or constitution is purely immanent, determined by neither divine clockmaker nor biology. Let us now see how this plays out on the level of philosophy.

The World of Signs

It is the sociological implications of the mechanical worldview that Maistre most forcefully rejects, both for society itself and for the knowledge of society. The gist of his social critique of Enlightenment naturalism is this: a purely mechanical paradigm that defines all being as natural and all nature as mechanical cannot account for social order, and the effort to do so can only lead to disastrous results. The symbolic, imaginary, and religious dimensions of society, which Maistre treats in his discussions of sacrifice and political theology, remain a dead letter for eighteenth-century naturalism. "These truths are not at all proven by calculation or by the laws of motion. . . . These are truths that man can grasp only by the *mind of his heart* [Luke 1:51]," that is, by hermeneutics (Maistre, *Soirées*, OC 5:128). Maistre's radical gesture was to extend the sphere of "these truths" even to science itself, arguing that knowledge of nature cannot be purely mechanical and that the origins of science are found outside science itself.

This is part of his general strategy of defending arcane traditions against the pretensions of modern reason and its disenchantment of the world. His critique of the mechanical world picture and the corresponding technological view of science may thus seem wholly retrograde. Yet, first, the criticism of such views, from Hegel to Heidegger and Vico to Voloshinov, has characterized modern thought as much as those views themselves. Second, we shall see, Maistre's emphasis upon the symbolic dimension of knowledge led him to anticipate the latest historiography on the "irrational" dimensions of early modern science and especially the role of the hermetic tradition in its genesis.

Against the naturalism of the Enlightenment, Maistre consistently upholds a Neoplatonic vision of nature. The natural order is thus defined as "the ensemble of all the laws, of all the forces, of all the elasticities that *constitute* the universe" (Maistre, *Etude*, OC 1:318). This notion of nature as an elastic ensemble of qualities contrasts sharply with that of an aggregate of parts, a contrast with major implications for how we understand not only nature in the abstract but our place within it.

It is the reduction of the person to a purely quantitative mechanical model that Maistre most firmly rejects in Condillac, "who not for one instant ceased to reason according to an imaginary man. See, for example, his work on the statue. *What would happen if a statue received successively the five senses, and successively again all the sensations that depend on them?* It would happen that this is not a man." Against this empiricist model of personality formation through successive and discrete perceptions Maistre urges the simultaneity and cohesiveness of a formative environment, of the circumstances of the human constitution:

> From the first moment of his existence, man is environed by all the ideas that pertain to his nature . . . from which it results that memory cannot represent any of them to itself as anterior or posterior, all are judged not only to exist but to *coexist* and to commence together at the same time; thus there is no *first impression*, no *first idea*, no *first experience*, and everything is simultaneous.—Ecce Homo! (*Examen*, OC 6:59–60n)

Indeed, Maistre's Neoplatonic position is much closer in spirit to Ficino's idea of a living statue endowed with speech by amulets and hieroglyphs that draw down invisible spiritual influences. Although this idea is no doubt less rational than Condillac's, there is perhaps a certain truth in viewing the beginning of mental life not as the product of the mechanical collision of nature with the brain in perception but as the influx of a *society of spirits*, a qualitative transformation of irrational influences irreducible to quantitative models. Replace *society of spirits* with *spirit of society* or with *society* plain and simple, and one is perhaps closer to modern psychology than was Condillac.

It is this same qualitative approach, psychological and not physiological, that Maistre applies to understanding the mental life of animals. In a scene of great pathos the Senator describes the understanding of a dog and its limits. My dog accompanies me to a public spectacle, "an execution, for example." The dog

> sees everything I see: the crowd, the sad cortege, the officers of justice, the scaffold, the victim, the executioner, everything, in a word. But what does he understand of everything? That which he must understand in his *quality as dog*: he will know how to distinguish me from the crowd and find me if some accident has separated us; he will arrange himself in a manner not to be maimed by the feet of the spectators; when the executioner raises his arm, the animal, if he is nearby, may retreat in fear that the blow be for him; if he sees some blood, he may shudder, but as at the butcher's. There stops his knowledge, and all the efforts of his teachers, for centuries of centuries, will never carry him beyond that; the ideas of morality, of sovereignty, of crime, of justice, of public force, etc., attached to this sad spectacle, are nothing for him. All the signs of these ideas environ

him, touch him, press upon him, so to speak, but in vain. (Maistre,
Soirées, OC 4:249–50)

This account surpasses mechanist accounts both by its sympathetic insight into the life of a dog and by its evocation of a symbolic environment made up of sensible signs that makes violence meaningful as an attribute of sovereignty (also significant is the carnivalesque accent this dog's-eye view adds to the more serious treatments of sacrifice already discussed).

The antimechanistic tenor of this passage is heightened when the Senator proceeds to use the dog's experience as a metaphor of humans' relation to what is incomprehensible: nature is to man what man is to domestic animals. "Who will say that a volcano, a whirlwind, an earthquake are not for me precisely what the execution is for my dog?" One understands only what relates to one's constitution, "the rest is a closed letter. . . . No reason not to think that we may ourselves be *environed, touched, pressed upon* by the actions of agents of a superior order of which we have no other knowledge than that which relates to our current situation" (Maistre, *Soirées,* OC 4:253–54). In Maistre's notebooks, a first draft of the dog episode is followed by a comment that encapsulates his traditionalist critique of naturalism: "we accuse the ancients of *animating* all the parts of nature; perhaps posterity will accuse us of *killing* all of them" (Maistre, "Extraits F," 418).[15]

These remarks, like so many in Maistre's work, may be taken in the direction of either mysticism or sociology. The difficulty is to understand the interweaving of these two tendencies in such a way as to neither reduce Maistre's argument to mere mysticism nor ignore his borrowings from the mystical tradition. To answer this difficulty, it is necessary to look more closely at his idea of the symbolic unity of that world with which science is concerned and then, in light of this, proceed to his sociology of knowledge with its emphasis upon the symbolic origins of science.

Maistre's understanding of the world as something that exceeds mechanical functioning is neatly expressed in the Chevalier's phrase, "this great whirl of a world [Descartes's *tourbillon*] that is also a great book" (*Soirées,* OC 4:160–61). This definition, while affirming the dynamism introduced into the world picture by Descartes, insists upon a textual or hermeneutic supplement to naturalist interpretations and at the same time upholds the legitimacy of the given world as not just any book but a great one, that is, as something meaningful, complex, and exemplary.

This idea of the world as text is often given a theological overtone, above all by the Count of the *Soirées*, which is as compatible with Catholic orthodoxy as it is with Cabala. "All created beings prove by their syntax the existence of a supreme writer who speaks to us by these signs. In effect, all these beings are letters the reunion of which forms a discourse that proves God . . . for there cannot be discourse without a speaking soul, nor writing without writer." The Cabalist element is put into relief as the Count continues, but so is the relevance of the textual metaphor to a comparative understanding of cultures. Number, he tells us, "is written in all parts of the universe." The number three, for example,

> is written in the stars, on the earth; in man's intelligence and body; in fable, in the Evangel, the Talmud, the Vedas; in all religious ceremonies ancient or modern, legitimate or illegitimate, aspersions, ablutions, charms, invocations, exorcisms, spells, black or white magic; in the mysteries of the Cabala, of theurgy, of alchemy, of all secret societies; in theology, in geometry, in politics, in grammar, in a thousand rhetorical formulae. (Maistre, *Soirées*, OC 5:97)

These remarks point to an understanding of measure common to all societies through which the world is ordered. Upon this textual logic alone, Maistre will argue, may more rationalized logics of the world be built. All order is founded upon intellectual bases, not mechanical ones. In a radical gesture, Maistre extends this claim to science itself, of which the historical origins are found in traditional symbolic practices.

The Mystical Origins of Science

Maistre's critique of the Enlightenment naturalism led him to a surprisingly up-to-date view of the history of science, one that argues that the basis of scientific thought must be sought in cultural traditions generally considered foreign to its development. Of all the major traditionalists, Maistre was the only one to concern himself with the scientific tradition. Here again, the thoroughgoing nature of his traditionalist argument led to rather untraditional conclusions, as he revealed the origins of the power of science in what science itself would consider scandalous and impure.

The special object of his criticism was the Enlightenment's idea of science as a salvific knowledge that, in Gnostic fashion, confers power on its possessor and returns him to authenticity. Against the "heart hardened by pride and a glacial philosophy" (*Soirées*, OC 5:137) of Enlightenment naturalism, Maistre provides three interrelated arguments. First, modern science cannot be understood simply as a revolt against imprisonment in the medieval universe, for science has a long history that, not coincidentally, has its roots in the dark ages. Second, man cannot place himself by means of science outside and above nature as an engineer-in-chief because knowledge of nature itself is at bottom symbolic. Our relation to nature is founded upon recognition, *connaissance* as against *savoir*, and is thus irreducible to the bare alternative of bondage or mastery. Third, science is not itself salvation from bondage, for it creates a tutelage of its own.

Maistre's provocative historical thesis that science derives from theological antecedents is neatly stated by the Count of the *Soirées*, who tells us that the sciences have only come to their high degree of development "because the universities were at first only schools of theology and because all the sciences *grafted* upon this divine subject have manifested the divine sap by an immense vegetation. The indispensable necessity of this long preparation of the European genius is a capital truth that has totally escaped modern discoursers" (OC 5:186).[16] Maistre thus altogether rejects the idea of science as a radical break from previous modes of thought.

Against d'Alembert's assertion that the Scholastics had "enervated the sciences by their minute questions," he thus responds that, while not scientific, scholastic thought prepared the basic tools for rational thinking about nature. Pointing out the inconsistency of d'Alembert's position, Maistre asks in his *Examen de la philosophie de Bacon*, "How could they enervate what did not yet exist? They felt their way awaiting daylight; they prepared the human mind, made it sharp, unbound, penetrating, an eminent friend of analysis, of order in ideas, and of clear definitions. It is they, in truth, who created a *Novum Organum*; they were what they needed to be; they did what needed to be done."

If the Scholastics asked some futile questions, he continues, they resemble a man who would use a capstan to harvest his cabbages: "one would doubtless have reason to laugh at the operation, but I see nothing in it that would alter the reputation of the capstan" (Maistre, *Examen*, OC 6:50–51). This passage is remarkable for its assessment of both the productivity and the limits of medieval thought. While Maistre might seem to wholly underestimate the limits of premodern thought, the "reputation" defended here is that of the *capstan* and most definitely not of the means of cabbage production. His remark asserts the existence of reason among the Scholastics; it by no means defends the medieval worldview in its entirety, the absurdity of which is very much emphasized.

Equally striking is Maistre's emphasis upon the contributions of alchemy to the history of science. He especially underlines how the technical innovations of the alchemists prepared and made possible a more rational theory of matter. The alchemists, for example, made the production of glass a

> principal object of their mysterious labors and their pious science. On their knees before their furnaces, and purified in advance by certain preparations, they supplicated him of whom fire has always been the most brilliant emblem among all peoples to render them masters of this active agent and the mass it maintained in fusion. Finally they gave us glass, that is, instead of a rebellious rarity they made of it a vulgar substance, docile to the wishes of man.

Once it had thus become "vulgar," the physical properties of this vitreous substance could be readily deduced (Maistre, *Examen*, OC 6:69–70). Here Maistre hints at a notion of the thematic origins of scientific discovery in nonscientific traditions that he will make central to his theory of knowledge.

This claim becomes more pronounced in his treatment of Renaissance nature philosophy and above all of Kepler, upon whom Maistre was among the first to acknowledge the influence of numerology and Neoplatonism. The Senator of the *Soirées* asserts that Kepler "only arrived at that immortal discovery [the Third Law of planetary motion] in following I know not what mystical ideas of numbers and celestial harmony that accord very well with his profoundly religious character but that for cold reason are only pure dreams." The author clarifies in a footnote that

> it is more than probable that Kepler would never have thought of the famous law that immortalizes him, if it had not emerged, as though of itself, from his harmonic system of the heavens, founded . . . on I know not what Pythagorean perfections of numbers, figures, and consonances; a mysterious system that occupied him from his first youth to the end of his days, to which he related all his works. (Maistre, *Soirées*, OC 5:182)

The Senator proceeds to contrast Kepler to the mathematicians of recent times, who "may be *powerful counters*: they handle with a marvelous dexterity that one cannot admire too much the instruments placed in their hands; but these instruments were invented in a century of faith and religious factions, which have an admirable virtue for creating great characters and great talents" (Maistre, *Soirées*, OC 5:184).

In his book on Bacon Maistre summarizes his general perspective on the history of science: all origins are symbolic, mythical, religious, even those of science. "All science began in the temples, and the first astronomers were above all priests. I do not say that one should recommence the ancient initiation and transform the presidents of our academies into hierophants; but I do say that all things recommence as they commenced" (Maistre, *Examen*, OC 6:473). The desire for truth, Maistre implies, is something extravagant, something that exceeds the norms of objectivity to which it eventually gave rise. How then does scientific knowledge begin?

In response to the Chevalier's counterargument that, just as a musician may calculate harmonies without being pious, "Kepler could well have discovered his laws without believing in God," the Senator tries to clarify his position. He does not at all claim that "every discovery must depart directly from a dogma like a chicken from an egg" (a formulation that comes close to parodying the Count) but rather that there is no causality in matter, that causes thus must be sought elsewhere, and that "only religious men can and want to depart from the realm of matter" (Maistre, *Soirées*, OC 5:192–93). Let us try to make some sense of this.

The last of the *Soirées* is concerned with the philosophy of science, and the unfinished work ends with a seven-page footnote on the Newtonian system that itself ends in an ellipsis—this is a gauge of the seriousness with which Maistre confronted the issue. In this footnote he presents "a few ideas" as "simple doubts," following the maxim that "there is no science that need not render account to metaphysics and respond to its questions"—an argument before the fact against positivism as well as a riposte against Enlightenment mechanical naturalism (Maistre, *Soirées*, OC 5:268).

One of these doubts, which Maistre reiterates in his private notebooks, in his work on Bacon, and through the mouths of both the Count and the Senator, is that the concepts of matter and cause are mutually exclusive. Matter enters into activity only through movement, and because movement is always an effect, a material cause would be a contradiction in terms. Concerned as it is with matter in motion, "discovery in the natural sciences consists solely of discovering new facts [the Count mentions the circulation of blood and the sex life of plants] or in relating unexplained phenomena to already known primary effects, which we take for causes" (Maistre, *Soirées*, OC 4:254). Thus Newton was able to describe a host of previously unexplained phenomena with his idea of gravity, but "about the cause of gravity, the lackey of the great man knew as much as his master." Newton himself never claimed gravity to be a physical thing but merely a mathematical description. In the wake of Newton, astronomers have been able to use the idea of attraction to describe accurately the behavior of heavenly bodies without having the least notion of what attraction is (Maistre, *Soirées*, OC 4:257–58).

At work throughout Maistre's polemic is not so much the Cartesian notion of a purely passive matter but the Neoplatonic idea of matter as secondary to or even a product of thought. "Matter can do nothing, and even is nothing but the proof of spirit," the Count informs us (Maistre, *Soirées*, OC 4:255). The more materially minded Senator (who, Mauss might say, represents magic against the Count's religion) likewise claims that "the world is a simple assemblage of appearances, of which the least phenomenon hides a reality" (Maistre, *Soirées*, OC 5:180). This Platonic idealism provides the common ground between the two interlocutors' differences of opinion. Maistre himself (as it were) wrote in his correspondence that "the physical world is naught but the image, or if you prefer, the repetition of the spiritual world. . . . Everything has been made by and for intelligence. Matter itself, properly speaking, does not exist independently of intelligence."[17] In the *Soirées*, the Senator (here quite typical of Maistre's own thinking) appeals in the same breath to the authority of Saint Paul and of Charles Bonnet, the naturalist: "The world is a set of invisible things manifested visibly" (Hebrews 11:5) and "the world would be then only an assemblage of appearances" (*Philosophical Palingenesis*). What unites the Father of the Church and the eighteenth-century naturalist is a shared Platonic view of the natural world (Maistre, *Soirées*, OC 5:178).

Incompatible though it is with the naturalist world picture, Maistre's Neoplatonic nature philosophy is not necessarily backward in all its implications. His remarks on the origins of scientific knowledge resemble in an almost uncanny manner recent work, after the Kuhnian revolution in the history of science, on the thematic and subjective sources of scientific discovery. Maistre's emphatic insistence upon the priority of human subjectivity to scientific objectivity, even in the knowledge of nature, is perhaps the central argument of his critique of Bacon. The Neoplatonic character of this critique is evident in the remark that "it is most necessary to keep from passing over this word REAL; for it is one

of the arcana of the Philosophy of Bacon that physics alone is *real.*"
Against this "arcane" position, Maistre argues that "all the sciences,
without distinction, have their reality in the intelligence that possesses
them . . . and that matter itself is only *real* mentally" (*Examen,* OC
6:404n). Maistre thus advances the Platonic claim that intelligence is active, not a passive recipient of knowledge, "and, under this point of
view, is really *power* or *cause.* Here let us admire the human mind."[18]

More radically, Maistre claims that because the ordering principles
of nature are invisible and immaterial, scientific knowledge must begin
not in passive observation but in an act of recognition. This perspective, incompatible with the idea of science as the theoretical subjuga-
tion of a purely mechanical nature, stresses that it is the common nature
of nature and man that provides the basis of all science. Against Bacon,
Maistre argues thus that

> man can know the animal only by comparing it to the animality of
> man; he even only knows matter because he is matter himself, in vir-
> tue of the incomprehensible bond that unites the two substances. He
> recognizes in brute matter extension, impenetrability, weight, color,
> mobility, and so on, because all that is found in his *body,* which is also
> HIM, one knows not how; thus, in matter, he still only knows *himself.*
> (*Examen,* OC 6:107)

To perceive reason in the universe is only possible for reason—only reason can understand reason. It is precisely *understanding* (*connaissance*)
that makes science possible, an insight that underlines the transferential
nature of man's relation to the world. "We cannot understand (in all the
force of this word [*connaître*]) except what is *in ourselves,* and inasmuch
as the object to be known relates to us" (Maistre, *Examen,* OC 6:112).
Citing Black's remarks on the oxygen/phlogiston debate ("let us make
use of the new nomenclature, but always without believing that we
know better than before what fire is"), Maistre appends the statement,
inflammatory for positivist ears, that "we know fire, like every other
thing, by what it has in common with us. . . . To know it perfectly it
would be necessary to be fire" (*Examen,* OC 6:114n). The Neoplatonic
background of all this discourse on the subjective origins of scientific
knowledge is plain when Maistre writes that "all the truths are within
us; they are US [NOUS], and when man believes to have discovered
them, he does nothing but look inside himself and say YES." It is in this
remembrance and the intuition of affinities, not in experiment, that the

beginnings of scientific theories must be sought (Maistre, *Soirées*, OC 5:54n).[19]

Nothing could be further from the main current of Enlightenment naturalism. The mechanical world picture is taken by Maistre as the defining feature of the Enlightenment and, as such, is subjected to biting criticism. Thus the Senator: "Our century requires a mechanical astronomy, a mechanical chemistry, a mechanical gravity, a mechanical morality, a mechanical speech, mechanical remedies. . . . Is not everything mechanical?" (Maistre, *Soirées*, OC 5:193). While Maistre speaks respectfully of Descartes, in his private notebooks he observes that had the philosopher left us nothing but his mechanical explanations of nature, "he would pass for a novelist" ("Philosophie D," 551).

The insistence that the order upon which science is founded requires "an operating or cooperating intelligence" (a big "or"—see the next chapter) and that "the physical system is physically impossible" leads Maistre to sympathize with ancient traditions that attribute will, life, and even divinity to the planets. One of the more bizarre texts among Maistre's often bizarre work, his unpublished "Essay on the Planets," informs us denizens of the enlightened age that "we pass over" the claims of astrology "too quickly." While admitting the "extravagances" of astrology and chiding its tendency to idolatry, Maistre as a traditionalist cannot accept "that a great error profoundly rooted in the minds of all men of every age is not somehow attached to some true root." This truth, which Maistre announces an as "incontestable axiom," is that "everything has been created *by* and *for* intelligence."

"How antiquity hated that *dead* philosophy so beloved of modern taste." Against Enlightenment naturalism, which treats "the celestial bodies as brute masses absolutely foreign to life," Maistre marshals Homer, the Hebrew Bible, the Christian Gospels, and the patristics to support the claim that the planets are somehow alive. "The planets are and can only be dwellings or prisons of intelligence in general, just as the individual body of a man is only that of his individual intelligence." Against the possible Gnostic implications of this assertion ("dwellings or prisons" is rather ambiguous on this point), Maistre concludes with a long citation from Origen that is said to show that "this theory was an object of the Christian initiation" and that therefore "primitive Christians would have found no metaphor in that passage from one of the prophets, *the stars shine joyfully at their set times: when he calls them, they answer, Here we are.*" The question is whether Maistre himself "found no metaphor" in these ideas ("Philosophie D," 653–72).

What Maistre published on this subject was more conditional and circumspect. In his notes to the eleventh *Soirée*, he broaches the planetary question in the midst of a discussion of causality.

> If I were to turn in a circle upon a plain, and some distant observers were to say *that I was being acted upon by two forces*, and so on, they are certainly able to do so, and their calculations would be incontestable. The fact is, however, that *I turn because I want to turn* . . . It is absolutely the same in the system of the world: could this immense machine be directed by blind forces? Without doubt, on paper, with algebraic formulas; but in reality, not at all.

In pursuing these ideas, Maistre tells us, we will understand why "Sabianism was the most ancient of idolatries; why one attributed a divinity to each planet, who presided over and seemed to amalgamate with it in giving it its name; . . . why Origen said that *the sun, moon, and stars offer prayers to the supreme God*, . . . that *they too await the manifestation of the children of God, who are now subjected to the vanity of material things* [*Contra Celsius*, book V]" (*Soirées*, OC 5:273–74). On the subject of Sabian solar myth, Maistre argues in his notebooks that the correspondence between Mosaic and Mexican astronomies is the sign not of some previous European influence in the Americas, as Gomilla had claimed, but, rather, of a universal veneration of the sun found among all ancient "Oriental" traditions. As examples, he cites the Egyptians, Greeks, and Hindus (Maistre, "Philosophie C," 442). He claims to find the same divine astronomy in Plato and in the "numerical metaphysics" of Pythagoras. Astronomy, then, would begin in astrology. Of this intellectual order of the living cosmos, Maistre concludes that "if one calls it God, World, Olympus, or Heaven does not matter, as long as one recognizes it in the movement of the stars and recognizes that it has given everything to man, above all intelligence and number" ("Extraits F," 60, 68). Maistre's evident relish for these arcane beliefs derives from several sources: in part from a "mysticism for its own sake" about which little useful perhaps can be said; in part from the above argument, which founds all knowledge in symbolic recognition; and in part from sympathy for any theistic cosmology whatsoever, a sympathy that often drew Maistre beyond the bounds of orthodoxy.

On some level, however, he believes that such an animistic approach to nature is simply more realistic than the mechanical: "the system that animates all parts of nature, and that to Robertson and so many others is a production of the grossest barbarity; this system, I say, is perhaps closer to the truth than one believes. The idea of a nymph enclosed in a tree who lives, suffers, and dies with it is less absurd than our mechanical explanations of vegetation" (Maistre, "Mélanges B," 561). This polytheistic and pantheistic tendency always challenges Maistre's Catholic orthodoxy. In antiquity, he tells us (and one knows the authority of ancient traditions for Maistre), "The word GOD signified a *superior nature* and nothing else. In this sense we are still polytheistic" (*Examen*, OC 6:104n). And this, it is implied, is a good thing.

Science and Society

Maistre's chief objections to Enlightenment naturalism are not epistemological, however, but moral and political. "All systems that tend to degrade man find me obstinately incredulous."[20] He is far less concerned with the atheism of science and the development of a scientific worldview than with what he calls "practical atheism," the Gnostic disenchantment and amorality fostered by the reduction of the world to a machine.

"We shall become brutalized by science, and that is the worst form of brutality" (*Essai*, OC 1:277)—Maistre here attacks what Vico before him called the "barbarism of the academy." To begin with, the freedom of the sciences must not be understood as the only kind of intellectual freedom, which Maistre indeed sees as being in danger of eradication by the Enlightenment. In the *Soirées*, Maistre likens the reign of scientific experts to just what the Enlightenment had decried among the priesthood: the willful obscurantism of an ideological clique that acts against its announced goals.

> I do not know if I fool myself, but this kind of despotism that is the distinctive character of modern savants is only proper to retard science. It rests today completely upon profound calculations within the scope of a very small number of men. They have only to listen to one another to impose silence on the crowd. Their theories have become a species of religion; the least doubt is a sacrilege. (Maistre, *Soirées*, OC 5:275n)

The Senator thus concludes that "the European savants are in this moment a species of conspirators or initiates . . . who have made of science a kind of monopoly, and who only desire absolutely that no one know *more* or *differently* than they" (Maistre, *Soirées*, OC 5:238).

As the philosophes said of the priesthood, so Maistre says of the philosophes: their reign over minds is maintained by the ruses of rhetoric.

They may tell us that the mechanical account is simply the best that we poor mortals may attain to, "but it is unnecessary to be the dupe of this pretended modesty. Every time a savant of this last century takes on a humble tone and seems to fear to choose, one can be sure that he sees a truth he would like to hide" (Maistre, *Soirées*, OC 5:268n). The "scrupulous attention to never employ anything but mechanical expressions," the Senator explains, is an index of this bad faith; it is "precisely because" they are aware of the inadequacy of purely mechanical accounts that "they put, so to speak, words on guard against truths" (Maistre, *Soirées*, OC 5:238). Maistre goes so far as to argue that this monopolistic tendency of science has produced its own variety of mysticism: the insistence that matter alone can act on matter leads to the attribution to matter of "appetite, desire, tendency, aversion, antipathy, attraction, repulsion, etc.," from which Maistre concludes that "there is no-one so credulous as the incredulous" (*Examen*, OC 6:158, 246).

In this critique of what is now called scientism, Maistre closely resembles his precise contemporaries Goethe and William Blake. All three, if they have little else in common, utterly reject the number-crunching materialism of post-Enlightenment culture as a threat to man's humanity. "You see them bent over the earth, uniquely occupied with physical studies and laws, no longer having the least sentiment of their natural dignity" (Maistre, *Soirées*, OC 4:212). This remark of the Senator could come directly from either Goethe's or Blake's portrait of Newton. (Maistre himself greatly admired Newton, who was no stranger to mystical researches, while decrying the Newtonianism of the eighteenth century.) The Count adds that the natural sciences contain "something hidden that tends to degrade man and to render him a useless or bad citizen." In a footnote, the author clarifies the Count's remark as follows: "the study of the natural sciences has its excess as does every other. They are not at all and should not be the principal end of intelligence" (Maistre, *Soirées*, OC 5:187).

The ultimate moral basis of Maistre's critique is revealed in a passage very reminiscent of Blake in its ironic indictment of the naturalists' ridiculous pride.

> Our supposed wise men, ridiculously proud of some childish discoveries, write learnedly about fixed air, volatilize the diamond, teach plants how long they must live, swoon over a tiny petrification on the proboscis of an insect, and so on; but they take care not to condescend to asking themselves once in their lives what they are and what is their place in the universe. Everything is important to them except

the one important thing. . . . They have cured us of our prejudices, they say . . . yes, as gangrene cures pain. ("Mémoire," 106)

By identifying all truth with the truth of the natural sciences, Maistre claims, the Enlightenment has sidestepped the fundamental questions of ethics, which do not admit of technical answers or mechanical responses. It thus threatens to make men into automata. The overweening "rationalism" (today we would say positivism) that claims that "nothing can occur but that which occurs, nothing occurs but that which must occur . . . would lead us straight to fatalism, and would make of man a statue" (Maistre, *Soirées*, OC 4:212).

It is in keeping with the sociological thrust of all his work that Maistre insists that the natural sciences must be considered subordinate to ethics, politics, and theology. Progress requires that people become better, not necessarily more knowledgeable. Intellect and ethics do not necessarily coincide: "certain men, if they came to find what they seek, could well become more culpable instead of perfecting themselves. What then do we lack today, as we are the masters of doing well?" (Maistre, *Soirées*, OC 5:253).

This continually repeated claim that good knowledge is that which makes one better is highly questionable when it is extended, as it too often is in conservative polemics, to support an argument for the maintenance of ignorance in the interests of domination. While Maistre does at times approach this view, it is not a necessary implication of his argument. He indeed asserts that science is a positive sign of man's sacred character: "This need, this thirst for science that agitates man, is only the natural tendency of his being that carries him toward his primitive state and informs him of what he is. He *gravitates*, if I may thus express myself, toward the regions of light"—this from the Catholic Count (Maistre, *Soirées*, OC 4:66).

Maistre goes to great lengths to argue that science and religion are mutually beneficial. Employing an alchemical metaphor, he writes that "science is an acid that dissolves all but gold," which thus perfects "true" religion by purifying it of all dross (*Examen*, OC 6:158). In turn, the mark of this true religion is not inflexible doctrine but the fact that it "changes man, exalts him in rendering him capable of a higher degree of virtue, civilization, and science" (Maistre, *Du pape*, OC 2:427). The truth of the one, then, serves the truth of the other.

Maistre thus argues that religious belief is in no way incompatible with scientific discovery. Suppose that a fervent Christian and an atheist "discover at the same time the property possessed by leaves of absorbing a great quantity of mephitic (or unbreathable) air, the first will cry: 'Oh Providence, I admire and thank you!'; the other will say: 'It is a law of nature.' May someone indicate to me the advantage of the latter over the former, even regarding the single aspect of physical knowledge" (Maistre, *Examen*, OC 6:406). The Senator, in typical fashion, presses this argument to an extreme, claiming in a powerful passage that nothing so threatens knowledge of the world as does atheism.

> All inventors, all original men have been religious or even exalted men. The human spirit, denatured by irreligious skepticism, resembles a wasteland that produces nothing, or covers itself with spontaneous growths useless to man. Then even its natural fecundity is an ill; for these plants, mixing and interlacing their roots, harden the soil and form an extra barrier between the sky and the earth. Break, break this cursed crust, destroy these mortally vivacious plants, call upon all the forces of man, thrust in the ploughshare, seek deeply the powers of the earth to put them in contact with the powers of the sky. (Maistre, *Soirées*, OC 5:181)

This statement, most Heideggerian not only in its polemic with rationalization but in its very imagery (the final clause is indistinguishable from some of the more dubious passages of "The Origin of the Work of Art" or "The Question Concerning Technology"), is not well received by the Count, who treats it as an instance of Gnostic presumption. The latter "adopts with all his heart" the bringing together of heaven and earth, but for him, it seems, this task is incompatible with the Gnostic project of "breaking this cursed crust." Instead, he asserts that the bringing together of the sacred and the profane, the making heavenly of the earth, is achieved by conscience, not consciousness; it is a social, not a hermetic task (Maistre, *Soirées*, OC 5:189).

It was this social dimension of the scientific project that Maistre emphasized in his account of the nonscientific sources of natural science. Without some account of the extrascientific sources of scientific reason, the emergence of modern science can only appear a miracle, and a Galileo or a Newton becomes a magical and inexplicable being. Such a *creatio ex nihilo* of scientific thought is itself incompatible with the rational outlook that denies miracles in principle. In thus bringing to light the prescientific sources of scientific knowledge, Maistre's counter-Enlightenment aims tend to further the cause of general enlightenment.

Maistre's contribution in this regard was to push to a more radical level and a broader significance early conservatism's discourse of expe-

rience and the concrete to the point of a fundamental anthropology that
includes science itself within the domain of the cultural life-world understood as an environment of signs. Even though his religious emphasis may preclude wholly rational answers, to have perceived in its
proper depth a question where previously there was none was itself a
great accomplishment.

Maistre's denial of the omnipotence of science, moreover, was not
meant as a rejection of science as a whole. A fragment from his private
notebooks makes this clear. Maistre there agrees with Malebranche
about "the *necessary sciences* being the conduct of life and the perfection
of the mind." Yet he forcefully rejects the alleged consequence that all
natural science is therefore vain: "it would be hard to advance anything
more contrary to reason and experience" than Malebranche's claim that
"the mind of man is sufficiently inclined to study but is not inclined to
piety" (Maistre, "Philosophie D," 559, 557). It is not science itself that
is wrong with the Enlightenment but something else within it that dis-
torts its image and use of science. What is wrong with it then?

Gnosticism Again

What Maistre most opposed in the Enlightenment was its thoroughgoing and wholly unmediated separation of science from religion, fact
from value, the rational from the symbolic and imaginary, in which the
truth of all the latter terms is found only in the former. This separation
of spheres, which posed a major threat to Maistre's understanding of
political legitimacy and social order, led him to treat the Enlightenment
as a form of Gnostic revolt. Although he never directly applied this
word to the philosophes, it is Gnosticism that he rejects in their cosmic
dualism and their rejection of existing order, positions he assails with
the aid of the great anti-Gnostic theologians Origen, Clement, and Augustine.

In Pagels's words, "what Gnostics know is that the creator [the demi-
urge] makes false claims to power."[21] For the Gnostic the world is the
product and assemblage of illegitimate powers. Legitimacy therefore
must only be sought outside institutions, which are reduced to a domain of pure hypocrisy and usurpation. Irenaeus tells us that the Gnostics "maintain that they have attained to a height beyond every power,
and that therefore they are free in every respect to act as they please."[22]
Maistre interprets eighteenth-century thought as the reawakening of
these assumptions with all the threats they entail for the legitimacy of
the traditional European order. Against them he develops his Neo-

platonic and providential world picture. On what possible grounds, however, could he assert the provocative and seemingly ludicrous claim of a Gnostic Enlightenment?

Maistre's critique isolates two tendencies of eighteenth-century thought that together add up to a Gnostic rejection of the world. The first is its cosmic dualism. The Enlightenment's assumption of an irreducible opposition between the sphere of universal values and the sphere of existing order, he believed, encouraged a picture of traditional social life as simple tyranny. Pushed to a not uncommon extreme, this resulted in a notion of society as a closed sphere of compulsion, outside of which alone is to be found authenticity. What the Gnostics saw in the cosmos the Enlightenment sees in society: a prison of maleficent fictions, phantasmagoria, and ignorance created and jealously guarded by those cohorts of bumbling archontic powers, the priesthood and the nobility.

Thus Rousseau, Maistre's nemesis, asserts that civilization is a fall from grace, artificial, corruptive, and vain, a diversion from and mask for inner poverty. This degradation is not the work of natural man but of society, a false order that constrains innocents to do the bad. The first words of *Emile* ("All is well when it leaves the hand of the Creator of things; all degenerates in the hands of men") refer not to the Christian doctrine of a good creation and a fallen man but to a good nature and a fallen society, understood as corrupt and corrupting. The *Discourse on the Origin of Inequality* thus posits the existence of a human self prior to society whose primitive integrity and essential goodness are lost as man enters civilization and thus becomes evil—the primal instance of "making a being evil by making him sociable."[23]

This notion of civilization as a prison encouraged the appeal to an altogether new social world. This is the second Gnostic moment Maistre finds within the Enlightenment, its self-proclamation as a countermove to the design of the world, as an awakening and breaking of spells, as a redemptive knowledge that alone can return man to his authentic state. Against the illegitimacy of all this-worldly or "this-societal" norms, the philosophes appeal to a set of eternal verities and values immune to corruption by the contingencies and compromises of historical experience, independent, unsullied, and transcendent.

Thus in Diderot's "Traité de la tolerance," the voice of Nature occupies the place of the Gnostics' Hidden God, calling to man: "Cast out the Gods who have usurped my power, and return to my laws. Return to nature from which you have fled; she will console you and dispel all those fears which now oppress you. Submit to nature, to humanity, and to yourself again; and you will find flowers strewn all along the pathway of your life."[24] Here again one finds the existing state of affairs defined as an illegitimate usurpation with which compromise and reconciliation are impossible. The political tendency of Enlightenment naturalism as Maistre sees it is to emphasize the unnaturalness of a social sphere constructed and maintained by false knowledge that need only be sapped that truth and justice may triumph.

Maistre's criticism of this way of thinking everywhere underscores how our understanding of the order of nature is bound up with that of the order of society, how our idea of the natural world supports or undermines the legitimacy of the social world, in other words, the political consequences of the disenchantment of the world. Against the cosmic dualism of Enlightenment naturalism, we have seen him defend a Christian Neoplatonist vision of the world and our knowledge of the world. Against the asserted tyranny and injustice of the world, he will take up the cudgels for a providential interpretation of history. Everything we have seen so far should lead us to expect his argument for Providence will not be wholly confined to orthodoxy. What is most odd is this: while in this chapter we have seen Maistre endeavor to "redivinize" the natural world, in the following we will see him so "naturalize" the idea of Providence that it sometimes seems to amount to little more than the general order of things. Perhaps nowhere so much as in his reflections on this old theological commonplace does Maistre reveal himself as our contemporary.

Chapter 7

Providence

Some say that the things which happen take place according to a Providence; these are those who perceive the regularity and order of motion. Others say that no Providence exists; these are those who take notice of the irregularity and abnormality of the powers and of evil. Some say that what must happen happens. . . . Others say that what happens comes about according to nature. Others again say that the world is an automatism. But the great majority have turned to the visible elements, knowing no more than these. – "The Tripartite Tractate," in *The Nag Hammadi Library*

Maistre's idea of Providence unites the themes of the entire investigation thus far: sacrifice, punishment, symbolic order, legitimacy, and his polemic against naturalist thinking. On the face of it, nothing might seem less relevant to modern European thought. Yet the problem of a general order that includes disorder, which is how Maistre approaches Providence, is a doubly modern question. Division, conflict, fall, and the questions they pose for justice: these are essential elements of the sense and experience of modernity, as they were an essential context of Maistre's writing. His assertion that this discord has a harmony of its own, that disorder has its own order, is a distinctively modern idea, despite the traditionalist language of Providence in which Maistre dresses it and despite his use of it against the Enlightenment. It was precisely the Enlightenment's overly narrow understanding of order that Maistre considered Gnostic.

Thus far we have seen him attack the reduction of life to technology and of society to a sphere of compulsion, asserting against the call for a return to a clockwork nature that social life and knowledge of nature alike are at bottom symbolic. There is thus no natural nature to be restored, for nature thus imagined is a fiction. The project of a Gnostic "return" has thus been answered. What has not yet been contested, however, is what Maistre perceived to be the basic anticosmic stance of the Enlightenment, which asserts the human order to be a bad order of tyranny, evil, ignorance, a world order in which not only is man's essence displaced, but unjustly so. The justification to man of the ways of the world was one of Maistre's central preoccupations, motivated I would argue not so much by a mystical fascination with Providence for its own sake as by the attempt to refute what he understood as a revival of the Gnostic depiction of man's world as radically unjust and unjustifiable, in need of total renovation.

The identification of Enlightenment and Gnosticism has more recently been urged by Eric Vögelin, but with a rather different emphasis, in his *New Science of Politics*. For Vögelin what is Gnostic is the claim to knowledge of the course of the world by the critical "Gnostic intellectual," "Marxian mystics," and "activists . . . like Comte, Marx, or Hitler."[1] The tendency here is to identify every form of social criticism as Gnostic. That is rather dubious: those forms of criticism that seek the good within history are the very antithesis of the Gnostic view that treats worldly good as an oxymoron and thus seeks betterment outside existence as we know it. Vögelin's thesis of a Gnostic "invasion of Western thought" (134) during the Reformation and its alleged progeny the Enlightenment is something of a travesty of Maistre's critique of modernity, but a travesty to be found in certain moments of Maistre's work, those moments of closure that deny all legitimacy to any manifestation of Enlightenment; these moments, though, are contested by other elements of his work. Against Vögelin's thesis, one must argue that the hypostatization of the forces of order is no less Gnostic than that of change; to these conservative and radical hypostases, one might argue, correspond the ascetic and transgressive moments of Gnosticism.

As we have spoken of political theology, the set of issues raised here might well be called those of a "political theodicy." Indeed, the significance of theodicy is as abiding as the need to justify the existing cultural order against challenges to that order: "good order" must be understood as always capable of overcoming or at least limiting the incursions of the "bad" if society is to be legitimate. As the affirmation that individual ills are subsumed under the general good, some notion of theodicy is requisite to any society. "Political theodicy" thus poses the problem of the acceptable, of whether one is or is not to consent to the order of the world, to "cosmic policy" as it were.

The question is whether or not this acceptance may have a purely rational or even reasonable basis, distinct from Berger's identification of theodicy with sadomasochism, "the worshipper voluptuously grovelling in the dust before the god who punishes and destroys in sovereign majesty." Any rational politics requires that allegiance to society can be based (has been or will be based) on something other than voluptuous groveling. Otherwise, no rational construction of legitimacy is feasible: legitimacy would always remain illegitimate, order sado-masochistic, the only escape from which would be into anarchy and anomie. This problem was central to Maistre, who saw it raised by a "Manichaean" Enlightenment. He would accept Berger's claim that "the surrender of the self to society . . . ipso facto implies a theodicy" but would reject its corollary, that "theodicy constitutes an essentially sado-masochistic collusion" between oppressors and oppressed.[2]

Theodicy above all refers to the metaphysical questions of freedom and necessity in the creation of order. These are questions of constitution and legitimacy, of the coalescence and compatibility (or "compossibility," to speak with Leibniz) that define the worthy order that is a legitimate constitution. The particular province of political theodicy, following its Christian analogue, is the problem of the unity of the sovereign who redeems and the sovereign who enforces claims, the violent creator sovereign and the providential all-providing sovereign, the infliction of ills and the bestowal of goods. A Gnostic politics would radically separate the power that provides from the power that punishes. We have already seen Maistre argue to the contrary that sovereignty is one and good (or rather becomes so as the violence of its origins is masked by history) and that violence is a "general law of the universe" and thus involuntary on the sovereign's part: punitive justice is violent but necessary given the generalization of social violence. What is now at issue is the justice of the distribution of this violence and thus the legitimacy of the social world.

The first thorough rejection of Gnostic cosmology, and one that became normative in the Western tradition, was that of Augustine. His doctrine of the fall and inherited sinfulness of man answers to the problem posed to theology by the existence of the bad, without recourse to the Gnostic dualism of opposed good and evil world principles, by ascribing it to God's just punishment. Man's complete freedom carries with it complete responsibility for his status. This formulation allows Augustine, in the words of Hans Blumenberg, "to interpret the deficiencies of the world not as an original failure of the construction of the world for man's benefit, but rather as the result of God's subsequent intervention in his work in order to put nature in the service of justice with respect to man." That, Blumenberg observes, however, "would have to produce a new variety of Gnosticism."[3]

This "new Gnosticism" replaced the cosmic duality of good and bad gods with a human duality of an elect few and a condemned mass. Yet this is only to displace the question of how to conceive the justice of that absolute sovereign who would condemn the mass of men to eternal suffering on account of a lack of faith that is no longer a matter of choice but of predestination. In this argument, the justice of the world is asserted as a premise, not as a conclusion. We shall see Maistre answer that it is not from divine goodness that the goodness of the world must be inferred, but, rather, it is from the workings of the world, above all the social world, that a providential history may be surmised.

Seventeenth- and eighteenth-century France witnessed a reawakened Augustinianism in the guise of the Jansenists, whose conflict with the Jesuits formed an important context of Maistre's thinking. Following Augustine, these Puritans of the Catholic Church held that the natural world was utterly fallen and abnormal, that man, guilty of this fall, stands in need of utter abasement, and that God alone is good, and he is absolutely so.[4] This thorough rejection of the world bears some analogy to the Enlightenment rejection of the political world; it has led a recent scholar, Richard Popkin, to raise the question (only, however, to put it to rest) of a "Manichaean Enlightenment."[5]

Popkin is able to discount this thesis by viewing the question of a reawakened Manichaeanism purely as a doctrinal one, not one of subject positions, of ethics and practice; he thus sidesteps the issue of a "practical Gnosticism" that for Maistre becomes essential. While there certainly did not arise new Gnostic or Manichaean churches in the eighteenth century, people did begin to approach life as though the world were bad, profane, false: from this angle the issue becomes both broader and more significant. Such a total criticism of man's life-world (El Dorado aside) is found in the remark of Martin in *Candide*: "I avow to you that in glancing over this globe, or rather this globule, I think that God has abandoned it to some maleficent being" (Popkin 45). While such an avowed Manichaeanism was indeed uncommon, a subtler form of it was by no means incompatible, as Popkin argues, with the prevailing reformist optimism of the time: Manichaeanism does not entail a complete pessimistic fatalism but rather a putting of all hope in another world than this one; it sees life as illegitimate, not hopeless (a hopeless religion is a contradiction in terms). In Blumenberg's words, for Gnosticism "the downfall of the world becomes the critical process of final salvation, the dissolution of the demiurge's illegitimate construction." The Enlightenment cannot simply be identified with a turn from theological thinking, above all when it holds that the collapse of what is old itself guarantees a return to good order, to man's ineffable truth. It is just this sense of crisis and new beginnings that the project of modernity entailed for many minds that encouraged the growth of a "new Gnosticism" (Blumenberg 128–29).

Nowhere is the oscillation between Enlightenment and Gnosticism more evident than in Bayle's *Critical Dictionary*, for whom "properly speaking, history is nothing but the crimes and misfortunes of the human race." For Bayle, indeed, the "completely absurd and contradictory hypothesis" of two warring gods held by the Manichaeans can "explain experiences a hundred times better than do the orthodox." While Bayle finds the Manichaeans' saving of God's goodness at the expense of his power unacceptable, he believes that they are more reasonable in their refusal to attribute any failing into the very source of what is, or ought to be, good. For absolute goodness, use of the bad to expedite the good would be most improper. In fact, the Manichaeans have reason so much on their side that they can be combated only by faith. The monists "would be better off believing and keeping quiet" than in offering arguments easily refuted by experience. "Man's understanding must be made a captive of faith and must submit to it. He must never dispute about certain things. In particular, he must only fight against the Manichaeans by appealing to Scripture, and only by the principle of submission, as St. Augustine did."[6] Thus argues Bayle, often cited as the father of free thinking, of rational skepticism. His recourse to revelation as the only weapon against Manichaeanism is a forceful demonstration of the threat posed to Western self-assurance by a reawakened Gnosticism.

Bayle's claim that there is no rational refutation of Manichaeanism called forth a veritable explosion of theodicies in the early eighteenth century, of which Leibniz's is only the most familiar. Maistre's writings on Providence represent perhaps the last great effort in this classic philosophical genre. Here again, he marshals the categories of traditional thought against the pretensions of the Enlightenment. Yet Maistre's idea of Providence was hardly so traditional as all that. While like every providentialist he does insist that the world obeys final causes that tend toward the good, neither God nor His personal intentions appear anywhere in Maistre's argument.

Indeed, the notion of a higher intentional order of ends belongs not only to religious apologetics. One can almost say that there is "always a Providence," for example, in positivism's vision of the good future toward which we ineluctably tend: any teleological view of history as a meaningful process postulates some sort of "Providence." In this broader sense, one can find a certain providentialism in the Enlightenment and Illuminism alike: both hope and aim for, bank upon, the redemption of man through the transformation of nature by logos. In Cioran's words, illuminating in their very exaggeration, "to pass from a theological or metaphysical conception to historical materialism is simply to change providentialisms."[7] In the Count's more gentle formulation, "Whatever topic one treats one always speaks of her" (Maistre, *Soirées*, OC 4:17).

The classical formulation of the idea of Providence is found in the opening words of the conclusion to Bossuet's *Idea for a Universal History*, "in which it is shown that everything must be ascribed to a providence." "From the highest heavens God holds the reins of every kingdom and every heart in his hands. At times he bridles men's passions, at others he gives them free rein; and that is how he leads all of mankind."[8] Maistre's *Considérations sur la France* begins with a paraphrase of these words:

> We are all attached to the throne of the Supreme Being by a supple chain that restrains us without enslaving us. Nothing is more admirable in the universal order of things than the action of free beings under the divine hand. Freely slaves, they act voluntarily and necessarily at the same time; they really do what they will, but without being able to disturb the general plans. (OC 1:1)

Maistre's reworking is significant. As we shall see more clearly in the following chapter, he translates Bossuet's discussion of the ways of God into the ways of the French, and the image of Providence becomes the image of the workings of moral and political order. Providence and just dispensation are thus sought in this world, in society, whereas Bossuet grounds morality and justice in heavenly rewards and punishments alone. History thus becomes not merely an example, a stock of commonplaces, as it is in Bossuet's work, but, as "experimental politics," the means of addressing the ultimate questions of philosophy. Finally and most significantly, Maistre's account focuses on the "suppleness" of Providence, which is found in "voluntary slavery," "free domination," and the guidance of the will according to its own nature; these terms perhaps imply that what is ultimately at stake is ideology.

Gnosticism and Counter-Gnosticism

Just as the constancy of his counterrevolutionary stance was a matter of doubt to his fellow royalists, so too Maistre's religious orthodoxy, what one might call the consistency of his counter-Gnosticism, has been a matter of controversy. For good reason: Gnostic thinking exercised a continual hold on his imagination. As early as age seventeen, he characteristically at once acknowledges and contests the validity of the Gnostic thesis: "The bad is in the world. The bad cannot come from the good principle. There are thus two principles. But there cannot be equality between them: the first must necessarily remain the vanquisher of the second" (Maistre, "Extraits F," 67). The elaboration of this "necessarily," here simply urged in a somewhat desperate tone, will lead Maistre to his most profound metaphysical speculations.

Almost fifty years later, shortly before his death, he describes in the eleventh *Soirée* how man is not made for time, "something forced that only asks to end," and how unnatural is this world "stained" with the bad, degraded into matter, and ruled by division. This close attention to division—divided nations, divided souls—leads Maistre to what one could almost call a provisional Manichaeanism. His very rejection of the Manichaean argument itself insists upon the truth of cosmic dualism: "Manichaeanism, and error by consequence, does not consist of believing that there are two Principles, the one good and the other bad; for nothing is clearer, and Christianity in its entirety rests upon this truth. Error consists of believing them equal" (Maistre, "Extraits F," 73). That all of Christianity "rests upon" a truth that Maistre will find in Plato already reveals the heterodox character of his Catholic Neoplatonism.

The dualist tendency of Maistre's metaphysics itself rests upon the idea, borrowed by Origen from the Gnostics, of a precosmic fall into matter. In a notebook entry that in its underlinings and its contestation of theological authority points to his enthusiastic allegiance to Origen, he writes:

> St. Augustine has poorly understood Origen when the latter says that the cause of matter is not the goodness of God alone, but that the souls, having sinned in distancing themselves from the Creator, had merited to be enclosed in diverse bodies as in a prison according to the diversity of their crimes, and that there one has the world; that thus the cause of the creation had not been to do good things *but to stop the bad*. This opinion has *nothing in common with Manichaeanism*. (Maistre, "Mélanges B," 303)

This talk of merited imprisonment to stop the bad shows that we are concerned on a metaphysical level with what on the social level was addressed by the theory of sacrifice: the self-limitation of disorder.

Thus we are told, in a passage from his book on the French Revolution that brings together the two ruling metaphors of sacrifice and harmony, that the reign of duality is only temporary. "*All is evil*, since nothing is in its place. The keynote of the system of our creation has been lowered, and following the rules of harmony, all others have been lowered proportionately. *All creation groans*, and tends with pain and effort toward another order of things" (Maistre, *Considérations*, OC 1:39–40). Sacrifice and harmony, difference and unity, minor ills and the *summum bonum*: these problems of symmetry and compensation are the inseparable guiding concerns of Maistre's sociology and cosmology alike. These shared themes continually implicate in one another his social thought and his metaphysics. Their point of intersection is theodicy.

First, let's tackle the sacrificial theme. In a very Manichaean passage, again qualified by Origenist thinking, Maistre writes that nothing is more apparent than "the existence of two forces in the universe in continual conflict. Nothing good is unsullied or unaltered by evil. Every evil is repressed or assailed by good, which continually impels existence toward a more perfect state." When this impulsion is clarified, in a "wonderfully appropriate" borrowing from jurisprudence, as a "total restitution," one has a compressed statement of how Origenist political theology binds law to cosmology by way of sacrifice and the doctrine of reversibility. Just as with the executioner on the sociopolitical level, the existence of the bad is cosmologically justified as the autodestruction of evil. "The remedy for an abuse arises from another abuse, and evil, having reached a certain point, destroys itself . . . For evil is merely a negative quality having only the dimensions and the durability of the being to which it is attached and that it devours" (Maistre, *Essai*, OC 1:277–82). Just as with the sovereign's punishments, this autodestruction of the bad at once keeps the divine hands clean of direct contact with evil and clears the Creator of reproach for its existence, in spite of the fact that, in the last analysis, it is always he who works the wheels.

The same dualism/antidualism found in the cosmos is present in each person: the "centaur" nature of man that triggered the essay on sacrifice. The idea of such a being as man coming directly from the hands of the Creator, the Count remarks, is "so revolting that philosophy on its own, I mean pagan philosophy, divined" the "lamentable dogma" of original sin (Maistre, *Soirées*, OC 4:68, 71). Responding to the Chevalier's observation that everywhere one hears both that virtue is happy and that virtue suffers, the Count concedes that indeed "the

world obeys two forces," and that the same noise is heard following a
performance of Racine and one of Figaro. The author corrects the
Count in a footnote: one hears "*as much noise*, perhaps . . . but *not the
same noise*. Conscience does nothing like vice, and even its applause has
an accent." The author always intervenes when oppositional Gnostic
thinking becomes too dangerously intense. Most significantly, the very
opposition between Gnosticism and counter-Gnosticism (embodied in
the Senator and Count), which in most thought on Gnosticism itself
tends toward a radical dualism, is contested by the dialogic structure of
the book as a whole. The Count goes on to argue that there are in fact
two men in each person, one of whom praises the good life and one of
whom laments its sacrifices. These two men, however, are not equal:
one represents right reason and conscience, the other spite and envy;
the latter is "no longer the *man*, but *another man*" (Maistre, *Soirées*, OC
4:165–67).

It is the contest between these two people in each person that for
Maistre describes desire. "Man being constantly agitated by two contrary forces, the examination of this terrible law must be the beginning
of every study of man." This altogether "certain and palpable fact of the
moral world" defines for Maistre both the difficulties faced and the ends
sought in politics (*Soirées*, OC 4:303). Because one cannot force the will
("a forced will is a contradiction in terms"), the Count observes, man's
will "can only be agitated and led by *attraction*"; the difficulty is man's
"double attraction" from which "only the sage is free." The ethical and
political question thus becomes "how to hold man . . . to demand what
his nature abhors" (Maistre, *Soirées*, OC 4:334). Politics becomes a matter of education or edification, of creating a unitary will. The other person within oneself is to be mastered, appropriated to oneself. The Senator presents the same argument with his typical extravagance: "when
the double law of man will be effaced, and these two centers be confounded, he will be ONE; for having no conflict within himself, where
would he get the idea of duality?" (Maistre, *Soirées*, OC 5:172).

In a more speculative moment kept to his private notebooks, this
self-unification is the object of a meditation on Plato's double man
(later used by Freud as a fictive solution to the aporias of *Beyond the Pleasure Principle*). "When life or exterior generation will have become similar to interior or angelic life, there will be but one birth. There will be
no more gender. The male and the female will make but one and the
realm of God will arrive." The citations with which Maistre buttresses
this remark are revealing. First, he quotes the apocryphal words of Jesus

on when the Kingdom would come, reported by Clement "the contemporary of the Apostles": "when two things become one, when what is outside resembles what is inside, when the Male is confounded with the Female, and there is neither man nor woman." Comparing these words to Plato's in the *Symposium*, Maistre observes that "the two foreheads, the four legs, are products of the Greek imagination, but let's hold to the general principle." Finally, Maistre quotes John Hunter, the physiologist and "good materialist" whose vitalist theory of blood was cited in the essay on sacrifices: "the generative parts of the two sexes are pieces added after the fact" ("Mélanges A," 580–81).

Here we find the basic elements of Maistre's thinking on Providence: the defining disequilibrium of human existence torn between flesh and spirit, the consequent strife between unity and disunity, and a Christian Neoplatonism that seeks an answer to this impasse in a "general principle" found in the more extravagant moments of the Christian, Platonic, and "scientific" traditions.

This halting movement from division to unity is the keystone of Maistre's metaphysics, metahistory, and what he calls his metapolitics. "Everything being divided, everything desires unity." Because this unity can only be produced through "attraction," through desire, will, or consent, its achievement will come by way of the symbolic, through ritual and language. Such thinking leads Maistre to conclude that "the two great epochs of the spiritual world are without doubt that of *Babel*, where the languages divided themselves, and *Pentecost*, where they made a marvelous effort to reunite themselves" (*Soirées*, OC 5:168–69). This very unusual definition of Pentecost as an effort of language (i.e., of Logos), without a word of Christ, underlines the fundamental place of language in Maistrean philosophy.

These reflections on language lead to a discussion of unity and diversity that moves from ethics to a general theory of politics, where Maistre presents the production of a unitary social will out of divergent desires in wholly secular terms: "Vice separates men like virtue unites them. There is no act against order that does not beget a particular interest contrary to the general order; there is no pure act that does not sacrifice a particular interest to the general interest, that is, that does not tend to create a single and regular will in place of these myriads of divergent and culpable wills" (*Soirées*, OC 5:173). Here the terms unity, sacrifice, and will are brought together in a way that points toward a rational reconstruction of the laws of social order. What then is this "general order," the object of Maistre's political theodicy?

General Order

In Maistre as in Leibniz one finds a taste for symmetries, harmonies, and like figures that resist interpretation as mere accident, that suggest a meaning inherent in the world prior to all judgment. Eighteenth-century philosophy and natural science brought on an indefinitely vast expansion of the spatiotemporal horizons of knowledge; Leibniz was the last great figure to show full confidence in a cosmic order of nature (hence his alleged medievalism). The idea of the cosmos as a text, as a meaningful language of figures and numbers, was still markedly present in Kepler and Galileo, who sought signs of divine imprint in nature (though for Galileo as for Newton the truth of nature is independent of divine truth).

In a revealing passage, Maistre shows his concern to maintain some shadow of the belief in the universe as a cosmos, as a good order, while hinting at the transformations this belief will undergo in his work. The whole passage is an exemplary instance of his counter-Gnosticism, represented here by the Count. "They speak of *disorder* in the universe; but what is disorder? It is a derogation of *order*, apparently; thus one cannot make an objection of disorder without confessing an anterior order." The Count proposes as a metaphor of this situation "a vast cabinet of natural history shaken by an earthquake": everything is in a ramshackle state indeed, "shells have rolled into the room of minerals, and a hummingbird's nest reposes on the head of a crocodile." The very disarray, however, points to an original arraying, without which the disarray itself would be imperceptible.

> Order is as visible as disorder; and the eye, promenading in this vast temple of nature, reestablishes without difficulty everything that a dire agent has broken, falsified, soiled, or displaced. There is more . . . already a few beams are propped up, one has made inroads into the midst of the debris, and, in the general confusion, a crowd of *analogies* already have taken their places and touch one another. (Maistre, *Soirées*, OC 5:102–3)

Here one has *in nuce* all Maistre's theory of general order and Providence: its Neoplatonic basis, the thesis that the bad is a purely negative quality, the oscillation between natural and religious discourse, and the use of outlandish metaphors (temple of nature complete with ridiculous crocodile) that seem to hint that on some level we are dealing with fictions.

Most important in the above passage is the idea of general order as an unfixed order, a self-regulating and flexible structure of compensation in which "all the powers of the universe set limits to one another by their mutual resistance" (Maistre, *Du pape*, OC 2:154). Providence is deduced from the good order of the world (and not vice versa as in Augustine or Leibniz), the consistency of which through all of its transformations is held to be sacred. First of all, then, Providence denotes a higher pattern or coherence to be found in seeming disorder.

Yet Providence refers not only to coherence but to causality and to final causes in particular. It necessarily implies a directedness of events, a proportionality between ends and means, that exceeds the principles of human action. The Count thus observes that "man in his ignorance often fools himself about ends and means, about his forces and about resistance, about instruments and about obstacles. Sometimes he wants to cut an oak with a penknife, and sometimes he throws a bomb to break a reed; but Providence never falters, and it is not in vain that she shakes the world" (Maistre, *Soirées*, OC 4:127). Here the idea of Providence approximates the simple regularity of nature upon which science itself relies. The first thesis of general order is that the universe is a cosmos, that is, a well-constructed whole: "there is only order, proportion, relation, and symmetry in the universe. . . . Number connects all movements" (Maistre, *Examen*, OC 6:388).[9]

Yet Maistre the Neoplatonist adds that all order is intellectual order, and Maistre the religious thinker adds that this intellectual order must be the work of an active intelligence. These two essential claims of Maistrean theodicy are summarized by the Count. Number is order and symmetry

> for order is simply *arranged number*, and symmetry is only order perceived and compared. . . . Take away number and you take away the arts, the sciences, language, and by consequence intelligence. Bring it back: with it reappear its two celestial daughters, harmony and beauty; the cry becomes song, noise receives rhythm, the leap is dance, force is called dynamic, and traces are figures. (Maistre, *Soirées*, OC 5:93–94)

The question here is how this intellectual order is articulated with the natural order. Who does the "arranging": man, God, or necessity? Plainly it is not man alone, for then Providence to all appearances would be wholly superfluous. It cannot be necessity alone, for that would repeat the clockwork argument of the naturalists. Nor can it be divine will alone, for that would return us to the arbitrary and hence unjust God of Descartes. Whatever the case, the identification of these two orders, the cosmic and the intellectual, is necessary if the world is to be seen as a cosmos and the project of theodicy be fulfilled.

Sometimes Maistre seems to identify the general providential order with sheer necessity: "whatever is necessary exists," "nothing happens, nothing exists, without a sufficient reason," "carrying out, as everything must do, the designs of Providence" (*Du pape*, OC 2:417, 421). "Nothing happens by chance; everything has its rule and everything is determined by a power that rarely tells us its secrets. The political world is as regulated as the physical world; but as the liberty of man plays a certain role in it, we end by believing he does everything."[10] Such statements do little more than point to an objective if hidden structure in society as in nature: voluntarism, human or divine, is consistently downplayed. How does such a position differ, then, from the naturalism it was meant to oppose?

The necessity of which Maistre speaks is not at all a mechanical one. Instead, order is always described in terms of flexibility and suppleness: "I do not at all see those immutable laws of which one has said so much. On the contrary, I only see in nature supple springs, such as they must be to lend themselves, as much as is necessary, to the actions of free beings, that frequently combine themselves with the material laws of nature" (Maistre, *Soirées*, OC 4:221). Necessity thus includes a necessary component of elasticity. This combination of free actions with material laws according to a supple necessity defines the general order. General laws are unshakable, but laws "combine with one another in a thousand manners" (Maistre, *Soirées*, OC 5:29). The laws of this general order are laws of combination and distribution.

"That hidden force that we call nature has means of compensation that we can hardly doubt." Providence for Maistre is precisely this means of compensation, of counterbalancing and reestablishment, by which voluntarism is articulated with necessity and "the irregularities produced by the operation of free agents come to arrange themselves in the general order" (*Soirées*, OC 4:230).[11] This statement implies that providential order is most manifest in political disorder; just as theodicy responds to the existence of ills, Providence is most an issue with regard to catastrophe.

Order or harmony is a matter of counterbalancing, distributing, compensating for disorders and discords; these latter seem to be the moving force. This is emphasized in a passage on social harmony and "just proportions."

Social harmony, like musical harmony, obeys the laws of *just propor-tions* in *the keyboard of the universe*. Tune the *fifths* rigorously and the *octaves* will be dissonant, and vice versa. Since discord is inevitable, instead of eliminating it, which is impossible, we must moderate it by a general distribution. Thus, in all parts, *imperfection is an element of the perfection possible*. This proposition [like so many in Maistre] is a paradox in form only. (Maistre, *Essai*, OC 1:277–78)

This Neoplatonic image of the cosmic keyboard is important on sev-eral counts. First, it argues the futility of "rigor" and the virtue of "moderation" in confronting the inevitable existence of ills. Second, it argues that social justice is "proportional," a matter of distributions. Significantly enough, both of these arguments present just dispensa-tion as a matter of compensation, punitive or statistical. Let us begin with the second point.

Statistical distribution and the law of averages make up the *supple springs*, the flexible part of the cosmic law. "All the powers of the uni-verse set limits to one another by their mutual resistance," guided by "the laws of probability, which . . . must always be held as sovereign throughout the world." This claim, setting aside as it does all Neo-platonic numerological speculation, provides the objective basis of the claim that "number connects all movements" according, that is, to the compensatory distribution of probabilities (Maistre, *Du pape*, OC 2:130, 154). This argument for cosmic order, in accordance with the structure of what I have called his political theodicy, finds a direct ana-logue in Maistre's understanding of social justice.

Indeed, he presents the social distribution of benefits and harm as a variety of roulette: "It is of the greatest evidence that goods and ills are a kind of lottery where each, without distinction, can draw a white or black ticket." This is not the lottery of predestination, where the chance fall represents God's will; rather, it is a purely statistical distribution of probabilities. It is this aleatory and indifferent distribution that on this level of Maistre's argument defines social justice. Thus the Count an-nounces as a "great truth" that "a general law, if it is not unjust for ev-eryone, cannot be unjust for the individual . . . The just law is not that which takes effect on all, but that which was made for all; the effect on this or that individual is nothing but an accident" (Maistre, *Soirées*, OC 4:20).

Generalized to a cosmic level, this probabilistic nature of general laws refutes the Gnostic claim of an unjust dispensation. "Every hu-man, as human, is subject to all the misfortunes of humanity: the law is general; therefore it is not unjust" (Maistre, *Soirées*, OC 4:26). The objective character of this general law is underlined when the Count asks his interlocutors if, in the event of an earthquake, one would have it that "God would be obliged to suspend in our favor the laws of gravity, because this terrace bears at this moment three men who have never killed or stolen? No, . . . we would certainly fall and we would be crushed. It would be the same if we were members of the lodge of Bavarian Illuminati or of the Committee of Public Safety." Otherwise, the Count continues, pointing out the same difficulties in occasionalism as Leibniz had before him, "each instant demanding a miracle, miracle would become the ordinary state of the world" and "the exception would be the rule" (Maistre, *Soirées*, OC 4:25–26).

This justification of the world by chance refutes some of the specific claims of "political Gnosticism" (i.e., that the bad order of the world is willful) but not its general thesis. This latter task requires that the sacred order be articulated with the natural order. That this is so and how it might be done begins to be intimated when the general distribution is presented as one of sacrifices. "Elizabeth of France mounts the scaffold; Robespierre mounts it an instant later. The angel and the monster were submitted, upon entering the world, to all the general laws that rule it" (Maistre, *Soirées*, OC 4:26). Maistre's Providence is not for Panglosses!

Justice and Generality

The above argument from chance and probability presents the world as not unjust: that a good person suffers or a bad person prospers is unfortunate but not unfair. This is not enough for the needs of theodicy, however, which must present the cosmos as a positively just order. Virtue must by and large be happier than vice, innocence better recompensed than crime. "Any other hypothesis," the Count observes, "would lead directly to the destruction of the moral order, or to the creation of another world" (Maistre, *Soirées*, OC 4:28). How, then, is the indifferent order of chance identified with an order of justice?

It is just such a question of worldly justice that triggers the *Soirées*, which begin as the Chevalier expresses some doubt: "I would like to see, on this same barque as us, one of those perverse men born for the misfortune of society, one of those monsters who fatigue the earth. . . . I would ask him if this night seemed as beautiful to him as it does to us." The Count answers that "perverse hearts have never had beautiful nights or days," but the Chevalier persists: one hears every day that success goes to bad faith and immoral action. "If this were really so," he confesses, "I'd be a little angry that Providence had reserved the punishment of the bad and the recompense of the just entirely for another world" (Maistre, *Soirées*, OC 4:5ff.). Responses to this problem motivate the bulk of this, Maistre's masterwork, further confirmation if such were needed of the counter-Gnostic tenor of his thought.

Direct responses take several forms. First, the Count adduces the moral causes of illness, the maladies produced by idleness, choler, gourmandism, incontinence, and so on, and concludes that "moral vices can augment the number and intensity of maladies to a point that it is impossible to assign; and reciprocally, this hideous empire of physical ills can be contained by virtue within limits it is equally impossible to fix" (Maistre, *Soirées*, OC 5:84–88). This realm of indeterminacy, impossible to "fix" by reason, is always in Maistre the domain of the sacred.

The second argument asserts the benefits of suffering. The Senator would have it that suffering turns us to heavenly things and "disenchants us with the misleading charms of this unhappy life" (Maistre, *Soirées*, OC 4:172). The more enthusiastic Chevalier adds that "sufferings are for the virtuous man what combat is for the soldier: they perfect him and accumulate his merits," they make him sure of himself and his value. The virtuous man should thus do as the soldier who seeks out danger, for whom suffering is an occupation and death an adventure (Maistre, *Soirées*, OC 5:85). The Count, for whom such otherworldly arguments do not suffice, concludes that "every man suffers because he is man, because he would be God if he did not suffer. . . . Those who demand an impassive man demand another world" (Maistre, *Soirées*, OC 5:88).

These two subsidiary arguments, taken together, point to the third, comprehensive one. The first points to the containment of the bad by moral taboos, the second to the turn to the good through mortification. Thus we return to sacrifice and to sacred punishment, which serve as the keystone of Maistre's theodicy as they do for his political and social theory.

Maistre prepares his ultimate and most general argument for the thesis that innocence is not unhappy by asking the troubling question, "where is innocence, I ask you? Where is justice? Is it here, around this table? Good God, eh?" (*Soirées*, OC 4:185). Most of what we call innocence is reducible to custom, pride, circumstances, or impotence: "I never meditate this shocking subject," says the Count, "without being tempted to throw myself to the ground like a culprit who asks for mercy; without accepting in advance all the ills that might fall on my head, as a light compensation for the immense debt I have contracted to eternal justice" (*Soirées*, OC 4:188). With culpability, debts, compensation, and justice we return to sacrifice.

The ultimate refutation of all complaints against the justice of the world is that innocence does not complain: "The more a person approaches that state of justice that does not belong to our feeble nature, the more you will find him resigned even in the cruelest situations in life" (Maistre, *Soirées*, OC 4:192–93). Only a victim can be innocent of something, and to be rancorous, to want more and better for oneself, is already to be culpable. To be innocent is to be a willing victim.

It is in (or rather on) the person of the willing victim that "compensation" as statistical distribution is joined with "compensation" as reparation or reprisal. In his writings on sacrifice Maistre called this dual compensation in which the innocent suffer for the guilty *reversibility*. We can now see why Maistre argued this idea to be the foundation of the sacrificial economy, prior even to substitution. In accepting his chance lot of ills willingly, and only in so doing, the victim fulfills the society's need for sacred substitution and "really sacrifices for all men" (Maistre, *Soirées*, OC 5:130). That justice is thus based on chance (substitution) and even more on disproportionality (reversibility) is confirmed when the Count argues that if all crimes were immediately and directly punished, all good deeds recompensed, the virtuous act would no longer have anything "supernatural" about it; if the thief's hand fell off, he would merely "abstain from stealing as one abstains from putting one's hand under the butcher's hatchet." Immediate recompenses would provide a purely functional motivation for good that, as we have seen, is not enough to maintain society as something more than an instrumental order of functions and roles (Maistre, *Soirées*, OC 5:27). Here it seems, as it has seemed before, that the sacred is nothing but this disproportionality of chance that escapes instrumental understanding.

This, then, will be another and perhaps the most staggering of Maistre's alleged paradoxes: that the only guarantee of the justice of the law, general and penal, is the suffering of innocence. It is the existence of the willing victim that in the last analysis makes law legitimate and punishment just. Let us look more closely at this idea, which seems as contradictory as it is inhuman.

If the first premise of the justice of law is that there be a willing victim, the second is that everyone is guilty and that the innocent victim is thus only a limit case, an exception so unlikely that it affirms the rule.

The reasoning behind this Kafkaesque thought is that innocence is a negative quality and meaningful only in relation to a crime: one may be innocent of this, that, and the other, but the assertion of complete innocence would have to address itself to the totality of crimes and their generality in human conduct. Innocence is something indeterminate, an absence of attributes, and cannot be established on its own terms. This means that innocence, like guilt, is defined only in relation to a tribunal. All the difficulty, that is, all the conceptual paradox and real suffering of the innocent victim, arises from the consideration that this tribunal, because it dispenses justice, must be acknowledged as both just and irresistible.

If the powers of law and its tribunal are just, this means that the plaintiff only becomes a victim if she does not, because she cannot, respond to her charges, if she has no means of responding to those charges: the victim is defined by her silence. There is thus no means of establishing that one is a victim of law, for use of that means would imply that one has not been victimized but rather granted what is called due process.[12] This means that the only innocent victim is she who does nothing to stop her immolation. The victim who pleads her innocence is not a victim: she has lodged her claim as justice requires, and her subsequent punishment would then be an ill but not an injustice, for the legal tribunal is just. Moreover, any further protestation would occasion her guilt of the crime of lèse-majesté, of disputing the justice of legitimate authority.

This is truly an inhuman thought that, generalized to the social order as a whole, deprives the subject of any means of resistance against the wrongs of power. Yet the same thing must be said of this idea as was said of Maistre's assertion of the sacrificial sources of social unity, to which indeed it is plainly allied. It is perhaps not so much his ideas as political life itself that is monstrous. If Maistre were to have advocated this as a principle, as a good way to go about politics, it would reprehensible, even culpable. However, his position is rather that this is how politics works, this is how the divide is maintained between the rights of power and the duties of obedience, and that this is what power is: *the right to punish with impunity*. To cap this Machiavellian meditation, Maistre the conservative asserts that this basis of politics, if it is to serve moderation rather than chaos, must be accepted as well and good, for the rejection of power's necessary conditions, we have seen, simply returns us to those conditions in a more naked and elemental form. It is not that sacrifice (or judicial sacrifice of the victim of the law) is good, but sacrifice (and law) is something necessary that is taken as something good and thus binds society.

This is why the willing victim is the foundation of social order. Her quietist *don de soi* (gift of self) represents an unmotivated affirmation of order and law, the only sacrifice that is not a scapegoating sacrifice but rather an affirmation and justification of the violence occasioned by life in common. That social order thus rests upon the *pur amour* of the willing victim is not the invention of Maistre. If this argument seems wholly monstrous or strangely familiar (or both), it would do well to recall that it is found as a central motif of that primal scene of philosophy's confrontation with the tribunal: the death of Socrates. Against Crito's offer of escape, Socrates argues that the citizen must always defer to the judgments and guidance of the judge, the established authority on what is just and unjust, "the expert in right and wrong, the one authority, who represents the actual truth."[13] For the innocent Socrates to flee would make of him neither an innocent nor a victim, "not the least culpable of your fellow countrymen but one of the most guilty" (52a), and would indeed confirm the judgment of his jury in their verdict: such "a destroyer of the laws might very well be supposed to be a destructive influence on young and foolish persons," thus confirming the judgment made against him (53c).

These labyrinths of law and justice, of faith and fiction, will continue to solicit us throughout this chapter; let us conclude this section with a passage that brings together justice, sacrifice, the innocent victim, and teleology in the interests of counter-Manichaeanism. Properly enough, the passage uses the metaphor of a balance, the very image of proportionality, compensation, measure, and justice. This bare proportionality must be supplemented, however, if Manichaeanism is to be refuted: Maistre's providential argument must show that the good not only exists in equal measure with the bad but ultimately tips the balance. It is the task of the willing victim, the Count concludes, to provide just this supplement.

> On one side, all the crimes, on the other, all the satisfactions; on this side, the good works of all men, the blood of martyrs, the sacrifices and tears of innocence accumulating without cease to create an equilibrium with the evil that, since the origin of things, throws in the other basin its poisoned floods. It is necessary that in the end the side of health carries it away, and to accelerate the universal work, the expectation of which *makes all beings groan*, it suffices that men desire it.

Thus, when asked why innocence suffers in this world, "we can respond: she suffers for you, if you so desire" (Maistre, *Soirées*, OC 5:213). What is most disturbing about this remark (and this observation might be extended to Maistre's thought as whole) is less its inhumanity or mysticism than its claim to truth. That the innocent victim suffers for us, like its associated claim that everyone is guilty, is an assertion that points to the real existence of a structure of social debts and responsibilities that bind us irrevocably to the people with whom we make up a society. To deny the presence of these bonds may well be more delusionary and more dangerous, more "reactionary," than to assert them.

General Politics

Maistre's theodicy argument bears directly upon his social and political philosophy, the main concern of this investigation. Most broadly, the idea of a general dynamic order of compensatory distributions informs his understanding of history as a political cosmology, a differentiated and dynamic ensemble of nations:

> The imaginary world of Descartes represents well enough the reality of the political world: each nation is a particular vortex at once pressing and pressed upon; the "whole" is only the combination of these vortexes, and the nations among themselves are like the individuals who compose them. . . . Everything serves a purpose, everything is in its place; everything forms part of the general organization, everything marches invariably toward the goal of association. (Maistre, *Etude*, OC 1:544–45)

Here the order of nations replaces that of souls in what could almost be called a political apocatastasis.

General order plays not only a descriptive or axiomatic role in Maistre's political theory but also a normative one. Legitimate power keeps to its proper place in the general order, and the criteria of legitimacy are the very characteristics of that order: measure, balance, and moderation. In one of his earliest essays Maistre wrote that "power, when it is in its place, always possesses, more or less, a certain moderation and, so to speak, a certain modesty . . . It acts smoothly with a tranquil force that forms its general character."[14] This model of legitimacy as moderate and harmonious, willfully nonmechanical but not for all that organic, still guides Maistre's thinking twenty-five years later in *Du pape*: "All legitimate actions, of whatever kind, are always imperceptibly carried on. Wherever there is noise, tumult, impetuosity, destruction, and so on, it may assumed that crime or folly is at work" (OC 2:341). This harmonious nature of legitimacy, like the general order of Providence, is a result of general distribution: legitimate power "guides men by general rules, designed not for such a case or such a man, but for all cases, for all times, for all men" (Maistre, *Du pape*, OC 2:167–68).

Such harmony was nowhere more evident for Maistre than in the seventeenth century, the "great century of France," when, in the Senator's words, "Religion, valor, and science being placed, so to speak, in equilibrium, there resulted that lovely character that all peoples have proclaimed by unanimous acclamation as the exemplar of the European character. Remove the first element, the ensemble . . . would disappear" (*Soirées*, OC 5:19). We are now in a position to better understand this centrality of religion to Maistre's political philosophy.

As the above citations intimate, the providential character of the general order is not in the interests of unbridled authority. Unlike instrumental definitions of order, Maistre's idea of Providence makes the sovereign subject to a higher jurisdiction. That Providence is the measure and not man is what provides a standard for judging men and societies, for criticism of inordinate power. It serves, that is, as a nonhuman, transcendent, and hence binding principle distinct from the arbitrary idea of a particular man or class, a higher justice irreducible to established legal forms. The sacred in Maistre refers to precisely this irreducibility. His Neoplatonic philosophy of ideal hierarchies and supersensible harmonies presents an order higher than sovereignty itself, which is thus not above the law. The sacred in Maistre's philosophy is neither altogether in this world, incorporated by divine right in the ruler and his appanages, nor wholly outside it, leaving the world to will-to-power. It is at once high enough and low enough to serve as a binding normative limit to power and to allow justice to be brought to bear on history.

Here we find the dual significance of Maistre's providential general order. First, it refutes the Gnostic charge that this world is fundamentally bad. Such a position legitimates violence, whether revolution against an archontic elite or exploitation of one's nonelect subordinates. Second, Maistre's approach avoids the best-of-all-possible-worlds notion held by Leibniz that forestalls all criticism. Maistre holds instead that all equilibriums or constituted harmonies are of value, while none are fully harmonized, free of the violence that demands compensation. Justice and legitimacy are measured by how closely they approach ideal equilibrium.

This critical or normative role of Maistrean Providence distinguishes it from those theodicies, from Boisguilbert to Smith's Invisible Hand, that serve primarily as endorsements of existing inequalities. For Maistre, Providence is that general order that condemns every disordinate power to ultimate failure, since "error, by a divine and immutable law [the law of compensation] always destroys itself."[15] Good order rests upon harmonious distribution. In history, one thus always finds a providential return to equilibrium "when a too preponderant nation terrifies the universe." This return is effected by "two simple means: sometimes the giant cuts his own throat, sometimes a quite inferior power throws across its path some imperceptible obstacle, but which then grows one knows not how, and becomes insurmountable; like a weak branch, caught in the current of a river, produces a logjam that diverts it." That there is thus "always a certain equilibrium in the political universe" provides less an apology than a warning for the extension or abuse of power (Maistre, *Soirées*, OC 5:30).

According to this "most evident" law of the "temporal government of Providence" that "each active being exercises its action within the circle that is traced for it, without ever being able to leave it," political excess always destroys itself (Maistre, *Soirées*, OC 4:249). This means that political order ultimately must rest upon justice, since "justice of its nature produces peace, as injustice of its nature produces war."[16] The political consequences of this general theory of excess, compensation, and equilibrium are laid out in the following passage:

> How many faults power has committed! and how much does it ignore the means of preserving itself! Man is insatiable for power; he is infinite in his desires, and always discontent with what he has, he only likes what he does not have . . . There is no man who does not abuse power . . . But the author of nature has placed limits on the abuse of power: he desired that it destroy itself once it passes these natural limits . . . To conserve itself power must restrain itself, and it must always keep a distance from that point where its final effort will lead to its final moment. (Maistre, *Etude*, OC 7:549–60)

This general theory of order is responsible for the depth and subtlety of Maistre's political analyses but also for their occasional folly. Both insight and a certain danger, a danger of what one might call "excessive moderation," are present in the following passage on revolutions:

> Every sensible man should defend (even without virtue and for his own self-interest) the king *he has* and the sovereign family *he has*. I do

not know whether I should laugh or cry when I hear speak of a *change of dynasty*. To have an angel, I would be tempted by a little revolution; but to put one man in place of another, one must be possessed . . . Shed torrents of blood to have Germanicus and Agrippina, worthy to reign; and to compensate you, they will give you Caligula. In eight or ten generations, all the good and bad qualities of human nature appear and compensate one another, so that every forced change of dynasty is not only a crime, but a stupidity.[17]

Such remarks tend to refute the dangers commonly imputed to Maistrean thought on the basis of his discourse on sacrifice; indeed, the moral of his reflections on Providence and sacrifice alike is that bloodshed must be kept at a minimum.

This passage, however, points to another danger that is more real if less immediately threatening, one shared by the conservative tradition as a whole, namely, political quietism, a passivity before a political order that is good simply because it exists. Even before the revolutionary crisis put a premium on order for its own sake, Maistre had written in "Lettres d'un royaliste savoisien" that political happiness is the product of "peace, tranquillity, of respect for the ancient maxims of Government and for those venerable customs that turn laws into habit and obedience into instinct" (OC 7:160). Such a habit to obey may well be the foundation of all power; this produced "instinct," one must add, however, is also the basis of abuses of power. Maistre's early phrase, "do everything for the general order" ("Lettres," OC 7:156) is a useful maxim against the more narrow-minded forms of Western self-assertion; it is subject to abuse when construed as a call for passivity toward whatever immediate "order" one may find oneself in.

This danger is plain in a passage that may be considered Maistre's last word on counter-Gnosticism. These words of the Count could not be more valid with regard to the general order, to the world as a whole, but they are equally false if applied to a particular order, to a particular state:

> Here we are, then, placed in an empire the sovereign of which has published once and for all the laws that rule everything. These laws are, in general, marked by wisdom and even by a striking goodness: some nonetheless (I suppose in this moment) appear hard, even *unjust* if one wishes. Granted that, I ask all the discontented, what must be done? Leave the empire perhaps? Impossible: it is everywhere, and nothing is outside it . . . What signify, in effect, sterile or culpable

complaints that furnish man with no practical consequence, no light
capable of enlightening or perfecting him? (Maistre, *Soirées*, OC
5:106)

This, then, is the limit to the openness and modernity of Maistre's social thought: a political quietism that encourages passivity before a sacred order and that strongly discourages active intervention in politics.

It is this quietism—and not some alleged adoration of violence—
that is the source of Maistre's resonance with the case of Heidegger: a
stance of passive expectancy toward destiny. Yet it is important to remark two essential differences between these men: first, Maistre's waiting was among the exiles and not among the executioners; second, as I
will show in what follows, his fascination with the sacred is far more
qualified by irony and by pragmatism than is Heidegger's. Moreover,
irrational passive expectancy in matters of politics is far more universal
than any derogatory finger pointing would tend to imply: such a stance
is by no means limited to royalists and fascists, and it thus cannot serve
as proof of some underlying identity between them. That political quietism is so widespread, of course, by no means makes light of its dangers—quite the contrary. Other elements of Maistre's politico–religious vision, moreover, prove critical of this political reverence. Before
turning to his explicit political positions, however, we must first ask
just how reverent his religion really was.

Fact or Fiction?
Any treatment of Maistre's theory of Providence must consider, however briefly, the question of his religiosity, a hotly debated topic in
Maistrean scholarship and one of great interest for the history of sensi-
bilities. What makes Maistre's religious thought significant for historians is how it embodies the transformation of Old Catholicism into
the New Catholicism of the nineteenth century. In it one finds traces of
Pascal, Saint Francis de Sales, and Fénelon but also anticipations of
Lamennais, Baudelaire, and Renan. His Catholicism is thus "epochal"
in the triple sense of the term: as representative of his period as a whole,
as a transition, and as a hiatus between more stable forms.

Maistre's religious traditionalism differs significantly from that of
other members of the "immortal retrograde school," above all in its
markedly intellectual Neoplatonic and Masonic accent. He returns to
the pagan sources and elements of Catholicism found in Clement, Origen, and Dionysius, in cult and superstition, placing far less emphasis
on the antipagan purifiers of Christian theology. This spirituality,

moreover, seeks its lights not only on the margins of the Church in these Hellenistic hybrids but also outside the Church in non-European religions. Such universalism shows significant Masonic overtones. Noteworthy in this regard is the Senator's continual reference, in dialogue with the Count, to "your religion," "your Saint Thomas": if one attributes the Senator's remarks on blood and war to Maistre, one must do the same with this Masonic diffidence. (As I've argued above, however, it is rather the tension between the Count and the Senator that best represents Maistre himself.)

In short, Maistre's Catholicism had little or none of that intolerance that marked the Restoration, especially under Charles X. As all historians of the period have remarked, the intransigent conflict between Catholics and antireligious Republicans created cultural and intellectual tensions that marked all of nineteenth-century French intellectual history. Maistre is important both in his expression of these tensions (and their productivity) at an early stage of their development and in his attempt to create hybrid forms of religiosity before Catholicism and anti-Catholicism became irreconcilable.

One thus finds in Maistre an effort to reconcile the most primitive, ancient, and popular forms of Catholicism with the most abstract and elite Neoplatonism. He seeks this reconciliation in the realm of ritual, of which he offers a Neoplatonic theory of the primitive cult that becomes the paradigm for his political philosophy. What is remarkable about this is the lay tone, the altogether worldly approach to ritual and to theodicy, from both of which alike the figure of the Christian deity virtually disappears.

A radically transformed image of Maistre emerges when his social and political interpretation of religious beliefs and practices is applied to his own. In punishment, sovereignty, magistracy, and science, we have seen, he reveals their underlying scandal by reading them as cultic practices. It is hard to imagine that he never turned his sociology of religion upon his own religious allegiances. Indeed, *Du pape* offers precisely a sacred sociology of Catholic institutions, and, like other Masons, Maistre sought out the allegorical truths hidden behind biblical imagery. Yet these sociological and allegorical approaches to Christianity by no means entail that his religion was false or hypocritical, no more than his behavior as a magistrate was any less serious for his insistence upon the cultic basis of law.

In all Maistre's writing on religion, however, there seems to be a certain coolness or formality in marked contrast to, say, the fervent heterodoxy of Lamennais, who wrote to the comtesse de Senfft that, "for me, politics means the triumph of Christ, legitimacy means his law; my fatherland is the human race which he has redeemed with his blood."[18] There is none of this passion in Maistre. One might well even wonder if his Catholic traditionalism is something like that which Renan ascribed to France as a whole: "France is of all countries the most orthodox because she is the least religious. Had she been more religious she would have become Protestant" or, in Maistre's case, Jansenist.[19]

While there is no doubt that Maistre led a Christian life, that his religious practice was adequate to the demands of his time, Maistre's religion reflects the tendency toward the formalization of religious practices in the eighteenth century described by Michel de Certeau. Certeau argues that with the establishment of "alternative" reformed national churches, accompanied by the disappearance of heresy and the appearance of cross-denominational mysticism and piety, and with the socialization of the Christian creed into social and political ethics, convictions tended to become silent as churches came to emphasize more the formality of practices and the administration of rites and less their underlying beliefs. Certeau thus concludes that "analyses of the 18th century clergy all show this obfuscation of living meaning under the proliferation of administrative measures aimed at protecting or spreading patented discourse and deeds."[20]

Although there is little "patented" about religion in Maistre's work, his emphasis on its rites and institutions indeed points to a certain formality. Maistre's brother Xavier said of Joseph's habits in religion and work alike that they "went like the most perfect chronometer. This order and rule would seem to have to lead to dryness. But no, his heart and mind have all their freshness."[21] Madame Swetchine, Maistre's most illustrious convert from the Russian church, wrote that "the idea in him ruled everything and overcame his heart, more honest and upright than naturally pious."[22] As the example of his Russian proselytizing makes clear, Maistre's religiosity was quite sincere. Yet this sincerity remained wholly private; in his publications, it is always the public value of religion that is emphasized.

Thus Maistre's assertion of papal infallibility emphasizes an institutional infallibility necessary for the unity of the Church, not a personal infallibility of divine inspiration; indeed, he tells us that "if it were admissible to set up degrees of importance among the various divine institutions, I should place the hierarchy above dogma, so important is it for maintaining faith."[23] What struck Sainte Beuve about Maistre's piety was not his belief itself, but that he "comported himself in all actions and all judgments as if he believed them in reality"; this practicing what one preaches (what Maistre might call practical theism), Sainte Beuve continues, is "rarer than anything."[24] Maistre himself rejects "the exterior of religion taken for religion itself," arguing that "true religion" is gauged by how it "purifies and exalts man."[25] Yet this rejection of superficial religion itself uses the criterion of practical results as a test, in keeping with his sociological approach to the sacred.

So much for seriousness. For all his Old World Catholicism, Maistre's treatment of the ultimate questions of religion is characterized by a lightness of touch that, as much as its Masonic overtones, reveals its eighteenth-century background. An illuminating example is how the Senator begins the third *Soirée* by "proposing a difficulty" to the Count, "Bible in hand; this is serious, you see" (OC 4:157). Such half-serious, half-playful references to the gravity of canonic religious thought reappear continually. Thus the remark "fortune is a woman, she only loves young men" tries to say something meaningful about Providence in the form of jest (and, moreover, in words borrowed from Machiavelli).[26] Such personification, above all of abstract feminine nouns like "Providence," is another marked trait that points to a self-consciously mythical or fabulous dimension in Maistre's thinking.

The received wisdom on the genres of Maistrean writing refers to a division of authorial labors between brothers: Joseph would write no fiction and Xavier no fact. This distinction is belied by the carnivalesque theatricality of the following passage, which argues a most serious claim about the workings of Providence in a most unserious and unorthodox manner:

> Human idiocy and perfidy are two immense blind men of which Madame Providence makes use to arrive at her goals, as an artist makes use of a tool to execute his works. Does the file know that it is making a key? All the execrable and laughable personages who act in this moment on the world's stage are files. When the work is done, we will prostrate ourselves to receive it from the hands of the Great Worker.[27]

This passage is remarkable in many aspects: its definition of creation as loss, as "honing"; the absurdity of its metaphor, "the personages are files," with its surrealist overtones that anticipate Rimbaud ("too bad for the wood that finds itself a violin"). Here one finds a transition not only from Old to New Catholicism but from Old to New Writing, in which classical references are supplemented by a carnivalesque surrealism. Significant too is the description of Madame Providence as alternately artist, toolmaker, and playwright: all three designations refer to history as a creation, and two refer to the realm of the imaginary as the locus of this creation.

Maistre's personification of Madame Providence must be compared with another text in which he takes up a friend's reference to his wife, Françoise, as "Madame Prudence," the "supplement" to the "easygoing senator" who has "what I regard as the eighth gift of the Holy Spirit: that of a certain loving persecution by which *it is given to her* to torment her children from morning to night *to do, to refrain,* and *to learn,* without ceasing to be tenderly loving. How does she do it? I have always watched without understanding it."[28] While the previous passage personified Providence, bringing it down to earth by comic and practical metaphors, this text raises his wife to the level of sacred if again humorous allegory.

Maistre's Catholic orthodoxy has been questioned by Omodeo, Scherer, Faguet, and others. Exemplary of such questioning are the remarks of Rohden, that Maistre was "more a theologian than a Christian, more a jurist than a theologian," and of J. C. Murray, that "the manner in which Maistre considers religion can be considered as that of a good sociology and that of a good political theory, but it is far from being a good theology."[29]

Maistre's distance from "good theology" is nowhere clearer than in an early passage from his notebooks on the cosmic dualism of the good and evil principles. It begins by asserting the universality of this belief, revealed by a comparative study of religions:

> The Banians, Parsis, Magi, Manichaeans, and so on, and the Christians, without even perceiving it, all admit this dogma. The Evil Principle is here called *Devil,* there *Ahriman,* elsewhere *Manitou.* The word makes no difference. The opinion of the two Principles is, in effect, very natural, and if it were less generally adopted one would have to be surprised.

Then, following his penchant for ancient Oriental wisdom, Maistre traces this universal belief back to Egypt. "Everything that the Philosophers later published about the good and bad Principles, everything said of it by the Persians after Zoroaster, . . . the Chaldeans, . . . and the Greeks—all of that derives its origin from that ancient Theology of the Egyptians enveloped under the story of Typhon and Osiris." A series of Vichian meditations on universal mythology follows that identify Typhon with Noah, Moses, or Esau. Not only does the young Maistre thus adduce the Egyptian origins of Christian theology (recall that "Christianity in its entirety rests upon this truth"), but he proceeds to explain the origin of this Egyptian theology in wholly, even wildly, naturalist terms: "Typhon, well understood, signifies nothing but the Flood [of the Nile], Enemy of the Sun and the Earth; and it is only by Metaphor that one has made it the Symbol of the bad principle" ("Mélanges A," 618–20). While the comparative, Neoplatonic, Orientalist, and historicist accents of this extended passage certainly reveal a mind bent upon origins and ultimate truths, they hardly testify to an orthodox piety or a sacrifice of the intellect.

Most Maistrean scholars describe his religious development according to the standard "libertines grown old" trajectory: after a youthful crisis of faith, Maistre returned to the Catholic fold. Thus Robert Triomphe argues that a brief antireligious period in his adolescence was followed by a "conversion" during his late teens.[30] Darcel, seconded by Lebrun, finds an early crisis soon resolved by a Pascalian bet on faith.[31] The question is what kind of "return" this was. Lebrun's conclusion that "any heterodox impulses . . . were soon checked and of minimal significance for his later thinking" is subject to debate: we've seen how Maistre's enthusiasm for Origen, for example, pervaded his thinking from start to finish.[32] While Maistre's writing on religion did undergo some changes, the most dramatic transformation was that he came to place more and more emphasis on religious sociology and less and less on religious truth, a development difficult to construe as "faith."

As we have seen, when he does not present Providence in fabulous terms, Maistre shows it to be an objective structure independent of all wills, a structure of legitimate relations with its own immanent laws. The idea of Providence as an altogether nonmiraculous distribution often seems to refer less to a fact than to a principle, that is, a principle of consistency or standard of measurement. Thus the personal figure of a deity may be and indeed is left out of the picture entirely (Madame Providence aside). In Maistre's work, political theodicy operates on an imminent and sublunary plane without direct divine intervention; the sacred always appears within a human (and often all too human) frame. Providence is always considered with regard not to divine intentions but to the future of France or the Revolution, always against a background of political questions.

Whether it is a matter of sacrifice or of political theology, Maistre's great contribution to political theory is his treatment of the political nature of religion and the religious aura of politics. In an unfinished passage elided from the *Considerations on France*, perhaps for its insistent worldliness, he tells us that Catholicism's

> characters are imprinted on our flags, our coinage, our medals of honour, our buildings, and all our monuments. It animates, vivifies, perpetuates, and infuses our legislation. It sanctions our customs; it presides over our treaties . . . It was the great family title and the proof of a common kinship. The hideous hand of revolutionary genius came to efface this sacred formula, and it has destroyed . . .[33]

This discourse of the vivifying imprint points to the essential and yet somehow exterior place of religion in Maistre's thought (it also, of course, points to its Neoplatonic background).

The essentially political thrust of Maistre's religious argument is emphasized in a passage remarkable for its combination of skepticism, realpolitik, and admiration for Christianity. Why must we accept the truth of Christianity? "Because it has been proven well enough by history" (that is to say, by "experimental politics")

> that religion is necessary to the peoples, and that the Sermon on the Mount will always be regarded as an acceptable code of morals, it is important to maintain the religion that has published this code. If its dogmas are fables, it is necessary at least that there be *unity of fables*, which will never happen without *unity of doctrine* and authority, which in turn becomes impossible without the supremacy of the sovereign pontiff. If I were an atheist and a sovereign, I would declare the pope infallible, by public edict, for the establishment and security of peace in my estates.[34]

Such treatment of religion, and even of Providence itself, as purely a question of civil politics, as a necessary myth, dates back to Maistre's master, Plato. In very similar if somewhat harsher terms, Plato tells us that were he a legislator "I would inflict a penalty little short of capital on any inhabitant heard to maintain that there are wicked men who lead a pleasant life."[35] Civil order depends upon a belief that justice is not a purely otherworldly phenomenon. Even were this but a fiction, Plato argues, there would be no "more useful fiction than this . . . for the sake of its effect on the young" (663e). With regard to belief in one's national dogmas in general and in Providence in particular, Maistre cites this same work of Plato: "one must believe these things on faith from the legislators and the antique traditions, at least if one has lost the spirit." To underline that this assertion of the religious basis of politics is a political and not a religious claim, Maistre adds, "Legislators, listen well." That this is to avoid the question of truth claims entirely need not concern us, Maistre tells us, for "happily *the truth of a fable* is of little import" (Maistre, "Sur les délais," OC 5:418n, 393n).

Once again, Maistre's notebooks only exacerbate these doubts, further emphasizing the fictive yet necessary character of religious "mythology." In a passage that long postdates the passing religious crisis hypothesized by historians, Maistre tells himself that "all religions have a mythology . . . eternal punishment. Never would I touch a false legend, so long as it is useful. Parables—evil rich. Prodigal son. Is it false? What does it matter . . . Dissertations against the truth of these facts almost resemble a treatise against the truth of *Telemaque*" ("Religion E," 157–58).

If Maistre writes elsewhere that "there is nothing so true as fable," it is to refer to the practical truth of myth, the very real force it exerts on people's conduct independent of its veracity.[36] Such practical truths are for Maistre as for the conservative tradition as a whole more significant than the truths of theory; it is with the former that the defenders of Order defend themselves against the latter. These guiding received ideas, I have argued, however, are not the province of conservative thought alone; they are a necessary concern for any sociology of the everyday, a form of sociology that finds many of its roots in the counter-Enlightenment tradition.

It is Maistre's position on the border between political partisanship and social theory that makes him such a challenging figure for intellectual history. When he remarks of the myths of the origins of power that "these are fables, one will say. I know nothing about that, in truth; but the fables of all peoples, even modern peoples, cover many realities," his disclaimer is that of the traditionalist. His insight into political myth, however, is that of a theorist of ideology, an impression reinforced when he explains why fables thus "cover" realities: the "founders of peoples spoke so much of the role of God" because "they felt that they had no right to speak in their own name" (Maistre, *Etude*, OC 1:331). This kind of insight derives less from Burke than from Machiavelli or from Vico, for whom, as for Maistre, myth is "true history."

Ultimately, what makes Maistre's religious argument still relevant is its sociological, philosophical, and not merely reactionary intent. "These reflections are addressed to everyone, to the believer as to the

skeptic . . . Whether you laugh at religious ideas or whether you venerate them makes no difference: true or false, they form no less the
unique basis of all durable institutions" (Maistre, *Considérations*, OC
1:56). That the pragmatic result of this religious sanction has nothing to
do with truth or falsity, one might add, is the "unique basis" of any theory of ideology.

These ideological concerns define the place of Christianity in Maistre's social theory. The victory of logos over matter is the telos of the
Christian message (a victory contested by the Gnostics). In Maistre,
this victory becomes the model of ideological hegemony, of the force
that ideas exert on material life, of authority as against brute force. True
or false, he finds it uniquely suited for this task.

It is perhaps strictly undecidable just how much Maistre's Christianity was heartfelt and how much a theoretical fiction, or again, how
much he adhered to Gospel truth and how much to "universal prejudice." In practice, he argues, the difference is inconsequential. This
pragmatic criterion itself might raise doubts on this score. Certainly it
reflects his fundamentally sociological interest in religion. Many of
Maistre's best interpreters have read the subtext of his treatment of
Providence to be that fables must be maintained to avoid the conflict
that rationalization would bring. What makes Maistre something other
than a simple reactionary, however, is that he does not merely insist
upon but rather theorizes and even sometimes goes far to demystify the
"mysteries" upon which government rests.

An alternative interpretation of Maistre's religious reticence, which I
have meant to show also has its reasons, would be that the world, outside the logosphere of human fables, is *inhuman*, that the good order of
the universe is not oriented toward man, that it differs from the fables
that rule human thinking, and yet that it has its own structure of "general laws." In that case, what all societies hitherto have been built upon
does not because it cannot derive from reason. This same doubt and the
same reticence to express it are found in a passage cited from an author
not commonly associated with Maistre: Montesquieu. "Even if justice
were to depend upon human conventions, this truth would be a terrible
one, and we should have to conceal it from ourselves."[37]

This truth was brought into the center of political debate by the
French Revolution. What to do when faced with such a "terrible" situation was a question answered differently by revolutionaries and counterrevolutionaries. In the following chapter I mean to show that Maistre, while ultimately siding with the latter, was even more unusual a

counterrevolutionary than he was a Catholic. He refused to see the Revolution in Manichaean terms, treating it instead as a sacrificial crisis and a manifestation of Providence. This providential interpretation set him at odds with both revolutionary and counterrevolutionary camps, Manichaean as they tended to be in their judgments of one another's illegitimacy. The sacrificial reading, on the other hand, asserts that the Revolution was before all else a symbolic crisis, thus anticipating both the arguments and the doubts of today's avant-garde historians, who are thus, perhaps, less avant-garde than they may seem.

Chapter 8

Revolution and Counterrevolution

To shift around things is not what is most difficult; but to shift senti-
ments, to acquire new ones, to be enriched by invisible things, there
is the problem. A sentiment not yet experienced, a new manner of
considering life, it is for this that it is necessary to let loose torrents of
blood. – Quinet, *La Révolution*

There has been no object of greater historical controversy than the
French Revolution. The historiographical storms that surround it often
resemble more a doctrinal than a scholarly debate. For the historical
imagination, the Revolution takes on its religious character as an unprecedented epoch of origins and transformations, bindings and un-
bindings (to say nothing as yet of blood)—the very definition of sacred
time. All interpretations of the Revolution testify to this sacredness;
differences arise as to whether it is a matter of sacred purity or impurity.
Owing to the profundity of political changes and philosophical questions it inaugurated, ultimate consensus on the significance of the Revolution seems most unlikely. Historiographic devotions, however,
have hampered understanding more than need be: *Admire all or be anathema!* says the Jacobin heritage, *Renounce all or be anathema!* says the
counterrevolution. The shortcomings for knowledge of this radical dualism have been pointed out by Quinet: "The Revolution is a Great Totality that must be accepted or rejected indiscriminately, without deliberation.—What? without criticism, without discernment make one
single mass of virtues and crimes, of light and darkness? . . . If one
aims to render democracy impossible, one could do no better."[1] Any
critical history of the French Revolution, Quinet implies, demands an
awareness of its equivocal significance: no criticism is called for where
the good and the bad are easily distinguished. Maistre is of interest here
not only for having applied a theory of sacrifice, of human equivocality
itself, to the events of the Revolution but also for his irreducibility to a
purely counterrevolutionary position. As one may anticipate, this irreducibility was the result of his understanding of the equivocal.

The standard treatment of Maistre's political thought starts from his
opposition to the Revolution, reads his work accordingly as a résumé of

reaction, and concludes in surprise that his recommended response to events in France was strangely moderate for such an archconservative. Having traced the main outlines of his thought in its own proper consistency, however, we can see that both his nuanced reading of the Revolution and his political moderation follow directly from his philosophical assumptions.

This chapter, then, addresses how Maistre applied his thinking to this founding event of modern politics. His theory of constitutions framed the Revolution as a fundamentally religious and symbolic event and, more specifically, as a sacrificial crisis. His providential interpretation of history sought an order within revolutionary disorder, an order of providential punishments and compensations that would define the revolutionary "mechanism." His traditionalist argument drew out its long-term origins. The resulting interpretation, we shall see, placed him sharply at odds with his fellow opponents of the Revolution not in spite of his philosophical position but because of it.

France

Like every philosophical conservative, Maistre approached politics from an historicist perspective that equates constitution with tradition. His interpretation of the Revolution thus begins with an assertion of the principle of historical continuity, that history "admits no leaps." On the basis of this principle he infers an immanent logic of historical processes: "The sixteenth and seventeenth centuries might be called the *premises* of the eighteenth, which in reality was only the *conclusion* of the two former. The human mind could not have risen, all of a sudden, to the degree of audacity that we have witnessed" (Maistre, *Du pape*, OC 2:530). This insight keeps Maistre from the common traditionalist distinction between the eighteenth century and its precedents as the difference between illegitimacy and legitimacy; he is thus more critical of the French monarchy and at least somewhat more lenient toward the eighteenth century. Philosophical conservatives like Maistre (one could also mention Lamennais in this regard) are of value for an understanding of the Revolution because they approach it as a long-term event resulting from centuries of development (the Reformation, absolutism, Enlightenment) and not, as do too often the Jacobin and anti-Jacobin historiographic traditions alike, as a momentary act of pure will or decision, an *acte gratuit*. Maistre finds the historical source of the crisis in France, we shall see, in the political and ideological bankruptcy of the ancien régime.

Maistre's first and last published books (*Considérations sur la France* [Considerations on France] and *De l'église gallicane* [The Gallican Church]) were both works on French history, concerned above all with the antecedents and consequences of the Revolution's social and intellectual dynamics. "The state of minds in France is the favorite of all my meditations."[2] France for Maistre is above all a nation of *states of mind*. France both dominates language and culture and is dominated by them. The art of the word is a French art, for better and for worse; this is why the Enlightenment was above all a French event. "Perhaps one does not know anything at all until the French have explained it. Eloquence applied to the most serious objects and the art of clarifying everything are the two great talents of this nation" (Maistre, "Fragments," OC 1:195). Sheer eloquence, however, may equally serve knowledge or seduction: "there is, in the power of the French, in their character, above all in their language a certain proselytic force that passes the bounds of the imagination. The entire nation is nothing but a vast propaganda."[3]

In Maistre's opinion it is this overwhelming power of its language that defines France's place in European politics. France lacks the military aptitude of her less refined neighbors; instead, it exercises the "much more honorable kind of domination, that of opinion." France "has received the scepter of fashion," which allows her to "reign over fantasies." This "monarchy" of the French language, its power over the European mind, establishes France as the defender of the social/symbolic European order. The ideological kind of power that France possesses "suffices to maintain the general equilibrium, not to trouble it in a sensible manner" (Maistre, "Fragments," OC 1:189–91).

The Revolution radically altered France's office as the ideological steward of Europe. What is most disturbing from Maistre's conservative point of view is precisely the power of the Revolution's ideas to maintain a general *dis*equilibrium that keeps Europe from returning to order. Its language and style make the French Revolution unique from all others in its impact on the European imagination, "the art by which the innovators knew how . . . to present things under the most deceiving points of view, to place honor and glory on the side of the new ideas, and ridicule on the side of the old maxims."[4] This "art" of the revolutionaries, however, was no mere artifice or sleight of hand.

In a piece of counterpropaganda addressed in 1793 to the inhabitants of occupied Savoy, "Lettres d'un royaliste savoisien," Maistre argues against those "much too severe judgments" of the Revolution and "insists much" on the seductiveness "even for wisdom" of the revolution-

ary ideas of social betterment. "Alas! who would not have been se-
duced! It is easy today to judge the Revolution, but then, it was even
easier to be fooled." He points to the errors of Piedmont's governance
of Savoy, especially the overzealousness of its "inquisition" against all
forms of dissent (Maistre, "Lettres," OC 7:87–88).

Maistre ascribes this ideological success of the Revolution to the
ideological failure of the monarchy. This failure is first of all manifest in
its decline into a rule of force, a "batonocracy" of abuses.

> It is necessary to have the courage to avow . . . that at the memorable
> epoch when the government of France began to shake, the govern-
> ments of Europe had grown old and their decrepitude was only too
> well known . . . A thousand abuses undermined the governments,
> that of France above all fell into corruption. No more cohesion, no
> more energy, no more public spirit; a revolution was inevitable.
> (Maistre, "Lettres," OC 7:84)

This courage to admit the inevitability of the Revolution singles Maistre out from the counterrevolutionary tradition.

In accordance with his theory of legitimacy, Maistre attributes the
political decline of the old order to the behavior of its elites. Their ideological surrender to the new ideas awoke and maintained the spirit of
revolution. "That bacchante, called *the French Revolution*, and which
even now [1820!] has only changed its garb, is the daughter, born of the
impious intercourse of the French nobility with the philosophism of
the eighteenth century." Indeed, Maistre claims that "the greatest mark
of respect and of profound esteem" that one could show the French nobility is "to remind them that the French Revolution—which they
would, no doubt, have redeemed with the last drop of their blood—
was, nevertheless, in a great measure their work" (*Du pape,* OC 2:439–
40n, xxxiii).

Here one catches a first glimpse of the sacrificial interpretation. By
forswearing the national dogmas, the nobility suspended the symbolic
constitution of France, returned it to the strife of political beginnings,
and thus called forth sacrifice. This abandonment of ideological foundations was the nobility's "crime and the origin of its ills. The universal
conscience, which is infallible, often without knowing it, has refused to
absolve the French nobles, and has refused them as apostates the compassion it owes them as unfortunates."

The apostasy of the Second Estate is matched by that of the First; to
the flippancy of the nobility is added the clergy's materialism. "No one

would deny that the priesthood in France needed to be regenerated. . . . Wealth, luxury, and a general inclination to laxity had caused the decline of this great body." The Revolution comes to the French Church as a "sifting" (the civic oath), a sacrifice (secularization and then the Terror), and finally a dissemination (exile) (Maistre, *Considérations*, OC 1:21–22).

The Revolution is thus before all else a spiritual crisis (and perhaps a regeneration). In order to understand the past, present, and future of that crisis, Maistre put to use the formidable theoretical apparatus we have outlined thus far. His traditionalist polemic traces its origins to the abstract individualism of Protestantism and the Enlightenment. His reading of the revolutionary dynamic follows the mimetic logic of sacrifice. His prognosis for recovery, for the counterrevolution and restoration, finally, is shaped by his providential philosophy of history. Let us take up each of these themes in turn.

Enlightenment

For Maistre the spirit of the Revolution is one with the Enlightenment. Not so much an event as an epoch, not even the century can contain it. "The French mind of the eighteenth century lasts forever, whatever the almanacs say" (Maistre, *Examen*, OC 6:43n). The Revolution incarnates the Enlightenment as "an entire age of criminal trifling" and puts its maxims into practice (Maistre, *Essai*, OC 1:234). That revolution and enlightenment constitute an epoch, however, means that they are not readily put behind one, that they have a future. Here we have the full ambiguity of Maistre's interpretation of the origins of the Revolution: on the one hand, the desire to blame the event on the allegedly outside forces of the philosophes and Protestants and, on the other, an effort to understand its long-term sources and consequences.

Maistre early understood the Enlightenment as not only a political project but also a product of politics, a product less of pure thought than of will to power. The Enlightenment becomes for him an age of combined bad faith, hubris, and inconsequence. All of these are equally marked in how "the unsuspecting, overweening self-confidence of the eighteenth century balked at nothing, and I believe it produced not a single stripling of any talent who did not make three things when he left school: a new pedagogy [*une néopédie*], a constitution, and a world" (Maistre, *Essai*, OC 1:243). This conceptual inconsequence, however, had great consequences for political life: "there is no established institution that might not be overthrown by the same means, judging it by an abstract theory" (Maistre, *Du pape*, OC 2:273). If the pride of the philosophes rested on bad faith, their bad faith rested on rancor. Here is found "the double and invariable character of modern philosophism, ignorance and effrontery" (Maistre, *Soirées*, OC 4:111). This is where the Enlightenment is original, unprecedented—not in substance but in sensibility, and a purely negative sensibility at that. Thus we have the difference between ancient and modern atheism: "ancient impiety never becomes angry. Sometimes it reasons; usually it jests, but always without bitterness." In contrast, Enlightenment impiety "is no longer the cold tone of indifference, of, at worst, the malignant irony of skepticism. It is a mortal hatred, the tone of anger and of fury" (Maistre, *Essai*, OC 1:303, 305). This means that it can only be destructive.

Maistre defines philosophy as "the science that teaches us the reason of things and that is more profound to the extent that we know more things." By this measure, the Enlightenment is "perfectly null (at least for the good)." This is because it is "purely negative, and instead of teaching us something, it is only aimed, by its own avowal, at disabusing man of all he believed to know, in leaving him nothing but physics." Such disabusing, for Maistre, itself constitutes an abuse of thought. Therein lies the difference between the seventeenth and eighteenth centuries. The philosophy of the first "is directed altogether toward the perfecting of man, while the second, in destroying the common dogmas, only tends to isolate man, to render him proud, egoistic, pernicious to himself and others" (Maistre, *Examen*, OC 6:455–57). Enlightenment sociability confuses the cynic with the sage and the epigone with the greenhorn; only the latter founds societies. In a most Vichian passage from the *Considérations sur la France*, Maistre denounces that barbarism of the academy that mistakes itself for a barbarism of origins: "Barbarous ignorance has no doubt presided over the establishment of a number of political systems, but learned barbarism, systematic atrocity, calculated corruption, and, above all, irreligion have never produced anything. Greenness leads to maturity; rottenness leads to nothing" (OC 1:53). The Revolution, then, fails because it is not "green" enough. Is that to say that it was not enough an event of the people? Maistre indeed asserts that "in the French Revolution the people have continually been enslaved, outraged, ruined, and mutilated by all factions" (*Considérations*, OC 1:117).

The claim that the Revolution has inaugurated the sovereignty of the people vaunted by the Enlightenment was itself an inconsequence uttered in bad faith. Against it, Maistre argues that there is always and everywhere a ruling aristocracy. "In all times and all places the aristocracy commands. Whatever form one gives to governments, birth and riches always place themselves in the first rank." Simply by definition, "the great offices will always belong (without exception) to the aristocracy." In principle, then, "pure democracy does not exist." It cannot, because "no human association can exist without domination of some kind" (Maistre, *Etude*, OC 1:430, 432, 464, 323). Thus Maistre warns that "whether the Americans want it or not, a nobility will be formed among them; as it will have no place in the constitution, what will be its effect? . . . Let's not rush into admiration" ("Fragments," OC 1:219).[5]

If there is always an aristocracy, its rule will be all the more arbitrary and harsh to the extent that its rights, duties, and powers are not fixed by law. For Maistre this is the basic difference between monarchy and democracy (and not, as for most royalists, the distinction between birth and wealth). In a monarchy the rapacity of the aristocracy is limited by the king, "by the universal supremacy of the monarch before whom no citizen is more powerful than another" (Maistre, *Etude*, OC 1:435). In a democracy, wealth and birth hold sway alone (another way of saying that democracies have no "constitution"). Thus, while Maistre concedes that in democracies there are "a great number of men with more freedom," he insists that monarchies grant "more liberty and equality to a greater number of men" (*Etude*, OC 1:437).

As did all men of his epoch, Maistre turned to the history of Rome to seek an analogy to the democratic transformations of the present. It was under the Republic, he argues, that Rome exercised the most absolute dominion over Italy and the rest of the Empire. At this time Rome itself was governed by "a fistful of men . . . barely two thousand property holders. It is to this small number of men that the known world was sacrificed." In all republics, what is called liberty "is nothing but the absolute sacrifice of a great number of men made to the independence and pride of the few." In contrast, even the vices of the cruelest of Rome's kings or emperors "weigh only on the capital cities, and at that only on the upper classes of the capital." Maistre imagines how a peasant under the reign of Tiberius "tranquilly guiding his plow, in the midst of the profoundest peace, would recall with dread to his children the horrors of the proconsuls and triumvirs of the Republic, and would be very little disquieted by the senators' heads that fell at Rome" (*Etude*, OC 1:503–4, 501, 513, 517). While in monarchies the few suffer for the one, in democracies the many suffer for the few; the former, Maistre argues, is more just.

Everywhere, Maistre pointed to the gulf that separated revolutionary discourse from reality. One of his first written responses to the Revolution was a lampoon of revolutionary rhetoric and its claims. This text, the "Discours du citoyen Cherchemot," assembled snippets of revolutionary writings into a collage that revealed the ludicrous inconsequence of their high pretensions. "What were we before the revolution? Less than beasts. What are we since the conquest of the rights of the people? More than men . . . Oh immortal revolution! the thrones have fallen; the people are kings; there are no more subjects!"[6] It is on this last point above all that Maistre concentrates his fire. Sovereignty remains no less foreign than ever to the millions of people in France who will never take part in decision making.

The defenders of the republic themselves admit that direct democracy is unfeasible; they uphold instead the rights of representation. In an almost humorous passage, however, Maistre points out the immense disproportion between representatives and represented:

> If one supposes 25,000,000 men in France and 700 deputies eligible every two years, and that these 25,000,000 men were immortal and that the deputies were named by turn, each Frenchman would find himself king about every 3,500 years. But as, in this amount of time, one cannot help dying from time to time, . . . the imagination is appalled at the number of kings condemned to die without having reigned. (*Etude*, OC 1:312)

Even indirect influence is denied the people, who in practice have little or no influence over the choice of "their" representatives: "The simple right of voting in a republic gives neither status nor power . . . One only counts in a republic to the extent that birth, alliances, and great abilities give you influence; he who is only a simple citizen is really nothing . . . The mass of the people thus has very little influence over the elections, as over other affairs. It is the aristocracy that chooses." The sovereignty of the people is thus purely "metaphysical" (*Etude*, OC 1:473–74). "Palpable" authority is completely in the hands of the so-called representatives. "These assemblies are purely a matter of form, and the scoundrel who presides calls himself *the people*."[7]

Like Tocqueville and the tradition of philosophical conservatism as a whole, Maistre finds the tyranny of modern life in its distinctive combination of absolutism and individualism. The removal from the political stage of all political actors but the person and the state has made of power a monolith.

What distinguishes Maistre's argument is its religious emphasis, which brings a sociology of religion and a political theology to bear upon the absolutism-individualism couple. The age of Enlightenment and Revolution is "Protestant," an era of "practical atheism." What defines it as Protestant is the destruction of all intermediary authorities and the reduction of ethics to personal conscience. "The bond of unity being once broken, there is no longer a common tribunal. . . . Everything resolves into private judgment and civil supremacy, the two things that constitute the essence of Protestantism" (Maistre, *Du pape*, OC 2:450–51).

Typical of his sociological concerns, Maistre takes issue with Protestantism on practical rather than doctrinal grounds. "Man has believed himself to be an independent being, and he has embraced practical atheism, which is more dangerous perhaps and more reprehensible than that of theory" (Maistre, *Essai*, OC 1:286). The practical atheism or "theophobia" of the philosophes insists that there is no superhuman standard and, "working without respite to separate man from God, has finally produced the deplorable generation that has done or allowed to be done all that we now see" (Maistre, *Soirées*, OC 4:284–85). Protestant freedom of conscience means in practice a freedom from ethics and social solidarity, an egoism the philosophes call individuality. "This system rejects every fixed and common belief. Dogma being subjected to man, it is examined, weighed, accepted, abdicated, as man pleases; the result is that every Protestant who affirms something speaks only for himself. . . How then could one expect an essentially impossible firmness of principles?" (Maistre, *Examen*, OC 6:504–5). The anarchic consequences of Protestant political theology are clarified in a passing remark on constitutions in which Maistre observes that "the Protestant system resembles that of a man who says that civil order has no need of judges, that to resolve conflicts the law alone is enough, that each person can read it and render justice himself" ("Religion E," 560). By founding itself upon Scripture and the individual rather than ritual and tradition, Protestantism has severed the social bonds that it has always been religion's task to provide. In this it is at one with the spirit of the Revolution and Enlightenment.

These long-term cultural origins pose the challenge of restoration. Such a state of society cannot last. Yet the three centuries of error that define the Revolution as an epoch make the prospect of a return to order most uncertain.

Protestantism, philosophism, and a thousand other sects, more or less perverse or extravagant, having prodigiously *diminished truths among men* [Psalms 11:2], it is impossible that mankind should continue long in the state they are at present. They are in agitation and labor, they are ashamed of themselves, and are seeking, with an indescribable convulsive energy, to make headway against the torrent of errors, after having abandoned themselves to them with the systematic blindness of pride. (Maistre, *Du pape*, OC 2:xxxvii)

In these remarks from 1819, Maistre still sees no sign of an end to the revolutionary epoch. In order to understand the present and future state of France, he turned to his theory of sacrifice and providential compensations. The resulting religious emphasis drew out the fundamental irrationality of events in France. Where other Catholic counterrevolutionaries merely pointed in horror at revolutionary excess, however, Maistre's theoretical reflections sought to grasp the logic of irrationality and once again to admire the order to be found in the midst of disorder.

Revolutions Holy and Unholy
The Revolution appears to its contemporaries and to its inheritors alike as a sacred moment, for some the most sacred moment, of European history. First of all, this is because it is taken to represent a total rupture with established ways of life, a fissure in time through which eternal values at long last flood into the everyday. The Jacobins were the first to present the revolution as a decisive break, once and for all, with the ancien régime. The less subtle among the conservatives also present the Revolution as a break, but as a break with reason or faith, an irredeemable lapse rather than a Parousia.

The Revolution came upon Maistre as a rupture: a revolution that had matured for three years in France appeared in Savoy overnight, under the guise of Terror and foreign invasion. It confronted him as an event in the fullest sense of the word: as a trigger, a blow of destiny in response to which he developed his philosophy. Maistre first experienced the Revolution as an impasse for thought. "This epoch resembles nothing, and history provides no given, no analogy to aid judgment." He underlines

the *divine bizarreness* of events. The confessor of Louis XVI, the heroic Edgeworth, dying at Mitau from a contagion caught in confessing, consoling, sending to heaven the soldiers of Bonaparte, at the side of Louis XVIII,—what a spectacle! *And what time was more fertile in miracles!* . . . Unhappily, one contemplates miracles, one admires them; but one does not command them.[8]

Maistre's theoretical achievement was to perceive a pattern to these "miracles," an order in irrationality.[9]

Auguste Cochin, a conservative critic of revolutionary society recently returned to vogue by the work of François Furet, observed that "the mistake of historians is to apply to the history of the men of the Revolution the methods and points of view of ordinary history, to judge individuals as if they were independent." There is little danger, in following Maistre's thought, to succumb to the perspectives of *ordinary history*, yet this remark raises an important difference between the perspective of the two conservatives. The "dependency" of which Cochin speaks derives from the artificiality of revolutionary society, which treats people as abstractions and seeks to "reduce them to a docile and perishable magma, such is the effect of machinism."[10] Maistre too speaks of a revolutionary machine but in a very different sense. If people have lost their independence, it is because the beneficent artificiality of social life has been lost, and men are subjected directly and without qualification to the "moral laws" of mimetic social order. Whereas for Cochin the Revolution reflected an oversocialization that left room only for abstract ideas of society, for Maistre it was the return to a primitive social life enthralled to sacred forces.

As something more than a mere political innovation, the Revolution took on the character of a sacred event. The Terror was justified by its adherents themselves as a messianic moment that required a certain cleansing violence. Maistre evokes this expectation of a political Parousia and the sacred violence of messianic politics in his descriptions of the "Angels of the Revolution": "*Liberty* and *equality* came to present themselves to you in the dress of two divinities; but soon enough throwing off this misleading garb, and deploying their fearful wings, they have glided over our unfortunate earth and shown the bloody rags and serpents of the furies" ("Lettres," *OC* 7:161–62). The Revolution is sacred because it is impure.

Like other counterrevolutionaries, Maistre constantly invoked this religious imagery as the sole means of expressing the experience of this event, overwhelming for all concerned. "The genie of confusion and disorder shakes his torches over France: he glides over that desolated ground; he refuses order to be reborn there and reigns over the debris . . . Never did the satellites of Nero, never did the victorious Algonquin command anything as terrible as the hideous spectacle with which you have frightened the universe since your dire emancipation."[11] This primitivism, more primitive than primitive society itself, makes for the "satanic" quality of the Revolution, which "departs from the ordinary circle of crime and seems to belong to another world" (Maistre, *Considérations*, OC 1:55).

These remarks return us to the theory of sacrifice. While crime is generally contained within its "ordinary circle" by punishment, under the ad hoc tribunals of the Terror punishment itself became a crime (and thus, we shall see, demanded its own compensation). Maistre attacked the Enlightenment–inspired version of the Revolution first by pointing to its irrational excess and second by reminding us that there is nothing older in the world than sacrificial crisis.

The Revolution, then, is a return to the primitive, to the chaos of origins. With political order placed in abeyance, the processes of sacred ordering come to the fore. The Revolution will thus be the object less of a sociology, a theory of social institutions, than of an anthropology, a theory of the prepolitical.

In his essay on sacrifices Maistre pointed to the suspension of the Christian political order that had replaced the regime of sacrifice as the beginning of revolutionary excess:

> An illustrious nation, arrived at the utmost degree of civilization and urbanity, nonetheless dared, in an access of delirium of which history gives no other example, to formally suspend this law [the Christian "law of love"]: what did we see? in the blinking of an eye, the mores of the Iroquois, and the Algonquins; the holy laws crushed underfoot; innocent blood covering the scaffolds that covered France; men curling and powdering bleeding heads; and the very mouths of women soiled with human blood. There you have *natural* man! Not that he does not bear within himself the inextinguishable seeds of truth and virtue; but without a divine fecundation, these seeds will never bloom, or will only produce unhealthy or equivocal beings. ("Eclaircissement," OC 5:387)

Maistre's rejection of a Rousseauian return to nature (a nature that, though sublime no doubt, is not what the romantics had in mind) alludes constantly to the limitation of sacred violence by the symbolic order of preestablished constitutions.

While all counterrevolutionaries dwell in this manner on gore and social irrationality, in the absence of an anthropological perspective they view this excess as simple madness or criminality rather than a sacred violence with its own logic. Maistre's merit is to bring to this sacred event a theory of the sacred. He understood the Revolution as a sacrificial crisis marked by mimetic strife, confusion of distinctions, and trespass of limits, as a transgression that called forth compensations.

Maistre's theory of sacred violence could not but pose the problem of revolutionary excess in a nuanced manner. Nowhere is this nuance (not to say ambivalence) clearer than in Maistre's discussion of the regicide. He hesitates over how to define the event, referring to it on the same page as a punishment and a murder (Maistre, *Considérations*, OC 1:142–43). Criminal or no, however, Louis remains for Maistre a victim, a sacrifice. Recounting the story of Louis's behavior before the Convention, Maistre comments that "the august martyr seems to be afraid to escape sacrifice, or to render the victim less perfect: what acceptance! and what would it not have merited?" ("Eclaircissement," OC 5:412–13). The subjunctive mood of this last phrase would seem to raise difficulties for Maistre's theory: are not all sacrifices compensated? We may anticipate that there might simply be too much in past or present French history to be compensated even by the death of a king.

Maistre's providential interpretation goes so far as to seemingly justify Louis's death: while the person may have been innocent, the crown was not, and Louis justly paid his forefathers' debts. Sometimes to kill a king, even an innocent one, is to do the right thing. While

> every criminal can be *innocent* and even *holy* on the day of his torment, . . . sovereignty is responsible for all the acts of sovereignty. All the debts, all the treaties, all the crimes oblige it. If, by some disordinate act, it organizes today an evil germ the natural development of which must bring on catastrophe in a hundred years, that blow will strike the crown justly *in a hundred years* . . . The king can only be born, he can only die once; he lasts as long as the royalty. If he becomes guilty, he is treated with weight and measure: he is, according to circumstances, warned, menaced, humiliated, suspended, imprisoned, judged, or sacrificed. (Maistre, *Soirées*, OC 5:167–68)

What must the ancien régime have been to merit Louis's death? Finding *weight and measure* in the indictment of sovereignty, Maistre goes far toward legitimating revolt. Revolution responds to the excesses of sovereignty; this and the converse movement, the return to legitimate sovereignty out of rebellion's excess, makes the Revolution a providential epoch of compensations. "*A certain accumulation of vices renders a certain revolution necessary* . . . Europe is paying ancient debts."[12]

Revolutionary Compensations: Terror and Providence

Perhaps every account of the French Revolution seeks some sort of providential explanation, a way of inserting its excesses into the history of a higher and more general good. Only those who would view the Terror either as the last word on revolution or as an inconsequence, as more of the same, deny it any providentiality (these are both Gnostic viewpoints, emphasizing the normality of evil). Typical of the need for a providential answer to the bloodshed of the Revolution is the remark of the Jacobin historian Louis Blanc: "What! Did not a sovereign law, a terrible law, attach evil to good as an absolute, irrevocable condition? . . . Man's special task is to prove that the NECESSITY FOR EVIL is a lie." That history hitherto has been founded on a lie is, of course, itself a Gnostic solution.[13]

The Terror appeared to Maistre as before all else a Gnostic challenge: history ("true metaphysics") must improvise a response to the "mixture" of innocence and guilt with which the Terror presents us. The problem that begins the *Considerations on France* is the same that triggered the *Soirées*: that vice and virtue are improperly recompensed. "If this dreadful destruction of mankind and especially this mixture of the innocent falling with the guilty still frightens certain imaginations and appears to require explanation, one can try to say something; but one must nevertheless caution that there is no assured route for the man who immerses himself in the paths of true metaphysics."[14] This absence of *assured routes* through the new epoch continued to trouble Maistre and his fellow royalists, though he was far more comfortable than they with the necessary improvisations (witness his letters, replete with consolations for the despairing and caveats for the overly assured).

His early responses mingled assurances and doubts. His understanding of symbolic order led him to believe in 1793 that the revolutionary regime could not remain: "an order of things founded upon atheism, immorality, theft, brigandage, murder, etc., cannot last. But when will it end? That's what one cannot know."[15] We shall see that as the years pass and above all when the Revolution is putatively over, Maistre became less and less confident that a new order of things had not been established.

The answer to the Gnostic challenge, we have seen, is Providence: "Poor Antoinette! My God, what a century and what monsters! I can well see that Providence will render justice, even by itself and without our involvement; but horrors have preceded and will precede Justice."[16] Following Maistre's idea of Providence, we may expect to see this justice result from an objective (if hidden) structure of social relations and moral laws. First, however, a providential interpretation must show that the Revolution indeed follows a just course. Such an argument would not appeal to the average counterrevolutionary, but Maistre did nothing to soften its bite.

Maistre's providential reading begins by arguing that there are fewer innocent victims of the Terror than one commonly believes. The Revolution is a product of the ancien régime: "every day I am more confirmed that it is made by the absolute monarchy."[17] While Maistre was well aware of the political faults of absolutism (see my afterword), his providential interpretation of history stressed the moral failure of the French monarchy. Its institutions were less hypertrophied than corrupt. And because mores are the very constitution of society, the monarchy had already dissolved before 1789. "When the innovators came to overthrow France, it only belonged to ancient history: the infamous Regency had gangrened this unhappy country to a point it is hard to express . . . Vice is of all times and places: but a corruption like that into which France had fallen only shows itself at the decadence of empires" (Maistre, "Fragments," OC 1:198, 200). This deep corruption meant that guilt for the excesses of the Revolution was general. If there was no unanimity of crime, there was one of indifference: "No doubt not all Frenchmen *willed* the death of Louis XVI; but the immense majority of people, for more than two years, *willed* all the follies, all the injustices, all the outrages that led up to January 21st" (Maistre, *Considérations*, OC 1:12).

Maistre's strong sense of this generalized responsibility of all the French and, more specifically, his criticism of the faults of the French monarchy kept him from the simple oppositions of guilt and innocence that too often mar the thinking of his counterrevolutionary comrades. "A given noble at Koblenz may have more reason for self-reproach than a given noble who sat on the left in the so-called constituent assembly . . . The French nobility has only itself to blame for all its troubles, and when it accepts this fact it will have taken a great step forward" (Maistre, *Considérations*, OC 1:151). The same holds true for that other nobility, the aristocracy of intellect, the Baillys, Lavoisiers, and other Enlighteners who fell to the Terror. Their deaths, Maistre argues, are human tragedies, but on the level of divine generality nothing could be

more just. "When a philosopher justifies evil by the end in view, when
he says in his heart, 'Let there be a hundred thousand murders, provided we are free,' and Providence replies, 'I accept your offer, but you
must be included in the number,' where is the injustice?" (Maistre,
Considérations, OC 1:9). The victims of the Revolution are thus not innocent. Maistre's providential interpretation still must show that the
relatively innocent are unsoiled by violence and that the guilty do not
benefit.

He thus reasserts the idea of the autodestruction of the bad: both the
victims and the executioners of the Revolution are guilty. "That which
is happening at the moment [the ritual purification of France through
sacrifices] can only be executed by an illegitimate power . . . But the
great work once accomplished, the instruments will become useless
and will be, by their very existence, an anomaly, a scandal to the world.
Therefore, etc., etc."[18] That evil is to do away with evil is at once the
Origenist background to Maistre's theory of sacrifice, his providential
explanation for the existence of the bad, and the basis of his understanding of the moral mechanisms of the Terror.

What is bad in the Revolution, Maistre means to show, is for the
best. This holds above all for the Jacobins, whose success was the sole
means of carrying out the providential task of punishing the French
while protecting France from its enemies. "All life, all wealth, all power
were in the hands of the revolutionary authority, and this monstrous
power . . . was both a horrible chastisement for the French and the sole
means of saving France . . . Once the revolutionary movement was established, only Jacobinism could have saved France" (Maistre, *Considérations*, OC 1:17–18). Jacobin ascendancy proved providential even in its
judicial murders. By punishing the enemies of order, the Terror itself
served the project of restoration: it left the hands of the monarchy free
of the blood of its opponents.

The excesses of the ancien régime called forth revolutionary violence
as its punishment, but this punishment itself, as befitting the crime, is
itself beyond proper bounds; thus the punishers themselves require an
extreme judgment, something disallowed to legitimate authority. All
destruction must be carried out by illegitimacy, even the destruction of
illegitimacy itself. The sovereign and the executioner must be kept separate at all costs.

> Here again we may admire order in disorder—the guiltiest revolu-
> tionaries could only be felled by the blows of their accomplices . . .
> Great crimes unfortunately require great punishments . . . Human-

ity still has not pardoned former French legislation for Damien's horrible punishment. So what could French magistrates have done with three or four hundred Damiens and all the monsters who are overrunning France? Would the sacred sword of justice have fallen as relentlessly as Robespierre's guillotine? (Maistre, *Considérations*, OC 1:13–14)

Here we find the "mechanism" of the Revolution by which it destroys its leaders. "The very rascals who appear to lead the Revolution are involved only as simple instruments, and as soon as they aspire to dominate it they fall ignobly." Sacrificial violence, in the absence of any sanctioned order, created a revolutionary dynamic independent of all actors. Society, if Terror could be called society, now works like a machine: it is only to this "society" that Maistre applies the machinist metaphors of Enlightenment social science. This is why the "most active personages" of the Revolution are precisely the most "passive and mechanical." "Everything has succeeded for them because they were only instruments of a force that knew more than they did. They made no mistakes for the same reason that Vaucanson's flutist never hits a wrong note." The Revolution thus *"goes all alone."* This manifestation of order within the utmost disorder, as well as the reference to an action that "goes" without actors, should alert the reader that we are in the presence of Providence: "never is order more visible, never is Providence more palpable, than when a superior action is substituted for that of man and it acts all alone" (Maistre, *Considérations*, OC 1:4, 6, 7). Providence mechanically compensates violence with violence until there is no more. Thus Providence is best sought in revolutions.

The first passage of the *Considérations*, after describing the supple divine chain that restrains men within their proper bounds, takes up this theme. "In revolutionary periods, the chain that binds man is abruptly shortened; his action is diminished, and his means deceive him. Then, carried away by an unknown force, he frets against it, and instead of kissing the hand that clasps him, he disregards or insults it" (Maistre, *Considérations*, OC 1:3). These remarks contest the alleged freedoms gained by revolutions: as returns to a primary, "mechanical" violence, these are moments of binding rather than loosing. Equally, this passage reappropriates the Revolution to theological discourse. To present the Revolution as providential, however, is to address a warning to the counterrevolutionaries, to all those who would disregard or insult the divine work.

The providentiality of the Revolution means that it was not unmotivated madness and monstrosity, that it even bears a certain undeniable legitimacy. This is perhaps the first surprise to result from Maistre's treatment of the Revolution: that it was a happy event. "The happiest of changes that occur among nations are almost always bought by bloody catastrophes of which innocence is the victim" (Maistre, "Eclaircisse- ment," OC 5:413). Indeed, the providentiality of the Revolution neces- sarily means that it is creative as well as destructive, an event with a le- gitimate future as well as an illegitimate past. Revolutionary bloodshed, "the horrible effusion of human blood," is "a terrible means; nevertheless, it is a means as much as a punishment . . . If Provi- dence erases, it is no doubt in order to write" (Maistre, *Considérations*, OC 1:27, 24). The resulting text will spell the future of the Bourbon res- toration.

Restoration: What Is a Counterrevolution?

Although restoration is one of the classical concepts of political theory, it has never received the attention that revolution has. Restoration and revolution are generally treated as contraries. That is a bit too simple. The idea of restoration does indeed always refer back to some prior vio- lent change, some illegitimate interruption of what is taken for good or- der. Yet this category is employed by Left and Right alike: one may have a restoration of rights just as one has a restoration of authority. In the broadest sense, restoration means the return of a lost political good, of a good of such inestimable value that its lack implies the illegitimacy of the given state of affairs. Thus for Edmund Burke the Glorious Rev- olution was precisely a restoration, a return to the ancient liberties of the English constitutional tradition, and it was as a restoration that he held this revolution to be legitimate.

Central to any understanding of restorations is their dynamic char- acter. Whereas the conservatism generally associated with the project of restoration implies preservation and the avoidance of change, resto- ration itself necessarily means a marked change, a resumption of conti- nuity, an active return to tradition, a rectification of recent history. This transformative character defines the essential conundrum of the politics of a restored regime: what was a crime yesterday is today a virtue, and what was a virtue is now a crime. How is legitimacy to be established and maintained in such a situation? Restorations, that is to say, are eras of adjustment, a coming to terms of the old and the new.

The refusal to adjust, to have anything to do with the intervening era, defines political reaction, which sees in this refusal the sole sign of legitimacy. Reaction thus easily tends toward a politics of resentment

that exacerbates the inherently agonistic character of restoration politics. To succeed, however, a restoration must in some part represent a
politics of malleable accommodation. In the years after 1814, however,
the respective representatives of revolution and counterrevolution tended toward opposing implacabilities, against any policy of pacifica-
tion, concession, or compromise. Historically, the Restoration regime
proved not an end to revolution but, rather, a counterrevolution that
prepared the ground for future revolutions.

The severity of France's break from its past defined the dilemma of
the advocates of restoration: on the one hand, a need to treat the Revolution as an illegitimate aberration in the history of French politics, on
the other hand, a need to acknowledge the deep changes wrought by
revolution, not the least of which was the requirement to justify monarchical institutions before the tribunal of reason established by the Revolution.

Before answering the question of what Maistre means by a restoration (and thus that of what kind of counterrevolutionary he was), it is
necessary to understand what obstacles he perceived in its path. What
must be countered, what restored, and how? The chief obstacle for any
royalist after 1800 was Bonaparte. Maistre's understanding of the political dynamics of the Empire, founded on his theory of legitimate
usurpation, is as subtle as that of anyone of his era, above all with regard
to the special strengths and weaknesses of the new emperor's position.
Maistre defines that position precisely as a hiatus between usurpation
and legitimacy.

Two errors, he argues accordingly, have distorted understandings of
Bonaparte: the first is to view his power as legitimate and established,
"which is only proper to discourage all the world, above all princes,"
and to grant the false principles upon which his power rests. The second error is to view him as a mere "culpable adventurer." The second
error (that of the royalists) is greater than the first, Maistre argues, referring to his theory of constitutions.

According to that theory, time, the recognition that time brings, will
be the difference between legitimacy and usurpation. Thus is posed the
great problem facing the Bourbon princes. "Time is a great element in
politics. A usurper one arrests today to hang tomorrow cannot be compared to an extraordinary man who possesses three quarters of Europe,
who has made himself recognized by all sovereigns, who has blended
his blood with that of three or four sovereign houses."[19] One thing is
certain, that Bonaparte has brought an end to the Revolution; what is

uncertain is what kind of an end this will be, a consolidation or a destruction. Either the house of Bourbon is finished, "worn out," and "it is good that government consolidates itself in France" under one ruler or another, or Bonaparte, by reestablishing hierarchy in France and refuting for the French the revolutionary principle of equality, is hastening the Bourbons' return.

What inclines Maistre toward the second supposition is Bonaparte's strength itself, for while legitimate authority rests upon recognition and obedience, Napoleon has sought only power and domination. Sovereignty has nothing to fear and usurpation nothing to gain from force of arms.

> What pretty things that lovable Corsican has done! . . . Without doubt Bonaparte could write his name beside that of the greatest princes, provide peace for the world, put himself at the head of the religious system of Europe, and wisely govern a France augmented by a quarter. Without doubt, but then he would be legitimate, and he would take root for always. In pillaging, trampling, ransacking, murdering, he provides the most legitimate hopes that he must disappear . . . He himself renounces the character of a legitimate sovereign: it is this delicate attention by which I am touched.[20]

Bonaparte's power is not one of names, norms, and recognitions but one of force and bodies, "military power disencumbered of every moral counterweight, unchained in the political world."[21] That is why he remains illegitimate, that is, temporary. His reign of force will call forth compensations. Maistre explains to Louis XVIII the foolishness of those sovereigns who would envy Bonaparte's power: "it's as though they envied the physical strength of a street porter."[22]

At other times he is not so sanguine, recognizing that Bonaparte, at least for the time being, indeed commands the respect that defines authority, the power to last. "As long as France supports Bonaparte, Europe will be forced to support him."[23] It is thus the Bonapartist spirit and the devotion of the French that pose the great threat, not military hegemony.

What is required is therefore a *counterspirit*: "One will have done nothing, if one has not brought to birth in France the spirit that wants no more of Napoleon."[24] Indeed, this warning threatens to make of the return of the Bourbons itself a "nothing," a reoccupation of the state apparatus without foundation in civil society. In 1815 Maistre thus says of Bonaparte that "unfortunately, his person alone has departed, and his maxims remain among us."[25] The authority of these maxims is a product of time, which now proves to offer the greatest challenge to the Bourbons, even if they are not used up.

> Everyone less than forty years old in France (that is, all the army and half the nation) no more recognizes the Bourbons than the Heraclides or Ptolemies. Since 1789, no moral and religious education, no nobility, no priesthood, no moral grandeur of any variety. War and nothing but war . . . In the colleges, academies, the theater, the church, as in the guards, one has heard speak only of Bonaparte.[26]

Thus is posed, as forcefully as possible, the necessity of ideological intervention, of a royal restoration of civil society to match that of the state.

Perhaps the most significant consequence of this ideological emphasis is that, whatever the hopes or plans of the exiled princes, the event of a restoration can be brought about only by the French people. Only the French can put an end to Bonapartism because they are its sole support. "In the final analysis, everything depends upon the French. If thirty million madmen want to defend [Napoleon], who will overthrow him? But there are ways to make them impatient."[27] Even after Waterloo, Maistre constantly emphasizes the hindrances to any meaningful or lasting restoration. Again, these hindrances are more spiritual than material, though no less concrete for all that: "the immense favor shown to Bonaparte by an immense number of men, the partisans he has left behind, the hopes he entertains, the fall in opinion of His Most Christian Majesty, the revolutionary ideas living and visible on all sides."[28] This state of affairs could not but redound upon the prospects of restoration.

It is indeed not the Bourbon but the Bonapartist throne that Louis XVIII has reascended. "The revolution was first democratic, then oligarchic, then tyrannical: today, it is royal, but always it follows its course." Yet restoration somehow entails letting the Revolution thus run its course: to resist it would only give it further momentum, would only exacerbate the mimetic crisis that the Revolution is for Maistre and call forth further compensations. Within the equivocal situation of restoration, "the art of the prince is to reign over [the Revolution] and to smother it gently *in embracing it*; to contradict it to its face or to insult it would be to expose oneself to giving it new life and to losing oneself at the same time . . . This is essential, vital, capital . . . If we remain or become an obstacle, *requiem aeternam*, etc."[29] This, to put it gently, was what the great majority of monarchists have failed to appreciate.

Maistre's understanding of the ideological dynamics of the Revolution set him at odds with his fellow royalists from the start. He underlines again and again that they have no idea of what a restoration requires. "Almost all errors spring from the misuse of words. It has been customary to give the name *counterrevolution* to any movement aimed at killing the revolution, and because this movement will be the contrary of the other, one concludes that it will be of the same kind. One should conclude the contrary" (Maistre, *Considérations*, OC 1:121–22). By these customary standards, it is implied, Maistre considers himself not a counterrevolutionary but in some sense the "contrary" of what goes by that name. The opponents of the Revolution are "as mistaken as to the remedies as they had been as to the illness" (Maistre, "Lettres," OC 7:131). In a famous maxim, Maistre asserts that "what they call the counterrevolution will be not a *contrary revolution* but the *contrary of revolution*" (*Considérations*, OC 1:157). Rather than a revolution in reverse, a shift from left-wing to right-wing violence, the counterrevolution can only be the reverse of a revolution. Restoration can only be a passage from violence to order, from sickness to health, vice to virtue.

The Restoration thus appears as a convalescence of sorts, with the proviso that the illness involved was deserved. "The Revolution made you suffer," Maistre writes to the people of France, "because it was the work of every vice, and the vices are very justly man's executioners." The Restoration, on the contrary, "far from producing the evils you fear for the future, will arrest those that devour you today. All your efforts will be positive; you will destroy only destruction." The Restoration will be what remains when evil has done away with evil. Maistre's understanding of political restoration thus follows Origen's idea of spiritual restoration as a death of death culminating in universal redemption. As does Origen in cosmology, so too does Maistre believe in politics that even the devils must be redeemed. "The usurper slew the innocent; the king will pardon the guilty. The one confiscated legitimate property; the other will be hesitant to disturb illegitimate property" (Maistre, *Considérations*, OC 1:144–48). Such a position was hardly calculated to endear Maistre with his superiors.

Maistre was remarkably open about his dissatisfaction with royal strategies that he viewed as utterly *counterproductive*.

> What were the royalists asking for when they called for their imagined counterrevolution, that is, one made abruptly and by force?

They requested, in fact, the conquest of France; they requested therefore her division, the annihilation of her influence, and the debase-
ment of her king—which is to say, perhaps three centuries of massa-
cres, the inevitable consequence of such an upset of equilibrium.
(Maistre, *Considérations*, OC 1:18)

Following his theory of compensations, Maistre insists that restoration means a return to equilibrium and consequently the avoidance of
retribution. Happily (or rather providentially), the stupidity of armed
counterrevolution is only equaled by its impossibility. Maistre allows
no illusions regarding the princes' armies: "militarily, the émigrés are
nothing and can do nothing" (Maistre, *Considérations*, OC 1:147). War
against the Revolution, Maistre concludes, is "perfectly useless," and
"health can only come from France." This is less because of the danger
of military defeat (though this too is certain) than that of allowing the
Legitimist party to legitimate the Revolution. Counterrevolution must
be something other than a *reaction* that would make of revolution its
permanent counterpart. What must be avoided at all costs is the revenge that would prolong or exacerbate the present crisis of mimetic violence.[30]

The ideological incapacity of the counterrevolution is greater than
the military one. "I have always said that if one could expect an efficacious resistance, it would arise from a nation that has not read our
brochures."[31] Maistre repeatedly argues that cultural counterrevolution
must precede political counterrevolution: power that lasts can only be
built on recognition. He thus seeks to refute "that principle equally
false and fatal: *it is necessary to win before recognizing the king*. The true
principle would be: *to win, it is necessary to recognize the king*."[32] This is
the sole means of royalist success: "the idea of making France bend by a
decided attack is an extravagance, but one can certainly *make it bored* and
lead it to do justice to itself."[33] The ideological task, then, is not to heat
spirits but to cool them. "The lightning that strikes down walls is
stopped by a taffeta curtain: pretty image of the revolution! Against it,
the true resistance is antipathy, but on all sides it has found conduc-
tors."[34]

Maistre's theoretical remarks on ideological restoration are supplemented by a remarkably prescient anticipation of how restoration
might actually take place, an account that repeatedly emphasizes the
mimetic dimension of political action. Restoration, Maistre argues,
will not be the product of popular deliberation but rather of recognition
and acceptance. "People will no more decree the monarchy's restora-

tion than they decreed its destruction or the establishment of the revolutionary government."[35] This passive acceptance, the only possible basis of restoration, has been prepared by the Revolution itself, understood as a sacrificial crisis. "The people were so crushed and intimidated by Robespierre's reign that any state of affairs where there is no longer uninterrupted killing seems happy and bearable . . . This feeling has outlived the infernal regime that created it . . . In a word, every Frenchman is happy enough so long as he is not being killed" (Maistre, *Considérations*, OC 1:126). Even excluding the Robespierrist interlude, the sacrificial dynamic of revolutions ensures that mass loyalties to the Republic will subside.

In a passage that presents what Bataille describes as the ecstatic curve of sacrifice, passing from increasing sovereignty to increasing abjection, Maistre argues that

> enthusiasm and fanaticism are not lasting phenomena. Human nature soon tires of this kind of ecstasy. So even supposing a people, and the French people in particular, may want something for a long time, it is still certain that they will not want it passionately for a long time. On the contrary, the peak of the fever having subsided, great outbursts of enthusiasm are always followed by despondency, apathy, and indifference. (Maistre, *Considérations*, OC 1:114)

When this apathy and indifference reach the decisive point, the bonds of loyalty to the Revolution will dissolve on their own, as if by magic: "an inexplicable blow, a magical blow . . . suddenly snaps" the disciplinary bond so that the revolutionaries "neither command nor obey; they no longer act together [il n'y a plus d'ensemble]" (Maistre, *Considérations*, OC 1:116). This magical snapping of bonds marks the end of the ritual of revolution.

The Restoration too will be structured in a ritual manner. As the reverse of a revolution it will be a mimetic crisis in reverse, a return to order founded on imagery, semblance, and rumor. Just as in ritual, it is not so much truth as what is taken for truth that guides collective action. As Maistre imaginatively anticipates the event, a rumor will spread that one city has opened its gates to the princes. While only a rumor, this rumor will be enough to induce the truth-effect that defines the action of ideologies. "It is soon learned that the news was false, but two other cities, believing it true, have given the example. Accepting the news as true, they have just submitted and decisively influenced the first, which had not thought of yielding" (Maistre, *Considérations*, OC

1:116). Consent to restoration is mimetically constructed in the very act of restoration itself.

That this consent is artificial or insincere makes no difference. "*Long live the king*, cry the loving and loyal. *Long live the king*, responds the republican hypocrite in dire terror. What does it matter? There is only one cry" (Maistre, *Considérations*, OC 1:117). It will happen with those who are hostile or simply indifferent "what happens with cowards in an assault; they certainly have to along with the others, then they say, *We have taken the town.—Damn, what a hot time!*—And one gives them crosses *pro virtute bellica*. What does that matter? Is the town any less taken?"[36] One major consequence of this theory of a mimetic restoration that resolutely ignores real political differences and even hands out crosses to cowards is that the Restoration, when it comes, must before all else show tolerance toward its opponents. One is almost led to think that a restoration by way of appearances will offer only the appearance of a restoration.

Indeed, even where Maistre appears to be most at pains to emphasize the temporary nature of revolutionary innovations, one finds an admission of real social transformation. "The crimes and exaggerations will pass: these excesses are no more natural to the body politic than is sickness to the animal body; they have only a term, short enough in relation to the duration of empires, but too long for the ephemeral beings who pass and who suffer" (Maistre, "Lettres," OC 7:38). This is nothing if not a statement of the limits of convalescence, and not only for the ephemeral. Only the crimes and exaggerations of the Revolution are said to pass; what is not excess, it is implied, will remain.

The lastingness of the Revolution, its possession of a future, is affirmed repeatedly and openly in Maistre's correspondence, if only hinted at in his public writings. "The more I examine what is happening, the more I persuade myself that we are assisting at one of the great epochs of the human species. What we have seen and seems to us so grand is only a necessary preparative. Must the metal not be founded before it is cast? These great operations are of a vast duration."[37] What kind of future, then, does Maistre envisage for the Revolution?

On 12 January 1793, days before the regicide and during a brief return to conquered Savoy, Maistre wrote in his journal, "Novus rerum nascitur ordo"; at that date he was not speaking of a return to paradise.[38] Twenty years later, in the midst of the Hundred Days, Maistre despairs of the Restoration's ability to achieve the sacred foundation that alone would give it solidity: a new political priesthood is nowhere to be found. "The ancient phalanx, already weakened by that which weakens everything, is at the point of disappearing entirely. Where are the successors, and who will receive the mantel of Elijah? That is the great question. I see much zeal, assiduity, and a spirit of conservation worthy of all kinds of praises; but I've looked hard, and nowhere do I see the creative flame."[39] This view of the future is also expressed in an earlier letter to Blacas that contains dark hints about the plans of Providence. "All our projects escape us like dreams; all the heroes disappear. I have retained as much as I've been able the hope that the faithful will be called upon to rebuild the edifice; but it seems that new workers throw themselves into the future and that Her Majesty Providence says: *Ecce! Nova facio omnia.*"[40] If Providence sides with the Revolution, then so too does legitimacy.

This awareness that his political desires may not coincide with future legitimacy makes Maistre unique among the counterrevolutionaries and very likely, in the detachment it encourages, accounts for the superiority of his understanding of the Revolution. "Whether or no our wishes are accomplished or whether inexorable Providence has decided otherwise, it is curious and even useful to study how these great changes occur and what role the multitude might play in an event whose date alone appears doubtful, never losing sight of history and the nature of man" (Maistre, *Considérations*, OC 1:112). Such pure curiosity, such openness to the future, was not what the royalist party was looking for.

Maistre's study of the Revolution quickly convinced him that its achievements were not to be gainsaid. A full return to the ancien régime would be "much more mad than putting Lake Geneva in bottles."[41] This is less because of any modification of the structure of the state than because of the transformation of the political culture that endorses those modifications. Traditional political theology is finished. "The red bonnet, in touching the royal forehead, made the traces of holy oil disappear . . . the charm was broken . . . Lengthy profanations have destroyed the divine empire of national prejudices" (Maistre, *Considérations*, OC 1:145).

The fundamental obstacle met with by the advocates of a French Restoration—an obstacle, again, of time—was the fact that by 1814 the Revolution itself had become a tradition. Everyone who had remained in France was to some extent "revolutionized"; in an indirect sense this was true even of those who had left. "Every great revolution always acts to a greater or lesser extent on even those who resist it and does not permit the complete reestablishment of old ideas."[42]

Indeed, it is those who resist this "great epoch" who most concern Maistre, for a "general Revolution" cannot be resisted with impunity. As early as 1793 he shows serious doubts about the ability of the Bourbon princes to effect a general restoration. In a letter that reveals the difficulties of his position on the fringes of the counterrevolution, Maistre writes to Vignet des Etoles, his superior in the Sardinian bureaucracy, that "to speak clearly (but this is only between us) I firmly believe that the Monarchy is irredeemably shaken (I mean the absolute monarchy) and that it has only one means to save itself: to modify itself and to gain the mind of the peoples. Unfortunately, this is not at all what it is doing."[43] What, then, was to be done?

In light of the foregoing, the elements of Maistre's strategy for restoration may be easily enumerated: reform not reaction, ideological action not force, flexibility not impatience. In an early and optimistic view, he presents reform as the means by which good is to come from present ills: "there is no doubt that the Sovereigns will occupy themselves with several systems of amelioration: the terrible jolt that has just tested Europe demands it absolutely" (Maistre, "Lettres," OC 7:155). Maistre continually upholds reform against the "deadly error" of being "attached too rigidly to ancient constructions," for it is the relative flexibility of constitutions that measures their longevity, a flexibility that the Bourbon princes evidently lack (Maistre, *Considérations*, OC 1:98). These princes, Maistre holds, "must disabuse themselves" of the "mad chimera" of "reestablishing the ancien régime. They must declare it publicly and frankly. Then they must attach themselves to their peoples by prudent concessions."[44] These remarks testify to a growing impatience toward royal backwardness, especially in things ideological. If the kings have failed ideologically with regard to the people, however, the nobility has likewise failed its kings: "The duty of every good Frenchman at this moment is to work untiringly to direct public opinion in favor of the king and to present his every act in a favorable light. Royalists must examine their consciences thoroughly on this point and permit themselves no illusions" (Maistre, *Considérations*, OC 1:108–9).

Finally, that reform and ideological transformation may do their work, patience is required. Restoration is not a matter of surgery but of convalescence, and the greater the crisis, the longer the recovery. "The surest thing is to count on the *longue durée*, for the entire world is modified by this shocking revolution, and works of this variety are not made in eight days."[45]

The difficulties peculiar to the ideological work of restoration are evoked by Maistre in the preface to *Du pape,* his first work published under the Restoration, in a passage that contrasts the revolutionary context of his first work with that of his last:

> At that time all honest men were at liberty to attack the brigands at their own risk and peril. Now that all the powers of Europe are restored, error having diverse points of contact with politics, there might happen to the writer who should not be constantly on his guard, the same misfortune that befell Diomedes under the walls of Troy,—that of wounding a divinity, whilst pursuing an enemy. (OC 2:xxii)

This allegory presents the fundamental problem for any politics that comes in the wake of crisis: what to do when friends and foes are no longer readily distinguishable. What the Restoration requires is a post-Gnostic politics, a politics not founded on the opposition of friend and enemy.

In an early text (1793), Maistre seems confident that such a reasonable moderation will guide the actions of a restored monarchy; for it to do otherwise would be to doff the guise of legitimacy for that of rebellion. Only clemency is proper to restorations: "it would be baseness to demand justice and a crime to perform it." Maistre thus advises the nobility to follow the example of the legitimate monarch and to assume the demeanor proper to a political priesthood:

> Kings never approach closer to the Supreme Being than when they pardon: approach the kings in pardoning in turn . . . There is only one role worthy of you, that of giving value to prayers of repentance . . . Burdened with the noble task of supporting the throne and reestablishing order, you would fall too much below your destiny were you to listen one instant to the voice of a wounded pride, which would dictate to you only vilifying complaints or grave faults against the social order. (Maistre, "Lettres," OC 7:127)

Twenty-seven years later, faced with the facts of Restoration politics, Maistre will decry "*the shocking self-assurance of the French Restoration.*"[46]

Nowhere is Maistre's rejection of the tactics of his contemporary royalists more forceful than in his rejection of the offer, extended by Vignet des Etoles in the midst of the 1793 Austro-Sardinian offensive, of a potential post as attorney general. The first words of this response hint at long-standing differences with the court: "even if I were thought of, which I do not at all believe [Maistre had been suspected of left-leaning sympathies], it appears that I would not be able to agree with the maxims adopted there." Such hints are rapidly transformed into out-right denunciations as Maistre condemns, for reasons moral and strate-gic, the very notion of counterrevolutionary bringing of charges:

> I tell you I would not want to take part in such a tribunal. What! The first idea of the king is to punish? Has one ever imagined anything so impolitic? While three fourths of Savoy are still under the knife, one amuses oneself by hanging in effigy! A pretty imagination in truth. You tell me not to get angry with anything; but, in the name of God, how can one not get angry when one sees such puerilities?

Needless to say, these are not the words of one's average royalist, and they were met with little appreciation in Turin.[47]

The response of the monarchy to Maistre's critique is signaled in Vi-gnet's reply: "Do you prefer revolutions?"—a reply that is emblematic of the Restoration's failure to bring an end to the revolutionary era of denunciations and counterdenunciations, to bring an end to Gnostic politics. It is precisely by pointing out this failure that Maistre, rather impertinently, responds to Vignet's question, in which he

> recognized one of the great misfortunes of the French Revolution; it's that a very great number of wise men have come to believe that there is no middle ground between the strangest political absurdities [those of the king!] and revolutions such as we have just seen them. I would not want either bad governments or revolutions. Between these two misfortunes there is a middle ground, that of a reasonable or tolerable government.[48]

A week later Maistre repeats the charge, underlining the ethical tasks of restoration. "The duty of the wise man is to hold the middle ground, and if I do not fool myself infinitely, you are, do not be displeased, at one of the extremes."[49] The policy of wise moderation, which grew di-rectly out of Maistre's philosophical conservatism, was nowhere to be found.

The bad faith that for Maistre defines revolutionary politics, how-ever, now appeared as much on the Right as on the Left. The mentality that gave rise to revolution "began for France in the Regency; the phi-losophes continued and redoubled it; the sovereigns and powerful men were their accomplices . . . What is deplorable is that it has overtaken us and that we all resemble them more or less as to political morality."[50] For the proponents and antagonists of restoration alike, political life has become an all-or-nothing affair, a zero-sum game. This makes of the Restoration an era unpropitious for authentic restorations. "I have heard of *ultras* and *citras,*" Maistre remarks. "God alone knows if there are *juxtas.*"[51]

Given such a disposition of political forces and given his loyalty to the project of restoration, Maistre's response to the situation could only be ambivalent. A comparison of two passages from his correspondence bearing upon the situation in France, each of which urges a distinct political position, allows us to perceive the nature and extent of this ambivalence. "If I sat in one of the two Chambers, I would defend to the last syllable this rag of a Charter, because there is no way to save France other than to walk with the King; otherwise the State will resemble a cart whose horses pull in different directions."[52] Here Maistre echoes the Ultraroyalists' denunciation of the Charter—it is a "rag," a "soap bubble." He nonetheless urges loyalty to the derided constitutional text, the institutions, and the royal family of the French Restoration as the only possible path toward reconciliation.

Two years later, we find a text that at first glance may seem to contradict this political ethos of centrism at all costs: "If I were French, I would be tempted to enroll systematically under one or the other of the exaggerated flags, so much am I persuaded that moderate systems are sure means to displease the two parties . . . It is a great humiliation for human nature that the wise man is sometimes forced to give himself the colors of madness." Here an extremist position is tentatively approached. Not only, however, does extremism remain on the level of temptation, but moderation remains the attribute of wisdom. Zealotry is described as madness and is to be embraced only as the artifice of a wiser moderation. Even more striking in this sketch of an extremist politics, Maistre leaves glaringly undecided which "one or the other of the exaggerated flags" he would be tempted to endorse. And in the midst of this adversarial temptation, Maistre reasserts the imperative to accept the framework within which these conflicts arise, namely, the constitutional Charter, even if it proves merely a temporary expedient. "A man who had the certitude that the Charter would no longer exist in ten years could conclude that it is unnecessary to defend it today: nothing, however, could be so false as this conclusion."[53] This completely false conclusion was that of the Ultras. As opposed to their device,

"Long live the king in spite of himself," Maistre would seem to uphold a program of moderation in spite of itself, that of employing even trumped-up zealotry toward the end of stable institutions. The restored aristocracy tended to do just the opposite, making use of the institutions established by the Charter to undermine those institutions, encouraging in the name of order a polarization of political forces that in many ways continued to shape French politics throughout the nineteenth century and beyond.

Very rarely, then, did Maistre admire the work of the Restoration. In at least one instance, however, he did endorse the strategy of the restored monarchy, providing in the process an idea of what a successful restoration would in his estimation have entailed. What he specifically applauds is the rejection of enmity as a political principle and, consequently, the appropriation of elements of the Revolution within the reestablished monarchical order. This, Maistre announces, is the general rule of restorations:

> There are in the peace treaty, in the discourses [of Louis XVIII], some absolutely revolutionary clauses; he makes use of his enemies with much talent, which is the great rule after revolutions. There is some Talleyrand in everything that is done: such a man beside the king of France is a strange spectacle, but it seems clear he has rendered great services to the good cause; the king will thus have made use of the gentleman and the minister while leaving the bishop to the judgment of God. Never will profound politics do otherwise.

A prudent reconciliation with one's erstwhile enemies that turns away from differences over ultimate values, a distancing from that sacrificial politics in which strangeness is an occasion for enmity—this is how Maistre defines the ending of the social crisis of revolution, the "strange spectacle" of restoration. "Health through our enemies, or else there will be none at all."[54]

From the perspective we have been sketching out, the Restoration proved hardly a restoration at all—not, as the Ultras would have it, because it was halfhearted but because it was too fervent. Instead of bringing an end to the Revolution, the Restoration confirmed its vitality. The Revolution, Maistre says, will end when people are bored with it.[55] They are not bored yet.

There is no happy ending to Maistre's interpretation of the Restoration. Within the sublunary sphere, short of Origenist speculations on total redemption and the reunification of all religions, any harmonization of the conflicts unleashed by the Revolution remains partial and provisional. Maistre's tragic understanding of history is signaled in his remark, "I die with Europe, I am in good company."[56]

Perhaps the best last word on Maistre's view of both revolution and counterrevolution is found in a passage from *Du pape*, the last major work published during his lifetime, on the endless struggles between popes and councils. "If men's eyes were not willfully closed, they would see that where there are mutual wrongs, it is the height of injustice to see them only on one side, that there are no means of avoiding these conflicts, and that the fermentation that troubles the wine is an indispensable preliminary to its clarification" (Maistre, *Du pape*, OC 2:312n). It is against such one-sidedness and toward moderation that all Maistre's political recommendations for a restoration of order are directed; only moderation can end the spiraling cycle of recriminations, reprisals, and compensations that marks the mimetic crises of empires.

Maistre here rejects the temptation of any Gnostic friend-or-foe politics, a rejection that should encourage us to see him not simply as an enemy of modern thought. On the contrary, his demand that we embrace creative ferment and his claim that from this strife comes clarification are fundamentally modern positions. His central philosophical project was to discover the laws of social fermentation, an order of tumult. Of Maistre's contribution to modern European thought, the least that can be said is that he added greatly to the ongoing intellectual strife that defines it. In this book, I have tried to say something more: that the ferment of Maistre's thinking on social excess and irrationality contributed significantly to the clarification of these highly obscure and equivocal subjects.

Afterword

Maistre's response to the Revolution and counterrevolution shows most clearly that he was a theorist and not an advocate of violence. His political thought represents neither a denial nor an embrace of violence but rather a search for possibilities other than violence despite its perhaps ineradicable presence in political life. He is essential to modern political discourse for having been among the first and most forceful to have pointed out as our task, above and beyond our particular political affiliations, the inclusion of unreason within a broader rationality, of difference within a broader identity, and of conflict within established institutions.

A fundamental recasting of Maistre's politics thus emerges from our study. His conservatism was not opposed to reform (he indeed presented reform as necessary to conservation) but rather to the violence of the new, to innovation that would break the bounds of conserved tradition. This is Maistre's traditionalism. Yet tradition in Maistre has proven an unexpectedly broad and open category that, we have seen, includes the least orthodox forms of Christianity along with the ideas of other traditional societies. This "strange spectacle" of Maistre's heterodoxy, his marginality to received doctrine and his ambivalence toward royal power, makes of him something other than a reactionary, someone who can continue to speak to our postrevolutionary dispensation.

While Maistre indeed shares the common elements of Catholic traditionalism, it is what he does with those elements that makes him unique. Barbey d'Aurevilly has pointed to the ground of this difference, at least in an allusive manner. For Barbey, Maistre is above all "the Genius of the *Aperçu*." Other conservatives—Bonald, Lamennais—"pose principles, and they chain them together; they raise buildings, these architects of truths." Maistre has no system, no "philosophy" in this strict sense. While I have tried to show that Maistre's thinking does make a meaningful unity, it is very true that he shows no *esprit de système*. In other words, Maistre was a theorist, a critical philosopher whose work exceeds the dimensions of mere apology or system building.[1]

What strikes all observers is the uniqueness of Maistre's tone among all traditionalists. Le Pappe de Trevern, a Catholic monarchist of the later nineteenth century, remarks that "if this excellent man had not been such a good Christian, if he had been incredulous, he could have done almost as much evil as Voltaire by the sarcasms, the irony, and the piquant turn with which his works are filled."[2] While Maistre's irony was limited less by his orthodoxy (which was hardly orthodox) than by a rejection of enmity uncommon among modern conservatives, still, this citation testifies to the uneasiness he arouses in his latter-day admirers. His indiscretion and impertinent tone as well as his thematization of social excess estranged him from Left and Right alike.

If Maistre did share the programmatic stance of his fellow conservatives, then he would indeed be the monster his opponents (and equally so his readers on the far right) make him out to be. His position would then be *Order through bloodshed! Back to human sacrifice!* I believe I have made it clear that this is not his stance. I would hold instead that Maistre's procedures of writing and thinking, in taking up fundamental conservative assumptions, at least begin to transform them into something different, from an apology of order to a theory of order, from what order must be to how order comes and goes. This theoretical dimension makes Maistre open to modern readings in a way that his fellow conservatives are not.

Maistre's distance from pure Reaction can be seen in how he never turns against change itself, never advocates pure repetition, although he does accept the basic conservative maxim that change must be founded on order. He does not reject "regeneration" but, philosophical conservative that he is, holds that it can only take place through the perfecting of ancient laws and customs.

One important factor that distanced Maistre from a purely reactionary defense of order was his consistent criticism of the absolutist tradition, whether democratic or royal. Before, during, and after the Revolution he repeatedly attacked the kings of Prussia, Austria, France, and Piedmont itself for their reliance upon force alone, upon "batonocracy," to maintain hegemony. In an unpublished essay written on the very eve of the Revolution he pointed out the resultant disunity of all the European monarchies, a disunity fostered and maintained by the conflict between feudal and absolutist authorities. What passes for political life, "it is unnecessary to observe at this hour," is only the

> formless debris of the collision between the feudal colossus and the
> royal power; the People, crushed between these enormous masses,

has not yet come out of its annihilation. This old state of war has produced a mutual defiance that is the radical vice of our governments. Jealous authority regards as crimes of lèse-majesté the least political discussions, and it is a crime to believe that the people have rights. From this derives the degradation of the people in the majority of monarchies, the inconceivable ignorance into which they have fallen about the things that concern them most.[3]

Another essay of the same date bemoans France's lack of representative institutions, critically contrasting the French parlements with the English parliament. Had it not been for the royal "revolution" that reduced the parlements to a purely judicial function,

> the king would have necessary counsel, the nation would be represented constantly, and its representatives would really be an integral part of sovereignty. But the parlements judged, and the nation was lost. In truth, the Estates were established, but this representation was neither habitual nor required; it remained at the arbitrary disposition of the king and became by consequence illusory.[4]

While perhaps questionable as history, Maistre's eulogy of the lost rights of the nation certainly represents good parlementary politics.

Maistre's opposition to the absolutist tradition thus grew out of his youthful career as a senator in the Savoy parlement. In his first public work, a speech delivered before the parlement in 1775 on the occasion of his monarch's entry into Savoy, Maistre's very praise of the king is couched in words that the latter could only take as a warning. Maistre contrasts his ruler to "those kings who have always fled effort, who arrive on the throne without firm principles, without views, without knowledge, and who only begin to reflect when the cry of peoples announces all is lost." To further underline this imputed difference, Maistre places on his sovereign's lips the words "I owe justice and protection to everyone." Warming to the subject, Maistre continues that "the last vestiges of feudalism must be eradicated . . . Victor [Victor-Amadeus III, 1773–96] will lead true philosophy by the hand; he will ordain it to blow upon the old formulas," and all remaining backwardness will disappear from Savoy. Maistre argues that the fundamental institutions of Savoy are sound, however. What testifies to this is the law that allows the parlements to suspend the registration of royal edicts, not only to make representations but to resist the sovereign. This kind of health was not terribly appealing to the king.[5]

The identical misjudgment was repeated twenty years later with regard to the French king. A book produced by émigré parlementarians, which he believed to have the approval of Louis XVIII, he describes as having "collected and developed the principles of the French monarchy." Maistre's argument cites those passages of the book most favorable to parlementary power as evidence against any absolutist essence of the French monarchy; for Louis, however, the text was a summary of the claims of the parlements not against absolutism but against the king (*Considérations, OC* 1:92ff.).

Fifteen years later yet, at the height of Bonaparte's power, Maistre described the despised emperor and the Sun King as veritable twins, likening the absolutisms of 1810 and 1710:

> Have your imagination, if you can, place the red bonnet of Napoleon on the head of Louis XIV, or the wig of Louis XIV on the head of the Corsican; once this effort is made, you will find many points of contact. Take away the revolutionary exaggeration, you will see, on both parts, a great and vainglorious nation forced astray, an abuse of power, outrageous desires, vast projects, poverty, depopulation, and vast humiliations, fruits of a union of forces pushed to an extreme.[6]

Maistre's opposition to absolute government, then, was consistent over his entire career, neither a mere liberal episode of his youth nor a counterrevolutionary change of heart.

Indeed, the metaphorics of Maistre's entire political theology derive from the constitutionalist tradition: not a discourse of the Sun King, despot by divine decree, but of harmony and orchestration, of the solar *system*, attraction, gravity, vortices, and so on. His "political cosmology" always emphasizes systemic interdependency, the mutual determination of positions. Such interdependency is manifest in his theory of constitutions, which emphasizes intermixings, hybridization, and fluctuation in the development of political forms. It is also evident, on a more practical level, in his politics of moderation, against the people who would have all freedoms, but also against the followers of the king who would give up none. Both these projects, he argues, are bound to fail, according to the principle that excess always draws forth compensations: repression leads to contestation just as revolution leads to terror. Accordingly, Maistre tells the people that abuses are not as bad as revolutions but tells the king that abuses make revolutions. This position, which opposes to the people's demands the benefits of authority and to royalist demands the benefits of liberty, is the parlementarian one.

Had the royalist restoration succeeded, rather than fallen in 1830 and again in 1848, the received picture of Maistre may well have been very different. For the royalist reaction he was a most questionable bedfellow. Available evidence points to the existence of a secret dossier, assembled by the court in Turin, on his involvement in Masonry and his critical opinions of the Sardinian monarchy. For a time he was suspected of involvement with alleged Masonic fomenters of revolt in Savoy.[7] His reputation as a spokesman of reaction was to a significant degree the work of later authors either unaware of or unwilling to admit the conflicts in the royalist camp and Maistre's difficult place within them. He only became widely read in the years 1840–80; the three major texts he published in his lifetime—the *Considérations*, the *Essai sur le principe générateur,* and *Du pape*—all infuriated the Ultraroyalists and their Gallican supporters, who would hear nothing of reform, moderation, or limits on royal authority.

Maistre's propaganda work for the monarchy met with no warmer reception. Of the fate of his "Lettres d'un royaliste savoisien," he writes to Vignet that "sometimes I laugh a philosophic laugh in seeing my work arrested in Turin (apparently as antiroyalist), and, at the same time, suppressed in Geneva upon a formal requisition by the commissaries of the National Convention."[8] This laughing tone later disappears: "insulted in Turin, confiscated in Chambéry, what the devil would you have me do?"[9] Eventually Maistre's frustration drove him to an almost threatening remark that underlines his ambiguous place among the counterrevolutionaries: "if I had written for the Republic, she surely would have caressed me much; the monarchy forbids my book and forgets me."[10]

Some such forgetfulness was necessary that Maistre acquire his reputation as a reactionary's reactionary, above all the forgetting of his forceful rejection of absolutism, militarism, intransigence, and retribution. As one thoughtful interpreter has observed, "in complete accordance with the principle he so often pointed out, that *the written word is silent, it cannot answer back*, Maistre was unable to repudiate the scoundrels who were one day to claim him as their master."[11] The afterlife of Maistre's work in this regard resembles Nietzsche's, whose works were with more sinister results appropriated by the Nazis in a similarly piecemeal and forgetful fashion.

Like Nietzsche too, however, Maistre cannot be completely absolved of his posthumous fate at the hands of Legitimists and the Action Française. Here, indeed, he stands self-accused. What he says of the philosophes applies equally to his own case: though they may disown the excesses of the Revolution, "since they have put forth maxims capable of giving birth to all crimes, these crimes are their work, because the criminals are their disciples" (Maistre, *Etude, OC* 1:414). Maistre's historical "crime" was to have not merely theorized order and political theology but to have endorsed them as well. It is this endorsement that ultimately leaves him open to charges of complicity with the excesses of order that were able to gain his posthumous approbation, if only forgetfully.

A fundamental question here, especially with regard to Maistre's status as either theorist or ideologue (so far as this pure opposition of roles is maintainable), is that of the formalism of his arguments, his treatment of practical issues in purely theoretical terms that ignore and at times indeed conceal the question of practical applications. His formalism, like that of much politicized thought, is not uncommonly motivated by a desire to mask unpleasant political realities. His apology for the Spanish Inquisition is exemplary of the long history of the iniquities of Catholic politics, from the destruction of heretics through allegiance with fascist regimes, that Maistre's abstract presentation conceals and sometimes seems at pains to do so.

The formalism of counterrevolutionary thought is most evident in its tendency to totalize, to seek a vision of a harmonious totality even in the midst of excessive disorder. In considering order and disorder, tradition and discontinuity, as correlates, as antithetical terms of an eventual synthesis, counterrevolutionary thought tends to presuppose both a synoptic gaze that encompasses them within the formal unity of a self-same and well-ordered tradition that will eventually incorporate all differences and disorders. This effort toward totalization is certainly to be found in Maistre; it motivates much of his sociological, historical, and anthropological project. Yet one also finds in his writing a sharp awareness of what remains incommensurable and nonintegratable, utterly lacking in counterrevolutionaries as disparate as Bonald and Ballanche. This supplement of disorder found within every order he calls the sacred and places it at the center of his political theory.

This challenge to formal totalization is even more marked in his textual practice. Maistre's writing incorporates extremely diverse traditions, among them what was for Maistre the most challenging other, the Enlightenment, with which, in his notebooks, he enters into a highly ambivalent dialogue irreducible to the friend or foe dyad. His writing, that is, is dialogical rather than monological. The *Soirées* in particular embody a confrontation of worldviews that proves ultimately unresolvable. This abiding tension and supplementarity, this absence of ultimate resolution, synthesis, or totalization, is what makes Maistre a modern figure and what allows his work to overflow its immediate context to be read from a variety of perspectives.

It would be foolish to deny the retrograde political intentions behind Maistre's critique of the Enlightenment, of Protestantism, of modern science. Yet I have meant to show that these do not exhaust the significance of his thought, that his work is intellectually important, and that, in sum, his theory of politics is as much guided by a concern for truth as for partisan politics. According to this theory itself, however, the reduction of practical politics to pure theory is impossible. This is evident not only in the idea of "unwritten constitutions" but, more fundamentally, in that of the inevitability of violence, which may be limited by institutions but not eradicated. This *remains*, this residuum that remains after the incorporation of conflict into stable institutions, is the domain of politics as the assertion of differing wills. By this same token, the purely theoretical dimension of Maistre's thought that I have been at pains to lay bare cannot describe the whole of that thought. Its political applications bring it into the sphere of conflict, of clashing desires.[12]

To the extent that Maistre's theory of political unity is guided by a desire for that unity, that his theory of sovereignty is motivated by monarchist loyalty, he belongs to the history of ideologies rather than that of social knowledge (to some degree, however, *some* such political motivation is found in every theory of politics). To the same extent, he remains responsible for the posthumous applications of his thought in the name of order and infallibility. There is no denying that Maistre intended his works to serve the project of restoration, to shore up the forces of order against revolt from below. Yet we have seen that he did not include the Ultras among those forces of order, in spite of their assumption of this title. Moreover, he was not in any simple way against the Revolution, which he viewed as a manifestation of Providence and with which he believed any future regime would have to compromise. In short, the restoration he envisaged for France was not that which the French Restoration proved to be, not because it was too lukewarm but too zealous.

I have not meant to argue that Maistre was no conservative, no ideologue; these facts have been all too well established both here and by previous accounts of his work. I have rather sought to demonstrate that he was not only a conservative ideologue but also a highly original theorist of order and ideologies, that not all his political theory is disguised political interest but instead deserves broader recognition in the history of social and historical thought. I would even be tempted to hazard the following conclusion: that Maistre ultimately belongs as much to the history of enlightenment as to that of obscurantism because the theory of social unreason itself belongs to the history of reason.

Notes

PREFACE

1. Two fine recent examples of the biographical approach are Lebrun, *Joseph de Maistre*, and Maistre, *Joseph de Maistre*. Examples of the ideological interpretation are found in the standard accounts of French conservatism: Roche, *Les Idées traditionalistes en France*; Bagge, *Les Idées traditionalistes en France sous la Restoration*; Godechot, *La Contre-Révolution*; Beik, *The French Revolution Seen from the Right*; Muret, *French Royalist Doctrines since the Revolution*; Rials, *Révolution et contre-Révolution au 19e siècle*; and Dimier, *Les Maîtres de la contre-Révolution*. The ideological interpretation reaches its apogee in Triomphe, *Joseph de Maistre*. A thorough review of the English-language literature on Maistre is provided in Watt, "The English Image of Joseph de Maistre."

2. Goyau, *La Pensée religieuse*, and Lebrun, *Throne and Altar*.

3. Schmitt, *The Necessity of Politics*, *Political Theology*, and *Political Romanticism*.

4. *La Revue des Etudes Maistriennes*. A number of important articles from this journal have been translated by Lebrun in *Maistre Studies*.

INTRODUCTION

1. Clement, *Romanticism in France*, 201, 207; Roche, *Les Idées traditionalistes en France*, 40; and Evans, *Social Romanticism in France*, 96.

2. Steiner, "Darkness Visible," 4. See also Steiner, "Aspects of Counter-Revolution."

3. Sollers, "Qui aura le courage?" 8. Maistre also receives great praise in Sollers's novel *Women*, 212–13.

4. Mouffe, "Radical Democracy," 38–39.

5. Habermas, "Modernity versus Postmodernity" and *The Philosophical Discourse of Modernity*.

6. Brandes, *The Reaction in France*, 269.

7. Berlin, "The Counter-Enlightenment," 21, 24.

8. Berlin, "Georges Sorel," 315–16.

9. Maistre, *Les Soirées de Saint-Pétersbourg*, *Oeuvres complètes* (OC), 5:40. Hereafter cited in text as *Soirées*. Unless otherwise noted, references to Maistre's works can be found in the OC.

10. Berlin, "Joseph de Maistre," 150.

11. Berlin, "Joseph de Maistre," 143.

12. Cioran, *Joseph de Maistre*, 9, 47.

13. Maistre, unpublished reading notes, "Philosophie C" (1807), MS, Maistre Archives, Archives Départementales de Savoie, Chambéry, 19. Hereafter cited in text as "Philosophie C."

1. FRENCH TRADITIONALISM

1. Blanc de Saint Bonnet, *La Restauration française*, 39.

2. For the bitterly contentious debates in France on the occasion of the revolutionary bicentennial, see Kaplan's magisterial account, *Farewell, Revolution.*

3. Régis Debray, *Que vive la République*, cited in Kaplan, *Farewell, Revolution*, 1:62.

4. Dupuy, "Ignorance, fanatisme, et contre-Révolution," 37–38.

5. Mazouric, "Autopsie d'un echec," 238.

6. Maistre, "Lettres d'un royaliste savoisien à ses compatriotes," OC 7:69. Hereafter cited in text as "Lettres."

7. Staël, *An Extraordinary Woman*, 1:126.

8. Staël, *An Extraordinary Woman*, 1:170.

9. Chateaubriand, *The Genius of Christianity*, 1:227–28.

10. Baldensperger, *Le Mouvement des idées*, 2:57.

11. Chateaubriand, *The Genius of Christianity*, pt. 1, bk. 1, chap. 14.

12. Cited in Chaussinand-Nogaret, *The French Nobility*, 6.

13. Cited in Taine, *The Ancient Regime*, 1:299.

14. Maistre, *Les Soirées de Saint-Pétersbourg*, ed. Darcel, 2:469.

15. Beik, *The French Revolution*, 51.

16. Gombrowicz, *Diaries*, 2:166.

17. Nietzsche, *The Gay Science*, 343.

18. Mannheim, *Conservatism*, 127–29.

19. Staël, *Considerations on the Main Events of the French Revolution* (1818), *An Extraordinary Woman*, 366.

20. For an excellent introduction, see Berlin, "The Counter-Enlightenment."

21. For a more global discussion of the varieties of traditionalism, see Balandier, *Anthropologie politique*, 202–5.

22. Marquard, *Farewell to Matters of Principle*, 15.

23. For Catholic theories of natural law, see the extensive treatment by Rommen, *The State in Catholic Thought.*

24. The best survey of Bonald's life and ideas remains Moulinié, *De Bonald.* For a more recent study with conclusions quite different from my own, see Gengembre, "La Doctrine pour et contre l'histoire."

25. Bonald, *Théorie du pouvoir*, 28.

26. Bonald, *Législation primitif,* 224–26.

27. For Lamennais's indebtedness to Bonald, see Vidler's intellectual biography, *Prophecy and Papacy.*

28. Lamennais, *Des progrès de la Révolution et de la guerre contre l'église*, vol. 9 of *Oeuvres complètes*, chap. 1.

29. Lamennais, *Nouveaux mélanges*, vol. 7 of *Oeuvres complètes*, 79.

30. Lamennais, *Essai sur l'indifférence*, vols. 1 and 2 of *Oeuvres complètes*, 1:40. Hereafter cited in text as *Essai*.

31. Lamennais, *De la réligion considerée dans ses rapports avec l'ordre politique*, vol. 8 of *Oeuvres complètes*, 267.

32. Lamennais, letter of 10 April 1832, cited in Le Guillou, *L'Evolution de la pensée religieuse*, 157.

33. Cited in Vidler, *Prophecy and Papacy*, 83.

34. Bénichou, *Le Sacre de l'écrivain*, 159–60.

35. George, *Pierre-Simon Ballanche*, 140.

36. Ballanche, *Essais de palingénésie sociale*, 3:172. Hereafter cited in text as *Essais*.

37. Ballanche, postscript, *Orphée, Oeuvres*, 6 vols. (Paris: Bureau de l'Encyclopédie des Connaissances Utiles, 1833), 6:356.

38. Ballanche, *Essai sur les institutions, Oeuvres*, 4 vols. (Paris: Barbezat, 1830), 2:172.

39. Cited in Bénichou, *Le Sacre de l'écrivain*, 167–68.

40. George, *Ballanche*, 49.

41. See, for example, Ozouf, "L'Idée et l'image du régicide."

42. Chateaubriand, *The Genius of Christianity*, 167.

43. Pareto, *Sociological Writings*, 225.

44. Nisbet, "Conservatism and Sociology."

45. Cited in Bénichou, *Le Temps des prophètes*, 172.

46. Nisbet, "De Bonald," 324, 330.

47. Beik comes to a similar conclusion: "disillusioned like Marx, they proclaimed from the other side of Liberalism the same brutal conclusions" (*The French Revolution*, 112).

48. Remond, *The Right Wing in France*, 35.

49. Bagge, *Les Idées traditionalistes en France*, 244–45.

50. Sternhell, *Neither Right nor Left*, 104.

51. Maulnier, *Combat*, in Sternhell, *Neither Right nor Left*, 12.

52. Drieu La Rochelle, in Sternhell, *Neither Right nor Left*, 249.

53. Valois, in Sternhell, *Neither Right nor Left*, 106–7.

2. SACRIFICE

1. Hegel, *Reason in History*, 54–55.

2. Merleau-Ponty, *Humanism and Terror*, xxxii.

3. Fontana, *Benjamin Constant*, 114.

4. Herzen, *From the Other Shore*, 134–35.

5. Wittgenstein, *Remarks*, 8e.

6. Lévi-Strauss argues that, unlike totemism, a classificatory system that establishes relations of homology between natural and cultural series, sacrifice is a dynamic system that brings into contact realms generally defined by their fundamental nonidentity: the sacred and the profane, the divine and the human, and, one might add, the human and the animal. (One might well question, however, whether totemism and sacrifice can ever be separated, even as ideal types: totemism

always has some sacrificial element, and sacrifice always has a totemic or fetishistic one.) Lévi-Strauss, *The Savage Mind*, 224–26.

7. Vernant, "At Man's Table," 42. Translation modified.

8. Durkheim, *The Elementary Forms*, 10.

9. Maistre, "Eclaircissement sur les sacrifices," OC 5:283–84. Hereafter cited in text as "Eclaircissement."

10. Maistre, "Sur les délais de la justice divine," OC 5:407. Hereafter cited in text as "Sur les délais."

11. Maistre thus cites John Hunter, who, in his *Treatise on the Blood, Inflammation, and Gun-shot Wounds*, argued that blood is alive and that "we grow out of it" (OC 5:297).

12. Heine, "The Romantic School," 44, 49.

13. For the ambiguities of Maistre's critique of Rousseau, see Garrard, "Rousseau, Maistre, and the Counter-Enlightenment." For Maistre's chief texts on the subject, see *Against Rousseau*.

14. Maistre, "Religion B," MS, Maistre Archives, Archives Départementales de Savoie, Chambéry, 455, 384. Hereafter cited in text as "Religion B."

15. For an introduction to the voluminous literature on this subject, see White, "The Noble Savage Theme as Fetish." The standard account remains Gerbi, *The Dispute of the New World*. On the controversial subject of the Enlightenment origins of modern "scientific" racism, see Mosse, *Towards the Final Solution*, and Eze, *Race and the Enlightenment*.

16. Duchet, *Anthropologie et histoire*, 160.

17. For a contemporary treatment of Hindu widow sacrifice that, from a post-colonial Marxist and poststructuralist feminist position, largely agrees with Maistre's interpretation, see Spivak, "Can the Subaltern Speak?" The best work on the subject, to my knowledge, is that of Lata Mani. See, for example, "Contentious Traditions."

18. Maistre, *Etude sur la souveraineté*, OC 1:322. Hereafter cited in text as *Etude*.

19. Maistre, *Considérations sur la France*, OC 1:33. Hereafter cited in text as *Considérations*.

20. Maistre, *Essai sur le principe générateur des constitutions*, OC 1:270. Hereafter cited in text as "Essai."

21. Desroche, *Jacob and the Angel*, 1.

22. Girard, *Violence and the Sacred*, 13.

23. Thus it is only now, after two millennia of misreadings begun by the evangelists themselves, that "the shattering truth contained in the Gospels can be understood," namely, that "the word of God says no to violence" (Girard, *Things Hidden*, 220, 210; see also 182–88).

24. Eagleton, *The Ideology of the Aesthetic*, 7.

25. LaCapra, "Violence, Justice, and the Force of Law," 1065.

3. PUNISHMENT AND WAR

1. "Mélanges B," MS, Maistre Archives, Archives Départementales de Savoie, Chambéry, 384. Hereafter cited in text as "Mélanges B."

2. Jean-Louis Darcel, "Genèse et publication des *Soirées de Saint-Petersbourg*," introduction to *Les Soirées de Saint-Pétersbourg*, ed. Darcel, 15–16.

3. Turner, *The Ritual Process*, 95, 100.

4. Cited in Artz, *Reaction and Revolution*, 144.

5. Descostes, *Joseph de Maistre avant la Révolution*, 1:93. For a more responsible and revealing account of the Black Penitents, see Darcel, "Des pénitents noirs." See also Lebrun, *Joseph de Maistre*, 7, 15.

6. Foucault, *Discipline and Punish*, 59–64.

7. For an especially strong version of this critique, see Taylor, "Foucault on Freedom and Truth."

8. "Eloge de Victor Amedée," cited in Descostes, *Joseph de Maistre avant la Révolution*, 1:307.

9. Maistre, letter of 15 January 1817 to the comte de Vallaise, OC 14:23–24. Maistre's antimilitarist position has been treated by Mandoul and Vermale.

10. "Eloge de Victor Amedée," cited in Descostes, *Joseph de Maistre avant la Révolution*, 1:308.

11. Bataille, "La Limite de l'utile," *Oeuvres complètes*, 7:264.

12. Bataille, *La Part maudite*, 71.

13. Maistre, "Théorie de religion," OC 7:310–12.

14. Bataille, "Schéma d'une histoire des religions," *Oeuvres complètes*, 7:436–38.

15. Hollier, *The College*, 23, 326, 402.

16. Bataille, *Visions of Excess*, 73.

17. Bataille, "La Limite de l'utile," *Oeuvres complètes*, 7:266.

18. Cited in Richman, *Reading Bataille*, 58.

19. See LaCapra, *Emile Durkheim*, chap. 1.

20. Comte, *Système de politique positive*, 1:67.

21. Comte, *Opuscules*, 263.

22. Comte, *Cours de philosophie positive*, 4:135n.

23. Conrad, "Books," *Joseph Conrad on Fiction*, 81.

4. SYMBOLIC POWER

1. Maritain, *Man and the State*, 24, 29.

2. Cited in Kertzer, *Ritual, Politics, and Power*, 163.

3. Schutz, *On Phenomenology*, 82.

4. Maistre, "Cinq paradoxes," OC 7:299.

5. Maistre, "Mémoire au duc de Brunswick," *Ecrits maçonniques*, 100. Hereafter cited in text as "Mémoire."

6. Walzer, "On the Role of Symbolism," 194.

7. Turner, *The Forest of Symbols*, 30.

8. Maistre, *Du pape*, OC 2:342–43. Hereafter cited in text as *Du pape*.

9. Heusch, *Le Pouvoir et le sacré*, 15, 18.

10. Balandier, *Anthropologie politique*, 99–101.

11. Maistre, "Extraits F," MS, Maistre Archives, Archives Départementales de Savoie, Chambéry, 19–113ff. Hereafter cited in text as "Extraits F."

12. Plato, *The Laws*, 659d.

13. Althusser, "Ideology and Ideological State Apparatuses," 168.

14. Evans-Pritchard, *The Divine Kingship*, 27.

15. Pasquier, *Les Recherches de la France*, cited in Keohane, *Philosophy and the State in France*, 45.

16. Maistre, "Fragments sur la France," OC 1:205. Hereafter cited in text as "Fragments."

17. Maistre, letter to comte de Bray, 16 January 1815, OC 13:26.

18. Compare Zizek's recent definition of ideology as "a kind of reality whose very ontological consistency implies a certain non-knowledge of its participants—if we come to know 'too much' . . . , this reality would dissolve itself" (*The Sublime Object*, 21).

19. Maistre, letter to the chevalier de Rossi, 15 August 1811, OC 12:55.

20. Maistre, "Mélanges A," MS, Maistre Archives, Archives Départementales de Savoie, Chambéry, 58. Hereafter cited in text as "Mélanges A."

21. Maistre, "Religion E," MS, Maistre Archives, Archives Départementales de Savoie, Chambéry, 51–53. Hereafter cited in text as "Religion E." Further on, Maistre concludes by asking, "Is all revelation in the New Testament? When one says one must believe in J. C., isn't one implying that either J. C. is here to speak to us or that he wrote the evangels himself?" (55).

22. On democratic mores, Maistre here cites Machiavelli's *Discourses*.

23. Maistre, "Réflexions critiques d'un chrétien dévoué à la Russie sur l'ouvrage de méthode du archevêque de Twer," OC 8:413–14. Hereafter cited in text as "Réflexions."

24. See also Maistre, *Lettres et opuscules inédites*, 2:114.

25. Vico, *The New Science*, sec. 661.

26. Maistre, "Le Caractère extérieur du magistrat, ou les moyens d'obtenir la confiance publique" (The exterior character of the magistrate, or the means of obtaining public confidence), OC 7:12. Hereafter referred to in text as "Discours."

27. Clement of Alexandria, *Stromates*, 232–33.

28. Schutz, *On Phenomenology*, 90.

29. Maistre, *Examen de la philosophie de Bacon*, OC 6:453, 474. Hereafter cited in text as *Examen*.

5. LEGITIMACY

1. Maistre, letter to the chevalier de Rossi, July 1804, OC 9:188.

2. Tom Paine, *Dissertation on the First Principles of Government*, cited in Kramnick, *The Rage of Edmund Burke*, 148.

3. Hume, *A Treatise on Human Nature*, bk. 3, chap. 2, sec. x.

4. Maistre, letter to Madame Swetchine, 31 July 1815, OC 13:124.

5. Maistre, letter to the comte de ★★★, 2 October 1809, OC 11:323.

6. Pascal, *Pensées*, 47.

7. Compare Machiavelli's explanation of why Numa "pretended he was intimate with a nymph": to reshape Roman society he had "need for the authority of God

. . . because he planned to introduce new and unwonted laws into the city, but learned that his own authority would not be enough" (*Discourses* 1:9, in *The Portable Machiavelli*, 208).

8. Bodin, *Six Books*, bk. 1, chap. 8.

9. Maistre, letter to the comte de Rossi, 29 March 1815, OC 13:51.

10. Rivarol, *Maxims et pensées*, 25.

11. Barth, *The Idea of Order*, 148.

12. Otto, *The Idea of the Holy*, 12, 26.

13. Lamennais, *De la religion considérée dans ses rapports avec l'ordre politique et civile*, vol. 7 of *Oeuvres complètes*, 241.

14. Montesquieu, *The Persian Letters*, 162.

15. Bossuet, *De la politique*, bk. 2, sec. 1.

16. Necker, cited in Barth, *The Idea of Order*, 67.

17. Schmitt, *Political Theology*, 12.

18. Maistre, "Discours sur la caractère extérieure du magistrat," OC 7:26.

19. Maistre, letter to Comte Pierre-Louis de Blacas, 20 September 1812, *Joseph de Maistre et Blacas*, 192.

20. Maistre, letter to Baron Vignet des Etoles, 28 October 1794, OC 9:80.

21. To cite a contemporary example, one could say that the Watergate hearings did not deny but rather upheld the legitimate authority of the presidency; Nixon was struck down not for being too strong a president but for exceeding the proper bounds of the office: the sacred character of the presidency was thus reaffirmed.

22. Maistre, letter to the marquis de Saint-Marsan, 16 October 1814, OC 12:463.

23. Maistre, letter to Comte Antoine d'Avaray, 3 July 1804, *Mémoires politiques et correspondance politique*, 128–29.

24. Maistre, diplomatic report, 20 October 1815, *Correspondance politique*, 2:132.

25. Pascal, *Pensées*, 47.

6. SCIENCE AND SOCIETY

1. Vartanian, *Diderot and Descartes*, 48.

2. Blumenberg, *The Legitimacy of the Modern Age*, 181–203.

3. Descartes, *The Philosophical Writings*, 2:21.

4. Marx, *Capital*, 1:338, 390n.

5. Elster, *Leibniz*, 59.

6. Mayr, *Authority, Liberty, and Automatic Machinery*, 26.

7. Cited in Vartanian, *Diderot and Descartes*, 206. On the Beast-Machine, see also Rosenfield, *From Beast-Machine to Man-Machine*, and Boas, *The Happy Beast*.

8. La Mettrie, *Man as Machine*, 128.

9. La Mettrie carried his naturalism to sometimes extravagant lengths, periodically entering into disquisitions on the twitching of corpses and removed pieces of bodies. He claims that strength of mind is manifest in the solidity of the brain: the brains of women, imbeciles, children, puppies, and birds are "softer" than those of the thinking man. If the deaf can be made to read and write, he asks, why not apes? One must choose, however, a *big* ape with an "intelligent face": such an

ape could well be made "a perfect man, a little gentleman" (*Man as Machine*, 140–41, 105, 95, 99–103).

10. Mayr, *Authority, Liberty, and Automatic Machinery*, 113.

11. Michelet, *The People*, 96.

12. Cited in Cioran, *Joseph de Maistre*, 26.

13. The underlined material is quoted from Rousseau, *Social Contract*, bk. 2, chap. 7. Compare the Cambridge Neoplatonist Ralph Cudworth, whom Maistre read closely. Cudworth explains that while human art achieves its work "but with a great deal of tumult and hurlyburly, noise and clatter, it using hands and axes, saws and hammers, and after this manner, with much ado, by knockings and thrustings, slowly introducing its form or idea (as, for example, of a ship or house) into the materials . . . Nature is different from mechanism, it doing not its work by trusion or pulsion, by knockings and thrustings, as if it were without that which it worked upon . . . Nature acts directly upon the matter, as an inward and living soul, or law on it" (*The Intellectual System*, 1:220).

14. Maistre, letter to the vicomte de Bonald, 1 December 1814, OC 12:466–67.

15. That the Senator's words first appear in Maistre's private notebooks is further reason to view the *Soirées* as an interior dialogue rather than the reproduction of actual discussions in which the Count alone represents Maistre's thinking.

16. The source of Western science in the symbolic and imaginary structures of Christian theology has been argued by Kojève in "Christian Origin of Modern Science."

17. Maistre, letter to Tchitchikov, 6 May 1810, OC 11:450.

18. "Philosophie D," MS, Maistre Archives, Archives Départementales de Savoie, Chambéry, 551. Hereafter cited in text as "Philosophie D." This remark is found among the hundred pages of notes on Viller's *Philosophie de Kant* (Metz: 1801).

19. Maistre's interpretation of the history of science anticipates, albeit in a more tendentious form, phenomenology's emphasis on the subjective sources of scientific discovery. As Merleau-Ponty puts it, "in order to perceive things, we need to live them," for perceptual knowledge occurs "only if the phenomenon finds an echo within me." Thus "every perception is a communication or communion." Awareness of this phenomenological dimension of knowledge, he observes, was long "hampered by the prejudices of objective thinking," which "severs the link between the thing and the embodied subject" (*The Phenomenology of Perception*, 316–25).

20. Maistre, "Extraits G," MS, Maistre Archives, Archives Départementales de Savoie, Chambéry, 216. Hereafter cited in text as "Extraits G."

21. Pagels, *The Gnostic Gospels*, 44.

22. Irenaeus, *Against All Heresies*, pt. 1, chap. 13, sec. 6.

23. Rousseau, *The First and Second Discourses*, 140.

24. Cited by Cassirer in *The Philosophy of the Enlightenment*, 135.

7. PROVIDENCE

1. Vögelin, *The New Science*, 112, 122.

2. Berger, *The Sacred Canopy*, 58, 54, 59.

3. Blumenberg, *The Legitimacy of the Modern Age*, 133, 57. On the politics of eschatology in the early Church, see Werner, *The Formation of Christian Dogma*.

4. On Maistre's place in the Jansenist-Jesuit controversy, see Lebrun, *Joseph de Maistre*, chap. 1.

5. Popkin, "Manichaeanism in the Enlightenment." On Jansenism's contribution to the disenchantment of the political world, see Chartier, *The Cultural Origins of the French Revolution*.

6. Bayle, *Critical Dictionary*, 147, 173, 186.

7. Cioran, *Joseph de Maistre*, 14.

8. Bossuet, *Idea for a Universal History*, 373–74.

9. This claim bears heavy Neoplatonic overtones. Compare the words of John Dee: "Whatever is in the Universe possesses order, agreement and similar form with something else" (*Propaedeumata Aphoristica*, sec. 9).

10. Maistre, letter to Baron Vignet des Etoles, 28 October 1804, *OC* 9:78.

11. This idea of a counterbalancing reestablishment, we shall see, decisively shapes Maistre's notion of what a counterrevolution or a restoration might be.

12. On the paradox of the plaintiff, see Lyotard, *The Differend*, 9–24.

13. Plato, "Crito," 48a.

14. Maistre, "Addresse à la Convention nationale," *OC* 7:50.

15. Maistre, letter to the archevêque de Severoli, 1 December 1815, *OC* 13:189.

16. Maistre, letter to the comte de Vallaise, 14 September 1815, *OC* 13:159.

17. Maistre, letter to the comte de Rossi, 25 August 1815, *OC* 13:140.

18. Cited in Vidler, *Prophecy and Papacy*, 198–99.

19. Renan, *Questions contemporaines*, 42.

20. Certeau, *The Writing of History*, 180.

21. Xavier de Maistre cited in *Le Correspondant* (Paris), 10 December 1902, 918.

22. Swetchine cited in Falloux du Coudray, *Life and Letters of Madame Swetchine*, 1:400.

23. Maistre, "Lettre à une Dame Russe, sur la nature et les effets du schisme, et sur l'unité catholique," 8 February 1810, *OC* 8:142.

24. Sainte Beuve, *Causeries de lundi*, 4:196.

25. Maistre, "Lettre a M. le Marquis ★★★ sur l'état du christianisme en Europe," 1 May 1819, *OC* 8:500.

26. Maistre, letter to the comte de Blacas, 29 May 1819, *OC* 14:172.

27. Maistre, letter to Mme. de Costa, 28 May 1793, *OC* 9:37.

28. Maistre, letter to Mme. Huber-Alléon, 26 September 1806, *OC* 10:206–7.

29. Rohden, *Maistre als politische Theoretiker*, 190; Murray, "The Political Thought," 77.

30. Triomphe, *Joseph de Maistre*, 67–82. See also Soltner, "Le Christianisme," 97–110.

31. Darcel, "Des pénitents noirs," 92–93.

32. Lebrun, *Joseph de Maistre*, 17–20.

33. *Considerations on France*, trans. Lebrun, 82n.

34. Maistre, letter to the archevêque de Severoli, 1 December 1815, *OC* 13:185.

35. Plato, *The Laws*, 662b.

36. Maistre, letter to the Comte Jean Potocki "sur la chronologie biblique," 5 June 1810, *OC* 8:122.

37. Montesquieu, *The Persian Letters*, 162.

8. REVOLUTION AND COUNTERREVOLUTION

1. Quinet, *La Révolution*, 47–48.

2. Maistre, letter to the évêque de la Fare, 9 March 1805, *OC* 9:358.

3. Maistre, letter to the archevêque de Severoli, 1 December 1815, *OC* 13:188.

4. Maistre, letter to the comte de Vallaise, 6 March 1817, *OC* 14:65.

5. These doubts about American democracy are repeated in a notebook entry from 1807, where he observes that "from a repugnance in the people to pay even the most necessary taxes, and from absurd notions of liberty incompatible with law, there is a great danger of the dissolution of the confederacy, and of the introduction of a restless, turbulent, and ungovernable oligarchy" (Maistre, "Mélanges A," 76).

6. Maistre, "Discours du citoyen Cherchemot," *OC* 7:368–69.

7. Maistre, letter to Louis-Amé Vignet des Etoles, 11 August 1795, in Darcel, "Les Années d'apprentissage," 122.

8. Maistre, letter to the chevalier de Rossi, 14 April 1806, *OC* 10:106.

9. Maistre, letter to Comte Pierre-Louis de Blacas, 4 June 1807, *Joseph de Maistre et Blacas*, 67.

10. Cochin, *La Révolution et la libre pensée*, 184, 169. On Cochin, see Furet's important essay in *Interpreting the French Revolution*.

11. Maistre, "Addresse de quelques parents des militaires savoisiens à la Convention nationale des français," *OC* 7:76.

12. Maistre, letter to the Comte d'Avaray, 30 July 1807, *OC* 10:447.

13. Louis Blanc, *Histoire de la Révolution Française*, cited in Orr, *Headless History*, 62.

14. Manuscript for *Considérations sur la France*, cited in Lebrun's translation, *Considerations on France*, 39n.

15. Maistre, letter to Vignet des Etoles, 5 May 1794, in Darcel, "Les Années d'apprentissage," 88.

16. Cited in Darcel, "Les Années d'apprentissage," 42.

17. Maistre, letter to Vignet des Etoles, 22 August 1794, *OC* 9:74.

18. Maistre, letter to the comte d'Avaray, 24 July 1807, *OC* 10:436–37.

19. Maistre, letter to the chevalier de Rossi, 19 January 1809, *OC* 11:195.

20. Maistre, letter to unspecified recipient, July 1802, *Lettres et opuscules inédites*, 1:13.

21. Maistre, letter to the chevalier de Rossi, 18 August 1810, *OC* 11:475–76.

22. Maistre, letter to King Victor-Emmanuel, 22 May 1811, *OC* 12:47.

23. Maistre, letter to the comte d'Avaray, 12 July 1807, *OC* 10:432.

24. Maistre, letter to Blacas, 24 December 1811, *Joseph de Maistre et Blacas*, 148.

25. Maistre, letter to the marquis de Saint-Marsan, August 1815, *OC* 13:152.

26. Maistre, letter to the comte de Rossi, 29 March 1815, *OC* 13:57.

27. Maistre, diplomatic report, 3 May 1813, *Correspondance diplomatique*, 1:332.

28. Maistre, diplomatic report, 24 August 1815, *Correspondance diplomatique*, 2:111–12.

29. Maistre, diplomatic report, 6 July 1814, *Correspondance diplomatique*, 1:379–80.

30. *Joseph de Maistre et Blacas*, 179.

31. Maistre, letter to unspecified recipient, 2 October 1809, *OC* 11:315.

32. Maistre, letter to the comte d'Avaray, 30 July 1807, *OC* 10:448.

33. Maistre, letter to the chevalier de Rossi, 15 August 1811, *OC* 12:60.

34. Maistre, letter to the comte d'Avaray, 12 July 1807, *OC* 10:434.

35. Maistre, letter to the comte de Castelalfer, 3 November 1815, *OC* 13:176.

36. Maistre, letter to the comte de Castelalfer, 3 November 1815, *OC* 13:176.

37. Maistre, letter to the évêque de la Fare, 9 March 1805, *OC* 9:358.

38. *Les Carnets du comte Joseph de Maistre*, 24.

39. Maistre, letter to the R. P. [Révérend Père] d'Ervelange-Vitry, 27 May 1815, *OC* 13:79.

40. Maistre, letter to Blacas, 4 June 1807, *Joseph de Maistre et Blacas*, 66–67.

41. Maistre, letter to Vignet des Etoles, 9 December 1793, *OC* 9:58.

42. Maistre, diplomatic report, May 1814, *Correspondance diplomatique*, 1:366.

43. Maistre, letter to Vignet des Etoles, 6 January 1794, in Darcel, "Les Années d'apprentissage," 73.

44. Maistre, letter to Vignet des Etoles, 6 January 1794, in Darcel, "Les Années d'apprentissage," 73.

45. Maistre, letter to Blacas, 24 December 1809, *Joseph de Maistre et Blacas*, 104.

46. Maistre, letter to Constance de Maistre, 21 February 1820, *OC* 14:205.

47. Maistre, letter to Vignet des Etoles, 4 September 1793, in Darcel, "Les Années d'apprentissage," 50.

48. Maistre, letter to Vignet des Etoles, 17 September 1793, in Darcel, "Les Années d'apprentissage," 52.

49. Maistre, letter to Vignet des Etoles, 24 September 1793, in Darcel, "Les Années d'apprentissage," 55.

50. Maistre, diplomatic report, 28 April 1815, *Correspondance diplomatique*, 2:67–68.

51. Maistre, diplomatic report, 5 July 1815, *Correspondance diplomatique*, 2:372.

52. Maistre, diplomatic report, 13 October 1816, *Correspondance diplomatique*, 2:268.

53. Maistre, diplomatic report, 5 July 1817, *Correspondance diplomatique*, 2:372.

54. Maistre, diplomatic report, 6 July 1814, *Correspondance diplomatique*, 1:376.

55. Maistre, diplomatic report, 8 October 1812, *Correspondance diplomatique*, 1:218.

56. Maistre, letter to the comte de Marcellus, 9 August 1819, *OC* 14:183.

AFTERWORD

1. D'Aurevilly, *Le* 19e Siècle, 83–84.

2. Cited in Goyau, *La Pensée religieuse*, 28.

3. Maistre, "Essai sur la vénalité des offices," dated 1788, from a manuscript volume entitled "Miscellanea," MS, Maistre Archives, Archives Départementales de Savoie, Chambéry, 267.

4. Maistre, "Essai sur les parlements," "Miscellanea," 273.

5. Maistre, "Eloge de Victor Amedée," cited in Descostes, *Joseph de Maistre avant la Révolution*, 1:293–98.

6. Maistre, letter to Blacas, *Joseph de Maistre et Blacas*, 277–78.

7. For the secret file, see Lebrun, *Joseph de Maistre*, 24.

8. Maistre, letter to Vignet des Etoles, 9 July 1793, in Darcel, "Les Années d'apprentissage," 36.

9. Maistre, letter to Vignet des Etoles, 24 July 1793, in Darcel, "Les Années d'apprentissage," 38.

10. Maistre, letter to Vignet des Etoles, 6 January 1794, in Darcel, "Les Années d'apprentissage," 73.

11. Murray, "The Political Thought," 86.

12. On the formalism of political theory, see Mannheim, *Ideology and Utopia*, 38ff.

Works Cited

MAJOR FRENCH EDITIONS OF MAISTRE'S WORKS

Oeuvres complètes. 14 vols. Lyons: Vitte et Perussel, 1884–86.

Les Carnets du comte Joseph de Maistre. Lyons: Vitte, 1923.

Considérations sur la France. Ed. Jean-Louis Darcel. Geneva: Slatkine, 1980.

Correspondance diplomatique. Ed. A. Blanc. 2 vols. Paris: Librairie Nouvelle, 1860.

Correspondance politique de Joseph de Maistre. Ed. A. Blanc. 2 vols. Paris: Michel Lévy, 1860.

Du pape. Ed. Jacques Lovie and Joannès Chetail. Geneva: Droz, 1966.

Ecrits maçonniques de Joseph de Maistre. Ed. J. Rebotton. Geneva: Slatkine, 1983.

Joseph de Maistre et Blacas: Leur correspondance inédite et l'histoire de leur amitié. Ed. E. Daudet. Paris: Plon-Nourrit, 1908.

Lettres et opuscules inédites. 2 vols. Paris: Vaton, 1851.

Mémoires politiques et correspondance politique de Joseph de Maistre. Ed. A. Blanc. Paris: Librairie Nouvelle, 1858.

Les Soirées de Saint-Pétersbourg. 2 vols. Ed. J.-L. Darcel. Geneva: Slatkine, 1993.

MAJOR ENGLISH TRANSLATIONS OF MAISTRE'S WORKS

Against Rousseau: "On the State of Nature" and "On the Sovereignty of the People." Trans. Richard Lebrun. Montreal: McGill-Queens University, 1996.

Considerations on France. Trans. Richard Lebrun. Montreal: McGill-Queens University, 1974, and Cambridge: Cambridge University Press, 1994.

Essay on the Generative Principle of Political Constitutions. Repr. of 1847 ed. Delmas NY: Scholars' Facsimiles, 1977.

Letters on the Spanish Inquisition. Repr. of 1843 ed. Delmas NY: Scholars' Facsimiles, 1977.

On God and Society: Essay on the Generative Principle of Political Constitutions. Ed. and trans. Elisha Greifer and Lawrence Porter. Chicago: Regnery, 1959.

The Philosophy of Bacon: Wherein Different Questions of Rational Philosophy Are Treated. Ed. and trans. Richard Lebrun. Montreal: McGill-Queens University, 1998.

The Pope. Trans. Aeneas Dawson. Repr. of 1850 ed. New York: Howard Fertig, 1975.

St. Petersburg Dialogues. Trans. Richard Lebrun. Montreal: McGill-Queens University, 1993.

The Works of Joseph de Maistre. Ed. and trans. Jack Lively. New York: Macmillan, 1965.

OTHER WORKS CITED

Althusser, Louis. "Ideology and Ideological State Apparatuses." *Lenin and Philosophy*. Trans. B. Brewster. New York: Monthly Review Press, 1971.

Artz, Frederick. *Reaction and Revolution, 1814–32*. New York: Harper and Row, 1934.

d'Aurevilly, Jules Amedée Barbey. *Le 19e siècle*. Ed. J. Petit. Paris: Mercure de France, 1964.

Bagge, Dominique. *Les Idées traditionalistes en France sous la Restoration*. Paris: PUF, 1952.

Balandier, Georges. *Anthropologie politique*. Paris: PUF, 1984.

Baldensperger, Fernand. *Le Mouvement des idées dans l'émigration française*. 2 vols. Paris: Plon-Nourrit, 1924; New York: Burt Franklin, 1968.

Ballanche, Pierre-Simon. *Oeuvres*. 4 vols. Paris: Barbezat, 1830.

———. *Oeuvres*. 6 vols. Paris: Bureau de l'Encyclopédie des Connaissances Utiles, 1833.

Barth, Hans. *The Idea of Order*. Trans. Ernest W. Hankamer and William M. Newell. Dordrecht: Reidel, 1960.

Bataille, Georges. *Oeuvres complètes*. Paris: Gallimard, 1976.

———. *La Part maudite*. Paris: Editions de Minuit, 1967.

———. *Visions of Excess*. Ed. and trans. Allan Stoekl. Minneapolis: University of Minnesota Press, 1985.

Bayle, Pierre. *Critical Dictionary*. Ed. and trans. Richard Popkin. Indianapolis: Bobbs-Merrill, 1965.

Beik, Paul. *The French Revolution Seen from the Right*. Philadelphia: American Philosophical Society, 1956.

Bénichou, Paul. *Le Sacre de l'écrivain: 1750–1830*. Paris: Librairie José Corti, 1985.

———. *Le Temps des prophètes*. Paris: Gallimard, 1977.

Berger, Peter. *The Sacred Canopy*. Garden City: Doubleday, 1967.

Berlin, Isaiah. "The Counter-Enlightenment." *Against the Current*. Ed. Henry Hardy. New York: Viking Press, 1980. 1–24.

———. "Georges Sorel." *Against the Current*. Ed. Henry Hardy. New York: Viking Press, 1980. 296–332.

———. "Joseph de Maistre and the Origins of Fascism." *The Crooked Timber of Humanity*. Ed. H. Hardy. London: John Murray, 1990. 91–174.

Blanc de Saint Bonnet. *La Restauration française*. Tournai: Casterman, 1872.

Blumenberg, Hans. *The Legitimacy of the Modern Age*. Trans. Robert Wallace. Cambridge MA: MIT Press, 1983.

Boas, George. *The Happy Beast in French Thought of the Seventeenth Century*. Baltimore: Johns Hopkins, 1933.

Bodin, Jean. *Six Books of the Commonwealth*. Ed. and trans. M. J. Tooley. Oxford: Blackwell, 1955.

Bonald, Louis Gabriel Ambroise de. *Législation primitif, considerée dans les derniers temps par les seules lumières de raison*. Vol. 1 of *Oeuvres*. 15 vols. Paris: Le Clerc, 1817–43.

———. *Théorie du pouvoir politique et religieux dans la société civile, démontrée par le raisonnement et par l'histoire*. Vol. 13 of *Oeuvres*. 15 vols. Paris: Le Clerc, 1817–43.

Bossuet, Jacques-Benigne. *De la politique tirée des propres paroles de l'écriture sainte*. Ed. Jacques Le Brun. Geneva: Droz, 1967.

———. *Idea for a Universal History*. Ed. Elborg Forster. Trans. Orest Ranum. Chicago: University of Chicago Press, 1976.

Brandes, George. *The Reaction in France*. Vol. 3 of *Main Currents in Nineteenth Century Literature*. 3 vols. London: William Heidemann, 1903.

Caillois, Roger. *Man and the Sacred*. Trans. Meyer Barah. Glencoe IL: Free Press, 1959.

Cassirer, Ernst. *The Philosophy of the Enlightenment*. Trans. Fritz C. A. Koelln and James P. Pettegrove. Princeton NJ: Princeton University Press, 1951.

Certeau, Michel de. *The Writing of History*. Trans. T. Conley. New York: Columbia University Press, 1988.

Chartier, Roger. *The Cultural Origins of the French Revolution*. Trans. Lydia Cochrane. Durham NC: Duke University Press, 1991.

Chateaubriand, François-René de. *The Genius of Christianity*. Trans. C. I. White. Philadelphia: Lippincott, 1856.

Chaussinand-Nogaret, Guy. *The French Nobility in the Eighteenth Century*. Trans. William Doyle. Cambridge: Cambridge University Press, 1985.

Cioran, E. M. *Joseph de Maistre: Textes choisis*. Monaco: Editions du Rocher, 1957.

Clement, N. H. *Romanticism in France*. 1939. New York: Kraus Reprint Corporation, 1966.

Clement of Alexandria. *The Writings of Clement of Alexandria*. Trans. William Wilson. Edinburgh: T. and T. Clark, 1867.

Cochin, Auguste. *La Révolution et la libre pensée*. Paris: Copernic, 1979.

Comte, Auguste. *Cours de philosophie positive*. Ed. Emile Littré. 6 vols. Paris: Baillière, 1887.

———. *Opuscules*. Paris: Leroux, 1883.

———. *Système de politique positive*. 2 vols. Paris: Dunod, 1883.

Conrad, Joseph. *Joseph Conrad on Fiction*. Ed. W. F. Wright. Lincoln: University of Nebraska Press, 1964.

Cudworth, Ralph. *The Intellectual System of the Universe*. 2 vols. New York: Garland, 1978.

Darcel, Jean-Louis. "Les Années d'apprentissage d'un contre-révolutionnaire: Joseph de Maistre à Lausanne, 1793–1797." *La Revue des Etudes Maistriennes*, no. 10 (1986–87): 7–135.

———. "Des pénitents noirs à la franc-maçonnerie: Aux sources de la sensibilité maistrienne." *La Revue des Etudes Maistriennes*, nos. 5–6 (1980): 69–95.

Dee, John. *John Dee, Essential Readings*. Ed. Gerald Suster. London: Crucible, 1986.

Dermenghem, Emile. *Joseph de Maistre mystique*. Paris: Editions de la Colombe, 1946.

Descartes, René. *The Philosophical Writings*. Ed. and trans. John Cottingham, Robert Stoothof, and Dugald Murdoch. 2 vols. Cambridge: Cambridge University Press, 1987.

Descostes, François. *Joseph de Maistre avant la Révolution: Souvenirs de la société d'autrefois, 1753–1793*. 2 vols. Paris: Picard, 1893.

———. *Joseph de Maistre pendant la Révolution: Ses débuts diplomatiques, le marquis de Sales et les émigrés, 1789–97*. Tours: Alfred Mame et Fils, 1895.

Desroche, Henri. *Jacob and the Angel*. Trans. John K. Savacool. Amherst: University of Massachusetts Press, 1973.

Dimier, Louis. *Les Maîtres de la contre-Révolution*. Paris: Nouvelle Librairie Nationale, 1918.

Duchet, Michele. *Anthropologie et histoire au siècle des lumières*. Paris: Maspero, 1971.

Dumézil, Georges. *Mitra-Varuna*. Trans. D. Coleman. New York: Zone Books, 1988.

Dupuy, Roger. "Ignorance, fanatisme, et contre-Révolution." *Résistances à la Révolution*. Ed. Roger Dupuy and F. Lebrun. Actes du Colloque de Rennes. 17–21 December 1986. Paris: Imago, 1987. 37–42.

Dupuy, Roger, and François Lebrun, eds. *Résistances à la Révolution*. Actes du Colloque de Rennes. 17–21 December 1986. Paris: Imago, 1987.

Durkheim, Emile. *The Elementary Forms of the Religious Life*. Trans. J. W. Swain. London: George Allen and Unwin, 1976.

Eagleton, Terry. *The Ideology of the Aesthetic*. Oxford: Blackwell, 1990.

Elster, Jon. *Leibniz et la formation de l'esprit capitaliste*. Paris: Aubier Montaigne, 1975.

Evans, David O. *Social Romanticism in France*. Oxford: Clarendon Press, 1951.

Evans-Pritchard, E. E. *The Divine Kingship of the Shilluk of the Nilotic Sudan*. Cambridge: Cambridge University Press, 1948.

Eze, Emmanuel Chukwudi. *Race and the Enlightenment*. Oxford: Blackwell, 1997.

Falloux du Coudray, A. F. P. *Life and Letters of Madame Swetchine*. Trans. H. W. Preston. 2 vols. Boston: Roberts Brothers, 1875.

Fontana, Biancamaria. *Benjamin Constant and the Post-Revolutionary Mind*. New Haven CT: Yale University Press, 1991.

Foucault, Michel. *Discipline and Punish*. Trans. Alan Sheridan. New York: Vintage, 1977.

Fret, François. *Interpreting the French Revolution*. Trans. E. Forster. Cambridge: Cambridge University Press, 1981.

Garrard, Graeme. "Maistre, Judge of Jean-Jacques." Diss. Oxford University, 1995.

———. "Rousseau, Maistre, and the Counter-Enlightenment." *History of Political Thought* 15 (spring 1994): 97–120.

Gauchet, Marcel. *Le Désenchantement du monde*. Paris: Gallimard, 1985.

Gengembre, Gérard. "La Doctrine pour et contre l'histoire." *Résistance à la Révolution*. Ed. Roger Dupuy and F. Lebrun. Actes du Colloque de Rennes. 17–21 December 1986. Paris: Imago, 1987. 342–51.

George, Albert. *Pierre-Simon Ballanche, Precursor of Romanticism*. Syracuse NY: Syracuse University Press, 1945.

Gerbi, Antonello. *The Dispute of the New World: The History of a Polemic, 1750–1900*. Trans. Jeremy Moyle. Pittsburgh PA: University of Pittsburgh Press, 1973.

Gierke, Otto. *Political Theories of the Middle Age*. Trans. Frederick William Maitland. Cambridge: Cambridge University Press, 1900.

Girard, René. *Things Hidden since the Beginning of the World*. Trans. Stephen Bann and Michael Metteer. Stanford CA: Stanford University Press, 1987.

———. *Violence and the Sacred*. Baltimore: Johns Hopkins University Press, 1977.

Godechot, Jacques. *La Contre-Révolution*. Paris: PUF, 1961.

Gombrowicz, Witold. *Diaries*. 3 vols. Trans. Lillian Vallee. Evanston IL: Northwestern University Press, 1988.

Goyau, Georges. *La Pensée religieuse de Joseph de Maistre*. Paris: Perrin, 1921.

Habermas, Jürgen. "Modernity vs. Postmodernity." *New German Critique* 22 (1981): 3–14.

———. *Philosophical Discourse of Modernity*. Trans. Frederick Lawrence. Cambridge MA: MIT Press, 1987.

Hegel, G. W. F. *Reason in History*. Translation of the introduction to *Lectures on the Philosophy of History*. Trans. Robert S. Hartman. Indianapolis: Bobbs-Merrill, 1953.

Heine, Heinrich. "The Romantic School." *The Romantic School and Other Essays*. Ed. and trans. Robert C. Holub and Jost Hermand. New York: Continuum, 1985.

Herzen, Alexander. *From the Other Shore*. New York: Braziller, 1956.

Heusch, Luc de. *Le Pouvoir et le sacré*. Brussels: Université Libre de Bruxelles, 1962.

Hollier, Denis. *The College of Sociology*. Minneapolis: University of Minnesota Press, 1985.

Hume, David. *A Treatise on Human Nature*. Ed. L. A. Selby-Bigge. Oxford: Clarendon, 1978.

Irenaeus. *Saint Irenaeus against the Heresies*. Trans. Dominic J. Unger. New York: Paulist Press, 1992.

Kaplan, Steven. *Farewell, Revolution*. 2 vols. Ithaca NY: Cornell University Press, 1995.

Keohane, Nannerl. *Philosophy and the State in France*. Princeton NJ: Princeton University Press, 1980.

Kertzer, David. *Ritual, Politics, and Power*. New Haven CT: Yale University Press, 1988.

Kojève, Alexandre. "The Christian Origin of Modern Science." *Mélanges Alexandre Koyré*. 2 vols. Paris: Hermann, 1964. 2:295–306.

Kramnick, Isaac. *The Rage of Edmund Burke*. New York: Basic Books, 1977.

LaCapra, Dominick. *Emile Durkheim*. Ithaca NY: Cornell University Press, 1972.

———. "Violence, Justice, and the Force of Law." *Cardozo Law Review* 11, nos. 5–6 (summer 1990): 1065–78.

Lamennais, Félicité de. *Oeuvres complètes de F. de la Mennais*. Paris: Daubrée et Cailleux, 1836–37.

La Mettrie. *Man as Machine*. Chicago: Open Court, 1912.

Lebrun, Richard. *Joseph de Maistre: An Intellectual Militant*. Montreal: McGill-Queens University Press, 1988.

———. *Throne and Altar: The Political and Religious Thought of Joseph de Maistre*. Ottawa: University of Ottawa Press, 1965.

———, ed. and trans. *Maistre Studies*. Lanham NY: University Press of America, 1988.

Le Guillou, Louis. *L'Evolution de la pensée religieuse de Félicité Lamennais*. Paris: Armand Colin, 1966.

Leiris, Michel. *Le Ruban au cou d'Olympia*. Paris: Gallimard, 1981.

Lévi-Strauss, Claude. *The Savage Mind*. Chicago: University of Chicago Press, 1966.

Lyotard, François. *The Differend*. Trans. Georges Van Den Abbeele. Minneapolis: University of Minnesota Press, 1988.

Machiavelli, Niccolò. *The Portable Machiavelli*. Ed. and trans. Peter Bondanella and Mark Musa. Harmondsworth: Penguin, 1979.

Maistre, Henri de. *Joseph de Maistre*. Paris: Perrin, 1990.

Mandoul, J. *Joseph de Maistre et la politique de la maison de Savoie*. Paris: Alcan, 1899.

Mani, Lata. "Contentious Traditions: The Debate on Sati in Colonial India." *Cultural Critique* (fall 1987): 119–56.

Mannheim, Karl. *Conservatism*. Ed. and trans. David Kettler and Volker Meja. New York: Routledge and Kegan Paul, 1986.

———. *Ideology and Utopia*. Trans. Louis Wirth and Edward Shils. New York: Harcourt, Brace, Jovanovich, 1936.

Maritain, Jacques. *Man and the State*. Chicago: University of Chicago Press, 1951.

Marquard, Odo. *Farewell to Matters of Principle*. Trans. Robert Wallace. Oxford: Oxford University Press, 1989.

Marx, Karl. *Capital*. Trans. Samuel Moore and Edward Aveling. 3 vols. New York: International Library, 1967.

Mayr, Otto. *Authority, Liberty, and Automatic Machinery in Early Modern Europe*. Baltimore: Johns Hopkins University Press, 1986.

Mazauric, Claude. "Autopsie d'un echec, la résistance à la anti-Révolution et la defaite de la contre-Révolution." *Résistances à la Révolution*. Ed. Roger Dupuy and F. Lebrun. Actes du Colloque de Rennes. 17–21 December 1986. Paris: Imago, 1987. 237–44.

Merleau-Ponty, Maurice. *Humanism and Terror*. Trans. John O'Neil. Boston: Beacon, 1969.

———. *The Phenomenology of Perception*. Trans. Colin Smith. London: Routledge and Kegan Paul, 1962.

Meschonnic, Henri. *Modernité modernité*. Paris: Verdier, 1988.

Michelet, Jules. *The People*. Trans. John P. McKay. Urbana: University of Illinois Press, 1973.

Montesquieu, Charles de Secondat. *The Persian Letters*. Trans. C. J. Betts. Harmondsworth: Penguin, 1973.

Mosse, George. *Towards the Final Solution*. New York: H. Fertig, 1978.

Mouffe, Chantal. "Radical Democracy: Modern or Postmodern?" *Universal Abandon: The Politics of Postmodernism*. Ed. Andrew Ross. Minneapolis: University of Minnesota Press, 1988. 31–45.

Moulinié, Henri. *De Bonald: La Vie, la carrière politique, la doctrine*. Paris: Alcan, 1916.

Muret, C. T. *French Royalist Doctrines since the Revolution*. New York: Columbia University Press, 1933.

Murray, J. C. "The Political Thought of Joseph de Maistre." *Review of Politics* 11, no. 77 (1949): 63–87.

Nietzsche, Friedrich. *The Gay Science*. Trans. William Kaufmann. New York: Vintage, 1974.

Nisbet, Robert. "Conservatism and Sociology." *American Journal of Sociology* (September 1952): 167–75.

———. "De Bonald and the Concept of the Social Group." *Journal of the History of Ideas* (June 1944): 315–31.

Orr, Linda. *Headless History*. Ithaca NY: Cornell University Press, 1990.

Otto, Rudolph. *The Idea of the Holy*. Trans. John Harvey. New York: Oxford University Press, 1958.

Ozouf, Mona. "L'Idee et l'image du régicide dans la pensée contre-révolutionaire: L'Originalité de Ballanche." *Les Résistances à la Révolution*. Ed. Roger Dupuy and F. Lebrun. Actes du Colloque de Rennes. 17–21 December 1986. Paris: Imago, 1987. 332–41.

Pagels, Elaine. *The Gnostic Gospels*. New York: Random House, 1979.

Pareto, Vilfredo. *Sociological Writings*. Ed. S. E. Finer. Trans. Derick Mirtin. New York: Praeger, 1966.

Pascal, Blaise. *Pensées*. Ed. and trans. A. J. Krailsheimer. Harmondsworth: Penguin, 1966.

Pippen, Robert B. *Modernism as a Philosophical Problem*. Basil Blackwell: Oxford, 1991.

Plato. "Crito." Trans. Hugh Tredennick. *The Collected Dialogues of Plato*. Ed. Edith Hamilton and Hamilton Cairns. Princeton NJ: Princeton University Press, 1961.

———. *The Laws*. Trans. A. E. Taylor. *The Collected Dialogues of Plato*. Ed. E. Hamilton and H. Cairns. Princeton NJ: Princeton University Press, 1961.

Plongeron, Bernard. *Théologie et politique au siècle des lumières*. Geneva: Droz, 1973.

Popkin, Richard. "Manichaeanism in the Enlightenment." *The Critical Spirit: Essays in Honor of Herbert Marcuse*. Ed. Kurt H. Wolff and Barrington Moore. Boston: Beacon, 1967.

Quinet, Edgar. *La Révolution*. Paris: Librairie Belin, 1987.

Remond, René. *The Right Wing in France*. Trans. J. M. Laux. Philadelphia: University of Pennsylvania Press, 1969.

Renan, Ernst. *Questions contemporaines*. Paris: Michel Lévy, 1896.

Rials, Stephane. *Révolution et contre-Révolution au 19e siècle.* Paris: Editions Albatros et Diffusion Université Culture, 1987.

Richman, Michele. *Reading Bataille: Beyond the Gift.* Baltimore: Johns Hopkins University Press, 1982.

Rivarol, Antoine de. *Maxims et pensées.* Paris: Silvaire, 1960.

Roche, Alphonse. *Les Idées traditionalistes en France.* Urbana: University of Illinois, 1937.

Rohden, Peter Richard. *Maistre als politische Theoretiker.* Munich: Verlag der Münchner Drucke, 1929.

Rommen, Heinrich. *The State in Catholic Thought.* London: Herder, 1945.

Rosenfield, Leonora Cohen. *From Beast-Machine to Man-Machine.* Oxford: Oxford University Press, 1941.

Rousseau, Jean-Jacques. *Emile.* Trans. Allan Bloom. New York: Basic Books, 1979.

———. *The First and Second Discourses.* Ed. and trans. Roger Masters. New York: St. Martin's, 1964.

Sainte Beuve, Charles Augustin. *Causeries de lundi.* 14 vols. Paris: Garnier Frères, n.d.

Schmitt, Carl. *The Necessity of Politics.* Trans. E. M. Codd. London: Sheed and Ward, 1931.

———. *Political Romanticism.* Trans. Guy Oakes. Cambridge MA: MIT Press, 1986.

———. *Political Theology.* Trans. George Schwab. Cambridge MA: MIT Press, 1985.

Schutz, Alfred. *On Phenomenology and Social Relations.* Ed. Helmut R. Wagner. Chicago: University of Chicago Press, 1970.

Sollers, Phillipe. "Qui aura le courage de dire que c'est en France qu'a été inventée la terreur moderne?" *Le Quotidien de Paris* 16 July 1984: 8.

———. *Women.* Trans. Barbara Bray. New York: Columbia University Press, 1990.

Soltau, Roger. *French Political Thought in the 19th Century.* New York: Russell and Russell, 1959.

Soltner, Jean-Louis. "Le Christianisme de Joseph de Maistre." *Revue des Etudes Maistriennes* 5–6 (1980): 97–110.

Spivak, Gayatri. "Can the Subaltern Speak?" *Marxism and the Interpretation of Culture.* Ed. Cary Nelson and Lawrence Greenberg. Urbana: University of Illinois Press, 1988. 271–313.

Staël, Germaine de. *Considerations on the Main Events of the French Revolution.* 1818. *An Extraordinary Woman: The Selected Writings of Germaine de Staël.* Ed. and trans. Lillian Folkenflik. New York: Columbia University Press, 1987. 359–73.

Steiner, George. "Aspects of Counter-revolution." *The Permanent Revolution.* Ed. Geoffrey Best. London: Fontana, 1988. 129–53.

———. "Darkness Visible." Rev. of *Joseph de Maistre* by Richard Lebrun. *London Review of Books* 24 November 1988: 4.

Sternhell, Zeev. *Neither Right nor Left.* Trans. David Maisel. Berkeley: University of California Press, 1986.

Taine, Hyppolite. *The Ancient Regime.* Trans. John Durand. New York: H. Holt, 1876.

Taylor, Charles. "Foucault on Freedom and Truth." *Foucault: A Critical Reader.* Ed. David Hoy. Oxford: Basil Blackwell, 1986.

Triomphe, Robert. *Joseph de Maistre: Etude sur la vie et sur la doctrine d'un matérialiste mystique.* Geneva: Droz, 1968.

Turner, Victor. *The Forest of Symbols.* Ithaca NY: Cornell University Press, 1967.

———. *The Ritual Process.* Ithaca NY: Cornell University Press, 1977.

Vartanian, Aram. *Diderot and Descartes: A Study of Scientific Naturalism in the Enlightenment.* Princeton NJ: Princeton University Press, 1953.

Vermale, François. *Joseph de Maistre émigré.* Chambéry: Dardel, 1927.

Vernant, Jean-Pierre. "At Man's Table: Hesiod's Foundation Myth of Sacrifice." *The Cuisine of Sacrifice among the Greeks.* Ed. Marcel Detienne and Jean-Pierre Vernant. Trans. Paula Wissing. Chicago: University of Chicago Press. 21–86.

Vico, Giambattista. *The New Science.* 3rd ed. *Selected Writings.* Ed. and trans. Leon Pompa. Cambridge: Cambridge University Press, 1982.

Vidler, Alec. *Prophecy and Papacy.* London: SCM Press, 1954.

Vögelin, Eric. *The New Science of Politics.* Chicago: University of Chicago Press, 1952.

Walzer, Michael. "On the Role of Symbolism in Political Thought." *Political Science Quarterly* 82 (1967): 191–204.

Watt, E. D. "The English Image of Joseph de Maistre." *European Studies Review* 4 (1974): 239–59.

Werner, Martin. *The Formation of Christian Dogma.* Trans. S. G. F. Brandon. New York: Harper and Bros., 1957.

White, Hayden. "The Noble Savage Theme as Fetish." *Tropics of Discourse.* Baltimore: Johns Hopkins University Press, 1978. 183–96.

Wittgenstein, Ludwig. *Remarks on Frazer's Golden Bough.* Ed. Rush Rhees. Trans. A. C. Miles. Retford: Brynmill Press, 1979.

Zizek, Slavoj. *The Sublime Object of Ideology.* London: Verso, 1989.

Index

Bénichou, Paul, 20
Benjamin, Walter, 85
Bentham, Jeremy, 142
Berger, Peter, 93, 167–68
Berlin, Isaiah, xv–xviii
Bible: Maistre's citations from, 41–42,
117, 132, 148, 208; Maistre's unor-
thodox use of, 61, 100–101, 157, 192,
244 n.21
Blake, William, 160
Blanc de Saint Bonnet, Antoine-
Joseph-Elisée-Adolphe, 1, 20, 21, 146
Blanchot, Maurice, xi
Blanc, Louis, 212
blood, 33, 104, 154, 217; as a principle
of life, 40–42, 114, 146, 175, 242 n.11;
shedding of, 116, 130, 184, 188, 190,
191, 202, 210, 216. *See also* punish-
ment; sacrifice; violence; war
Blumenberg, Hans, 139, 168–70
Bodin, Jean, 118
Bonald, Louis-Gabriel-Ambroise,
vicomte de, 7, 8, 14–17, 18, 20, 21,
22, 25, 36, 78; compared with Mais-
tre, 57, 231, 236
Bonnet, Charles, 155
Bossuet, Jacques-Bénigne, 50, 122, 171
Brandes, George Morris, xiv
Bray, Gabriel de, 62
Buffon, Georges-Louis Leclerc, comte
de, 54
Burke, Edmund, xiv, xvii, 196, 216

Caillois, Roger, 79–82, 84
capitalism, 25, 26, 80, 141
capital punishment. *See* punishment
Castoriadis, Cornelius, xi
Catholicism: Neoplatonic elements in
Maistre's, 147, 161, 172, 175, 189,
195; orthodoxy of Maistre's, ix, xix–
xx, xxi, 69, 134, 191, 236; pagan elements in Maistre's, 40, 47–49, 51,
159, 173, 189–90; significance of
Maistre's, 28, 189–98, 208, 231–32;

traditionalist, 10, 11, 13, 15, 16, 17,
18–19; unorthodoxy of Maistre's,
xvi, 39, 41, 50, 62, 151. *See also* pope;
religion
ceremony. *See* ritual
Certeau, Michel de, 57, 191
Chambord, Henri-Charles-Ferdinand-
Marie Dieudonné d'Artois, comte
de, 25
change: conservative view of, ix, 2, 22,
30, 85, 216–17; Maistre's understanding of, 40, 114, 121, 135, 146,
161, 202, 232
Charles X, 190
Charter (1814), 10, 27, 228–29
Chateaubriand, François-Auguste-
René, vicomte de, 6–7, 23, 27
Christianity: Alexandrian, 39; comparative approach to, 47–49, 57, 194;
idea of exile in, 5. *See also* Catholicism; religion
Chrysostom, Saint John, 49
Cioran, E. M., xv, xviii, 171
civil society, 14, 127, 218–19
civil war, 113, 129, 131
Clement, N. H., ix
Clement of Alexandria, 107, 109, 163,
175, 189
Cochin, Auguste, 209
College of Sociology, 79–82
colonization, 53–55
compensation: counterbalances excess,
43, 60, 70, 77, 79, 173, 177–79, 184,
185–88, 247 n.11; as debt paid by
guilt, 63; French Revolution viewed
in terms of, 200, 208, 210–12, 218,
219, 221, 230, 234; innocence as, 42,
45, 180–82; war as, 73, 75. *See also*
general order
Comte, Auguste, 82–84, 167
Condillac, Etienne Bonnot, Abbé de,
142, 148
Conrad, Joseph, 85

contained but not eradicated, 116, 126, 132, 237; of colonialism, 55; of executions, 63–71, 72; Maistre was a theorist of, not an advocate, x, xvi, xvii, xviii, 56–57, 61, 75, 189, 231; sacrificial, x, xiv, 32–60, 84–85, 93, 215; of war, 71–76. *See also* general law (of violence)

vitalism, 146–47, 175

Vögelin, Eric, 167

Voltaire, 37, 180, 232

Walzer, Michael, 90

war: Bonald on, 15, 17; Maistre's reflections on, 35, 50, 61–62, 71–79, 113, 187, 190; Maistre's warnings against, 86, 129, 219, 221, 233

Warburton, William, xiii

Weber, Max, 104

Wittgenstein, Ludwig, 33

Zizek, Slavoj, 244 n.18

In the European Horizons Series

The Consecration of the Writer, 1750–1830
By Paul Bénichou
Translated and with an introduction by Mark Jensen
With a preface by Tzvetan Todorov

A Modern Maistre:
The Social and Political
Thought of Joseph de Maistre
By Owen Bradley

Dispatches from the Balkan War and Other Writings
By Alain Finkielkraut
Translated by Peter S. Rogers and Richard Golsan
With an introduction by Richard Golsan